Tertullian of Carthage was the first western Christian to write an extended theology. A vigorous and humorous apologist, he defended Christians against the hostility of the Roman state. Within the church he gave great attention to the rule of faith or criterion of truth which he found in the gospel. His controlling canon declared the perfection of the divine plan for human salvation, in Jesus Christ, son of God, crucified saviour, but when this was applied to the lives of believers he was disappointed by Christian mediocrity. Consequently he turned to an account of original sin, the necessary fear of God, and apocalyptic hope.

A complex thinker, he has in modern times been rejected by both liberal Christianity and its secular critics, who in fealty to the Enlightenment believed that a passion for reason should lead to a quasi-mathematical system. The destruction of this belief by Gödel, Wittgenstein, Rorty and many others opens the way for an understanding of Tertullian's passion for opposites, contingency and rational argument.

Misquoted and misused, Tertullian now calls for sustained analysis and interpretation. This book offers a major re-appraisal of his theology and its influence on the shape of the western Christian tradition, particularly on Augustine.

TERTULLIAN, FIRST THEOLOGIAN OF THE WEST

TERTULLIAN,
FIRST THEOLOGIAN
OF THE WEST

ERIC OSBORN

Professor Emeritus, Queen's College, University of Melbourne
Honorary Professor, La Trobe University, Melbourne

CAMBRIDGE
UNIVERSITY PRESS

PUBLISHED BY THE PRESS SYNDICATE OF THE UNIVERSITY OF CAMBRIDGE
The Pitt Building, Trumpington Street, Cambridge CB2 1RP, United Kingdom

CAMBRIDGE UNIVERSITY PRESS
The Edinburgh Building, Cambridge CB2 2RU, United Kingdom
40 West 20th Street, New York, NY 10011–4211, USA
10 Stamford Road, Oakleigh, Melbourne, 3166, Australia

© Eric Osborn 1997

First published 1997

Printed in the United Kingdom at the University Press, Cambridge

Typeset in Baskerville 11/12½ pt

A catalogue record for this book is available from the British Library

Library of Congress cataloguing in publication data

Osborn, Eric Francis.
Tertullian, first theologian of the West / Eric Osborn.
p. cm.
Includes bibliographical references and index.
ISBN 0 521 59035 3 (hardback)
1. Tertullian, ca. 160–ca. 230. 2. Theology, Doctrinal – History –
Early church, ca. 30–600. I. Title.
BR1720.T3O82 1996
230'.13'092–dc21 97-49902 CIP

ISBN 0 521 59035 3 hardback

Contents

Preface

Newness is more than a matter of timing. It is not enough, says Tertullian, to arrive early and stand at the head of a queue, as people did each day outside the baths in Carthage. An originator has to be original. The new miracles of Christ were followed by a long line of imitators; but the novelty of Christ was his uniqueness rather than his priority in time. In a humbler way, Tertullian himself is not merely first in an occidental queue. He is 'astonishingly original and personal'[1] and is able to do theology, that laminated fusion of argument and scripture, in a way which breaks new ground. Strikingly, he wrote his own kind of Latin. He liberated Christian thought from its Greek beginnings by analysing and developing biblical concepts.

Thinkers are 'divided according to traditions, each member of which partially adopts and partially modifies the vocabulary of the writers whom he has read'. Traditions begin from 'the people with poetic gifts, all the original minds with a talent for redescription'.[2] Tertullian was an innovator, and, in length of influence, he has outstripped the modern creators, like Darwin and Freud, by nearly two millennia. It is therefore useful to elucidate his final vocabulary, the words and meanings which continually recur in his arguments.[3] Most of his words were not new, but the way he arranged them was. He purified a dialect, by framing a vocabulary which enabled him to challenge the opponents of his kind of Christianity.

---

[1] Jean Daniélou, *A history of early Christian doctrine before the Council of Nieaea*, vol. III, *The origins of Latin Christianity* (London, 1977), 341.

[2] R. Rorty, *Contingency, irony, and solidarity* (Cambridge, 1989), 76.

[3] Like any consideration of Tertullian's use of words, this study acknowledges the monumental work of R. Braun, *Deus Christianorum*, 2nd edn. (Paris, 1977).

xiii

> Our concern was speech, and speech impelled us
> To purify the dialect of the tribe . . .[4]

He did not see himself as an innovator, but as the defender of a gospel which had come through the apostles from God. Swept off his feet by the Christian scriptures (Clement of Alexandria had compared them with the songs of irresistible Sirens), he came to grief when he denied friction between his final vocabulary and any part of scripture. His writing was part of the effective history, as Gadamer puts it, of the bible. He makes it easy for his reader to find his final vocabulary by calling it the 'rule' and expressing it in a variety of striking terms: 'What in the end is for you the total disgrace of my God, is the mystery of mankind's salvation' ('Totum denique dei mei penes vos dedecus sacramentum est humanae salutis').[5]

There were three reasons why he was able to write such a sentence. First, he possessed the intellectual virtues of clarity and economy. He gave reasons and set out arguments. Interpreters with wide knowledge of early Christian thought[6] have singled out his intellectual quality as pre-eminent. To this strength he added the rarer gifts of paradox, metaphor and wit, all necessary for a thinker who fashions a language. Second, he had a sense of the power of words, because Jesus Christ was for him a word-event; the living voice of the gospel carried him along. At creation, God who had always been rational became verbal and the place had never been quiet since. Theology was a lively matter, displaying 'the limitless wealth of the word of God in its interpretation in the world during its passage through history'.[7] Third, he was engaged in vigorous controversy, where a kind of brilliance was needed. Most of what he wrote was directed against someone. He took on the Roman establishment, Marcion, Praxeas, indulgent bishops, Hermogenes and Valentinians; indeed he took on the world itself and insisted that things were going to be very different at the end. He did this because, like Paul, he was Heraclitean in mind and temperament – a message from God could not count on security but only on strife. To that divine Heraclitean word which ruled

---

[4] T. S. Eliot, Little Gidding, *Four Quartets* (London, 1944), 39.
[5] *Marc.* 2.27.7.
[6] Like Karl Holl and Jean Daniélou.
[7] Gerhard Ebeling, *The word of God and tradition* (London, 1968), 31.

through all things he was committed; the possessive adjective 'my' preceded 'God' and 'lord' in his decisive statements.

As first theologian of the West, he is one of those second-century writers who both absorb elements of philosophy into theology and also illuminate the relation between the New Testament and later creeds. His ideas have become more accessible in this century which has turned from systems to problems, from conclusions to argument. Tertullian's perpetual argumentation (*ratio* is his favourite word) enables us to understand his conclusions. The specific aim of this book is to analyse Tertullian's arguments and thereby clarify his meaning. Elusive and forever antithetical, he could be described as 'the laughing Stoic', were it not that he specifically disowned all schools of philosophy and appeared 'like a meteor'.[8]

Meteors make few friends, so Tertullian presents a challenge to his reader. Since the Enlightenment, no ancient Christian writer has attracted more hostility.[9] Many have been repelled by the rhetorical force with which he led his readers from theory to practice. This won his contests in the second century and loses them today. Few have seen how his metaphors created a new language. There is no alternative to extended analysis and the demands of analysis are severe. We begin from the claim that 'if we want to understand others, we must count them right in most matters'.[10] This is a strategy for getting hold of people's fundamental beliefs, for learning their language, identifying their common concepts and the use to which they put them.[11] There is no way in which we can understand what any writer is saying if we neglect his final vocabulary, if we isolate a proposition from the arguments which define its meaning. If (as most have done) we take the proposition 'it is credible, because inept' away from the argument where it occurs, we cannot but reject it and play the common game of 'telling men of straw that they have no brains'.[12]

---

[8] Daniélou, *Latin Christianity*, 341.
[9] Renan described his work as 'un mélange inouï de talent, de fausseté d'esprit, d'éloquence, et de mauvais goût'. *Marc Aurèle et la fin du monde antique* (Paris, 1882), 456.
[10] Donald Davidson, On the very idea of a conceptual scheme, in Davidson, *Inquiries into truth and interpretation* (Oxford, 1984), 197.
[11] Quentin Skinner, A reply to my critics, in J. Tully (ed.), *Meaning and context, Quentin Skinner and his critics* (Cambridge, 1988), 238.
[12] J. Passmore, The idea of a history of philosophy, *HThS*, 5 (1965), 13.

Philosophers have continued to show, from Wittgenstein on-wards, that meaning is inaccessible without context, language-game, final vocabulary, verbal constellation, dialect, universe of discourse or whatever imperfect name we choose to call it. The more useful theologians have said the same.[13] That is why this book seeks to identify the final vocabulary which Tertullian created and used in different arguments. Such an analysis assumes that Tertullian is talking sense and sets out the way in which he arranges words.

The book begins with Tertullian's canon of truth, the perfection of all things in Christ. Then, before going further in exploration of his arguments, it examines those slogans which have classified him as an opponent of rationality: 'What has Athens to do with Jerusalem?' and 'Credible because inept.' There is little point in struggling with his arguments if he set no value on reason. These puzzles resolved and his predilection for reason established, his apologetic reveals an Heraclitean respect for opposites and a Stoic confidence in every soul's innate awareness of God. His longest dispute was with Marcion, who separated the just God of the Old Testament from the good God who sent Jesus. His conflict with Praxeas produced the first extended statement of trinitarian doctrine. The brief account of prayer indicates the central themes of his thought and his use of the bible is decisive and only rarely disastrous. His account of sin runs into his account of the church which he claimed should be the spotless bride of Christ. The marked difference between his treatment of Hermogenes' argu-ment and Valentinian theosophy is worth investigation. His eschatology is highly developed and his expectation of the end is colourful and coherent. From his theology and his Stoicism comes an austere and provocative ethic.

Interpretation requires us, as Gadamer put it, to project our prejudgements against a text which destroys some and lets others stand. The process continues and nothing is secure. Fifteen years ago, I wrote that Tertullian 'never stops to think what his opponent

---

[13] J. Daniélou, on the limits of philological pedigrees, wrote 'Words cannot be divorced from their contexts, and a change of context inevitably alters the sense of a word.' *Gospel message and Hellenistic culture* (London, 1973), 329.

might mean'.[14] Now I am mystified by the way in which he listens to what his opponent says. In his *apologeticum* he accepts the Stoic world of opposites and innate knowledge of God. He feels and redefines Marcion's antitheses and Praxeas' monotheism. Even from Valentinians, who are foolish enough to think that all other Christians are foolish, he takes important elements of trinitarian theology.

Our limited conquest of conceptual parochialism will depend on the range of our prejudgements, a respect for the text and the stamina of friends. Beyond La Trobe University and Melbourne, I am grateful to colleagues in Cambridge and Tübingen, Lille, Paris, Strasbourg, Leiden and Pamplona, who have asked different questions. Especial thanks are due to those who read and criticized the penultimate draft: Luise Abramowski, Michel Spanneut and Albert Viciano. Michel Spanneut has, in his books and articles, kept the Stoic influence before patristic scholars over the last forty years. Andrew Lenox-Conyngham and David Rankin have helped at many points. Margot Hyslop, senior reference librarian at La Trobe University, has found many books and articles. Ruth Parr of Cambridge University Press has guided the manuscript through the process of publication with understanding and intelligence. Once again, I am indebted to the Alexander von Humboldt Stiftung for the generosity which brought me back to Tübingen.

No translation can do justice to Tertullian's splendid Latin. While I have often consulted the translations listed in the bibliography, I have rarely left them intact and have never been finally satisfied. This general acknowledgement expresses a general debt; my special appreciation is extended to Evans's *Adversus Marcionem* which I have frequently followed with minor alterations.

Since it is forty years from the appearance, at Cambridge, of my first book on second-century Christian thought, it is my privilege to thank Henry Chadwick and to remember with deep gratitude A. Boyce Gibson and William Telfer, who first set my fallible feet on the way of exploration.

[14] *The beginning of Christian philosophy* (Cambridge, 1981), 272.

Note on the text and list of abbreviations

TEXT

Quinti Septimi Florentis Tertulliani, *Opera*, Corpus Christianorum, Series Latina, I, II (Brepols, 1954)

TERTULLIAN'S WORKS

an.	de anima
ap.	apologeticum
bapt.	de baptismo
carn.	de carne Christi
cast.	de exhortatione castitatis
cor.	de corona
cult.	de cultu feminarum, libri II
fug.	de fuga in persecutione
Herm.	adversus Hermogenem
idol.	de idololatria
iei.	de ieiunio
Jud.	adversus Judaeos
Marc.	adversus Marcionem, libri V
mart.	ad martyras
mon.	de monogamia
nat.	ad nationes, libri II
or.	de oratione
paen.	de paenitentia
pall.	de pallio
pat.	de patientia

pat.	*de patientia*
praescr.	*de praescriptione haereticorum*
Prax.	*adversus Praxean*
pud.	*de pudicitia*
res.	*de resurrectione mortuorum*
Scap.	*ad Scapulam*
scorp.	*scorpiace*
spect.	*de spectaculis*
test.	*de testimonio animae*
ux.	*ad uxorem, libri II*
Val.	*adversus Valentinianos*
virg.	*de virginibus velandis*

ABBREVIATIONS

ACW	*Ancient Christian Writers*
AKG	*Arbeiten zur Kirchengeschichte*
ANCL	*Ante-Nicene Christian Library*
ANRW	*Aufstieg und Niedergang der römischen Welt*
Apoll.	*Apollinaris.* Civitas Vaticana
APQ	*American Philosophical Quarterly*
Aug.	*Augustinianum*
BVSGW.PH	*Berichte über die Verhandlungen der sächsischen Gesellschaft der Wissenschaften, Philologische-historische Klasse*
DK	H. Diels and W. Kranz, *Die Fragmente der Vorsokratiker*
EA	*Etudes Augustiniennnes*
EL	*Ephemerides Liturgicae*
GCS	*Die griechischen christlichen Schriftsteller der ersten drei Jahrhunderten*
Greg	*Gregorianum*
HTh.	*History and Theory*
HThS	*History and Theory, Supplement*
JAC	*Jahrbuch für Antike und Christentum*
JRH	*Journal of Religious History*
JThS	*Journal of Theological Studies*
LCC	*Library of Christian Classics*

LCL	*Loeb Classical Library*
LongSedley	A. A. Long and D. N. Sedley, *The Hellenistic philosophers* (Cambridge, 1987)
MH	*Museum Helveticum*
MThZ	*Münchener theologische Zeitschrift*
NAWG	*Nachrichten der Akademie der Wissenschaften in Göttingen*
NThT	*Nieuw theologisch tijdschrift*
Orph.	*Orpheus*
PG	Migne, *Patrologia Cursus Completus . . . series Graeca*
PhJ	*Philosophisches Jahrbuch*
PhP	*Philosophia Patrum*
PP	G. S. Kirk, J. E. Raven and M. Schofield, *The Presocratic philosophers*, 2nd. ed. (Cambridge, 1983)
REA	*Revue des études augustiniennes*
REG	*Revue des études grecques*
RET	*Revista española de teologia*
RevSR	*Revue des sciences religieuses*
RHE	*Revue d'histoire ecclésiastique*
RHPhR	*Revue de histoire et de philosophie religieuse*
RIPh	*Revue internationale de philosophie*
RQ	*Römische Quartalschrift für christliche Altertumskunde*
RSLR	*Rivista di storia e letteratura religiosa*
RSR	*Recherches de science religieuse*
RThPh.	*Revue de théologie et de philosophie*
SC	*Sources chrétiennes*
Schol.	*Scholastik*
SCO	*Studi classici e orientali*
StPatr.	*Studia Patristica*
StTh.	*Studia Theologica*
SVF	*Stoicorum Veterum Fragmenta*
ThPh	*Theologie und Philosophie*
ThR	*Theologische Rundschau*
TRE	*Theologische Realenzyklopädie*
TU	*Texte und Untersuchungen*
TWNT	*Theologisches Wörterbuch zum Neuen Testament*
TyV	*Teología y vida*

VC	*Vigiliae Christianae*
ZKG	*Zeitschrift für Kirchengeschichte*
ZNW	*Zeitschrift für die neutestamentliche Wissenschaft*
ZThK	*Zeitschrift für Theologie und Kirche*

Other abbreviations follow the *Abkürzungsverzeichnis* of
S. Schwertner (Berlin, New York, 1976)

CHAPTER I

Simplicity and perfection

'We also are religious and our religion is simple', objected the Roman proconsul to the martyr Speratus, at his trial near Carthage on 17 July 180. 'If you will listen calmly', replied Speratus, 'I shall tell you the mystery of simplicity.'[1] Tertullian was not the only African who liked paradox.[2] Speratus claims simplicity for Christians rather than pagans. He counters the accusation that Christians are secret and sinister, by asserting that their secret is simplicity. He draws on the New Testament account of the mystery of salvation. The writer to the Ephesians had been concerned to tell the nations of the unsearchable riches of Christ and to bring to light 'the economy of the mystery which has been hidden from all ages in the God who created all things' (Eph. 3.9). The church declares to heavenly powers the manifold (πολυ-ποίκιλος) wisdom of God (Eph. 3.10), which is the divine mystery. The end of salvation, the vision of Christ and the church present a great mystery (Eph. 5.32).

Tertullian's lust for simplicity, supported by superlatives, persists throughout his work and is a good place to begin a study of his thought. A fine exposition, which begins 'Tertullien déconcerte', goes on to insist that Tertullian took a simple and total choice when

---

[1] Speratus speaks in reply to the proconsul's claim, 'Et nos religiosi sumus et simplex est nostra religio.' Speratus says, 'Si tranquillas praebueris aures tuas, dico mysterium simplicitatis.' *Passio sanctorum Scillitanorum*, 3f. See *Acta Martyrum*, ed. H. Musurillo, *The acts of the Christian martyrs* (Oxford, 1972), 86.

[2] This term is commonly used of Tertullian in the sense of apparent contradiction (Cicero: 'admirabilia contraque opinionem omnium' (*Paradoxa Stoicorum*, 4)), rather than in the more complex logical sense (Zeno, Russell). See J. van Heyenroot, Logical Paradoxes, in P. Edwards (ed.), *Encyclopedia of Philosophy*, vol. v (New York, 1967), 45–51. The two senses will sometimes over-lap.

he became a Christian and that his complexity comes from his earlier intellectual formation; whether a study of his thought begins from either simplicity or complexity, it will discover a profound unity.[3]

A man of keen and violent disposition (*acris et vehementis ingenii*),[4] much of Tertullian's lively talk is concerned with clarifying what others have confused. Like Paul, he reiterates that he wants to know nothing but Christ crucified. Christ revealed himself, not as a tradition, but as truth (*virg.* 1.1). Truth is simple (*ap.* 23.7f.), but philosophers have mixed with it their own opinions (*ap.* 47.4) and sunk to a perversity (*Marc.* 5.19.8) which tortures truth ('unde ista tormenta cruciandae simplicitatis et suspendendae veritatis?' *an.* 18.7). The soul testifies in its simplicity (*test.* 1.6) and its evidence is simple and divine (*test.* 5.1). Truth leads to beauty so female dress should be marked by simplicity (*cult.* 1.2.4 et passim). When Valentinians accuse ordinary Christians of simplicity, he replies 'although simple, we nevertheless know everything' (*Val.* 3.5). He writes (*res.* 2.11) to strengthen the faith of simple believers, employing his rhetorical skill on their behalf against heretics (*res.* 5.1).

THE SIMPLE BEGINNING

The divine economy of salvation is reflected in Christian baptism, which points to past and future. Life begins at baptism; here Tertullian shows his yearning for what is simple, in 'the sacrament of our Christian water, which washes away the sins of our original blindness and frees us for eternal life' (*bapt.* 1.1). Yet simplicity never displaces reason. Those who do not examine the reasons behind simple baptism, and who stay with an unexamined faith, are vulnerable through their ignorance (*ibid.*). The wrong kind of simplicity needs instruction, guidance and protection (*res.* 2.11).[5]

---

[3] 'This unity lies behind the pseudo-paradoxes and pseudo-contradictions.' J.-C. Fredouille, *Tertullien et la conversion de la culture antique* (Paris, 1972), 485.

[4] Jerome, *vir. illust.* 57.

[5] In this bad sense, the greater part of the faithful are *simplices* (*ne dixerim imprudentes et idiotae*) who, having moved from many gods to one God, panic at the exposition of the trinity (*Prax.* 3. 1). The same people are uncertain about the value of martyrdom, find their doubts exploited by Gnostics (*scorp.* 1.5), and cannot answer objections against the madness of dying for God (*scorp.* 1.7).

Tertullian rejects the naïveté of those who want a proof-text which forbids their attendance at the games (*spect.* 3.1) and the artless heresy which abolishes all discipline (*praescr.* 41.3).

A heretical viper[6] has turned many away from baptism, through that common perversity which rejects anything simple. 'Nothing, absolutely nothing, hardens human minds as much as the obvious simplicity of what God does, and the contrasting greatness of what he thereby achieves. The unadorned fact, that with such radical simplicity, without pomp, without any special preparation, and indeed, at no cost, a man is lowered into water, is dipped, while a few words are spoken, and then emerges, not much (if at all) cleaner, makes it all the more incredible that he gains eternal life in this way' (*bapt.* 2.1). In striking contrast, idol worship uses every possible embroidery of ritual and every additional expense.

Fussy, wretched incredulity denies God's primary properties of simplicity and power, which should be received with wonder and faith. God is found by the simple in heart (*praescr.* 7.10) and he appeared to Elijah openly and simply (*apertus et simplex*, *pat.* 15.6). God is too simple to have worked a Docetist deception (*carn.* 5.10). For the unbeliever, there is nothing in such plain acts as baptism and the pretended effects are impossible: which illustrates how God uses foolish things to confound worldly wisdom and does easily what men find most difficult.

The subtlety of God's simplicity is linked with his wisdom and power, which derive stimulus from their opposites of folly and impossibility, 'since every virtue receives its cause from those things by which it is provoked' (*bapt.* 2.3). So strife becomes a second theme of Tertullian's thought.[7] He links it with Pauline paradox, and it is fundamental to the Stoicism which looked back to Heraclitus whom Justin saw as a Christian before Christ. Simplicity and weakness belong to God as his omnipotent rejection of earthly power and wisdom. Christians who follow this divine simplicity are little fishes (*bapt.* 1.3) who cannot live apart from the water of baptism. Here their faith is contracted to the one word

---

[6] The Cainite heresy which honoured Cain because he resisted the evil God of the Old Testament. Tertullian's snakes prefer dry places.

[7] See discussion of paradox in ch. 3 and of opposites in ch. 4.

ἰχθύς which stands for Ἰησοῦς χριστὸς θεοῦ υἱὸς σωτήρ (Jesus Christ, son of God, saviour).[8]

Repetition underlines simplicity and Tertullian employs it to reinforce his claims. More than this, his key words (goodness, reason and discipline) link together diverse things which are derived from one simple divine origin. Goodness explains every part of the creative act (*Marc.* 2.4.5). Reason is founded in God who is ever rational, and provides grounds for Tertullian's every argument (including his paradoxes) and for his constant attacks upon his opponents (*paen.* 1). *Ratio* is his favourite word. Discipline governs all details of conduct. The constant refrain of these themes provides unity in his writing.

Christians are plain people because they accept the world as God's creation. This means that they do not run off into seclusion, but live like others; they eat, dress, bathe, work, trade, sail, fight, farm and practise a craft. They do not observe the common religious rites; but they are no less human or reasonable for that (*ap.* 42.4). Their simple lives are matched in modesty by simple dress (*cult.* 2.13.3). They follow the New Testament aesthetic of 'putting on' Christ.

Simplicity, in Tertullian, sometimes exacts its price and affects his arguments. The sudden enunciation of God's name is, for most, not the testimony of a soul which is naturally Christian, but the testimony of a soul which is not very Christian. The appeal to lines of episcopal succession is controversial rather than an end to controversy and, in any case, Tertullian always wants to obey conscience rather than bishop. In his case the two rarely agree.[9] Above all, Tertullian seems to fail in his account of divine justice and love. In his rejection of Marcion, he claims that only retributive justice can discourage sin.[10]

These matters will be dealt with again later. The points to note at this stage are three. First, we must expect that a passion for simplicity might induce errors. Theology, like philosophy, is a

---

[8] To this formula we shall return in the second part of this chapter.

[9] Charles Munier, La tradition apostolique chez Tertullien, in Collected studies series CS341, Autorité épiscopale et sollicitude pastorale, *L'année canonique*, 33 (Paris, 1979), 175–92 (192).

[10] See below, ch. 5. Despite initial simplicity, Tertullian develops a complex argument here.

complex matter and those who cut corners suffer accidents.[11] Second, those who turn every corner arrive nowhere. Debate differs from argument. The orator who silences his opponent rarely uses adequate argument. Against the plea for fear as an essential deterrent against sin, Marcion simply shook his head and said 'Absit'; he was silent but not convinced. Third, theologians and other exponents of rational argument commonly make a few bad mistakes. By far the best example is Augustine, who dominated a culture for a thousand years, and whose argument for the liquidation of schismatics through the severity of love[12] is only matched, for unconvincing barbarity, by his accounts of predestination and original sin. These three dangers make an exploration of Tertullian's arguments obligatory.

INTRICATE APOLOGETIC

Tertullian's defence of simplicity will always have a twist of paradox, and qualifications of fundamental force. There are his own deep conflicts. How complicated was he? One writer[13] produced a book to probe the disorder of his personality, another composed a large tome to show the perversity of his ethics.[14] Many have followed the verdict that he is a troubled fideist.[15]

More disconcerting is the praise of his admirers. Even a sober scholar could write: 'Roman restraint, legal clarity and military discipline were transmuted into an intellectual and moral force in the ardent, aspiring mind and heart of Tertullian.'[16] Enthusiasm gallops away with another:

Ardent in temperament, endowed with an intelligence as subtle and original as it was aggressive and audacious, he added to his natural gifts a

---

[11] Gerhard Ebeling often set out his lectures in numbered chapters, sections, paragraphs and even propositions. When he once came to chapter 4, section 3, paragraph 5, proposition 2, he paused and said with a smile, 'Entschuldigen Sie, bitte, wenn ich alles zu einfach mache!'

[12] *On the Epistle of John*, 7.8. See my, *Ethical patterns in early Christian thought* (Cambridge, 1976), 179–81.

[13] B. Nisters, *Tertullian, seine Persönlichkeit und sein Schicksal* (Münster, 1950).

[14] C. Rambaux, *Tertullien face aux morales des trois premiers siècles* (Paris, 1979).

[15] See following chapters for discussion of A. Labhardt, Tertullien et la philosophie ou la recherche d'une 'position pure', *MH*, 7 (1950), 159–80.

[16] H. von Campenhausen, *The fathers of the Latin church* (London, 1964), 6.

profound erudition, which far from impeding only gave weight to the movements of his alert and robust mind... Harassed from without, the African Church was also torn from within by an accumulation of evils; apostasies, heresies, and schisms abounded. Up through the confusion were thrust Tertullian's mighty shoulders, casting off the enemies of the Gospel on every side. He was not formed for defensive warfare.[17]

It is regrettable that some scholars want to award prizes rather than to understand what is alien to them.

A recent and restrained assessment, which touches lightly on the ideas of Tertullian in favour of his history and his literary achievement, calls him a 'Christian Sophist'.[18] This is helpful, but uncomfortably ambiguous, since Tertullian spent much time attacking and repudiating what is commonly regarded as sophistry.

How complex is Tertullian? There is no lack of intricate argument, however forcefully it may be presented; worse still, in the interests of simplicity and speed, steps are often omitted and details which have appeared earlier are not repeated. We might call this 'Tertullian's Trick'; because often, when we think we have found a fallacy and caught him out, we find that he has answered our objection elsewhere. A good orator does not repeat detail. For his interpreters today, this should be less of a difficulty after fifty years of philosophical analysis; but some still look for systems and the fun of deconstructing them. Many manage to ignore the truth that conclusions are ambiguous without the argument which leads to them. In order to understand an author we must remember the cards he has already played.

To a remarkable extent, Tertullian respected conventional rhetorical forms which made his work more accessible to his contemporaries.[19] Tertullian faced a complex situation, where the culture of Greece and Rome, the religion of Israel and the new faith in Jesus came together in a mixture of conflict and agreement. Each component had internal diversity within which Tertullian had to choose. A critical eclecticism was characteristic of all parties. The importance of Tertullian for cultural history is immense, and

---

[17] B. B. Warfield, *Studies in Tertullian and Augustine* (Oxford, 1930), 3f.

[18] T. D. Barnes, *Tertullian, A historical and literary study*, 2nd edn (Oxford, 1985), 211–32.

[19] See R. D. Sider, *Ancient rhetoric and the art of Tertullian* (Oxford, 1971), and the work of C. Munier, J.-C. Fredouille and H. Steiner who sees this valuable area of study as 'wohl erschöpft'.

he may rightly be called the 'first theologian of the West', provided this does not limit his influence to the West or obscure his massive debt to Irenaeus.[20] Justin had anticipated him, by his move to Rome, and it is remarkable how much had been achieved. But Justin still writes in Greek and his ideas are difficult because undeveloped. His interest is that of an originator whose ideas are taken up and developed by others who add, alter and diverge. As a result, his own meaning is frequently uncertain.

Tertullian's achievement was not merely cultural and linguistic, but above all intellectual. For, 'despite his obvious originality, he displays those characteristics which are to be found throughout Latin Christianity: a realism which knows nothing of the Platonist devaluation of matter; a subjectivity, which gives special prominence to inner experience; and a pessimism which lays more stress on the experience of sin than on transfiguration'.[21]

Tertullian believed in change. Plato gave place to Heraclitus and the Stoics. The way up is the way down. All things change and all things renew themselves. Nothing ends except to begin again (*res.* 12). While Clement, for all his delight in Heraclitus, looked beyond the world of material things to Plato's intellectual realities (*strom.* 6.1), Tertullian saw reality in flesh and matter, and found truth in an unending series of paradoxes.

He began as an apologist and apologetic displays the contingency of theology and philosophy.[22] It begins from a faith to which objections are made by opponents or experiences of widely diverse kinds. Faith's defender must answer the several objections of A, B, C and D, with groups of arguments. Against A he must prove αβγ, against B he must prove αδεζ, against C he must prove γηθ and against D he must prove ικλμ. Now in at least some instances, α will conflict with λ, γ with κ, ζ with θ, and so on. Romans will not like his higher loyalty to Christ, radical Christians will not like his political conformism, some will find him too indulgent and others will find him too ascetic; either they will not dance when they hear

---

[20] Note the necessary qualification of G. L. Prestige, *God in patristic thought* (London, 1936), 97: 'He was very far, indeed, from being merely the father of Latin theology. His ultimate influence on Greek theological speculation was probably very considerable.'

[21] J. Daniélou, *Latin Christianity*, 341.

[22] See D. Allen, Motives, rationales, and religious beliefs, *APQ*, 3 (1966), 112ff., for a useful account of the logic of objection and rebuttal.

the pipes or they will not lament with those who mourn. When the Baptist neither eats nor drinks, he is demonic and when Jesus eats and drinks he is a glutton and a winebibber (Matt. 11.16–19).

However consistent the position of the apologist is, it will not appear consistent until there has been careful analysis and then it may look too complex.

They live in countries of their own, but simply as sojourners; they share the life of citizens, they endure the lot of foreigners; every foreign land is to them a fatherland, and every fatherland a foreign land. They marry like the rest of the world. They breed children, but they do not cast their offspring adrift. They eat together but do not sleep together. They exist in the flesh, but they live not after the flesh. They spend their existence upon earth, but their citizenship is in heaven. They obey the established laws, and in their own lives they surpass the laws... The Jews war against them as aliens, and the Greeks persecute them.[23]

To meet apparent inconsistencies, like Tertullian's denigration and exaltation of marriage and philosophy, apologetic needs linking argument (for which it may not have enough time) as well as a few general concepts (economy of salvation, logos) which maintain a scattered presence.[24] Tertullian goes further, so that these concepts embrace fundamental questions of theology. The remarkable thing is that, for all his vehemence, his ideas do hold together. He had a deep, abiding concern. As a Stoic, he began with an undefined consciousness of God.[25] As a Christian, he filled that concept with the gospel, the story of salvation which ran from creation to apocalypse. The golden thread which runs through his thought is the recapitulation of all things in Christ.

Apologetic presents an extreme case of the tensions faced by all philosophy and theology. Today, theologians are reluctant to distinguish historical from systematic theology because every theology is marked by its historical situation and specific questions. This move is mirrored in a wider reaction against the scientific

---

[23] *Ad Diognetum*, 5.
[24] A recent writer calls this 'polemical Christianity'. (A. J. Guerra, Polemical Christianity: Tertullian's search for certainty, *The Second Century* (1990), 108). He points out that Tertullian draws on five kinds of support for his position (scripture, reason, moral excellence, spiritual witness and tradition) and that he uses different combinations when he attacks different enemies.
[25] In modern jargon, 'a God-shaped blank'.

positivism which was the last gesture of Enlightenment epistemology. In a wide-ranging review of the human sciences, we find one common feature: 'a willingness to emphasise the local and contingent, a desire to underline the extent to which our own concepts and attitudes have been shaped by particular historical circumstances, and a correspondingly strong dislike – amounting almost to hatred in the case of Wittgenstein – of all overarching theories and singular schemes of explanation'.[26] An apologist, like Tertullian, is more likely to be understood in such an intellectual climate. For we have all learnt that within the most carefully argued and tidy system, there are polarities and contradictions which cannot be ignored. What Gödel showed for mathematics (that there is no self-sufficient, consistent autonomy) seems true of all rational systems.

What did Tertullian write? His many writings show the range of his apologetic.[27] In 197, he exhorts the martyrs (*mart.*), confronting the major challenge to faith which was the suffering of God's faithful people and defending the faith before a persecuting state (*nat.*, *ap.*). Between 198 and 206, he argues that faith is natural (*test.*), he confronts the Jewish attack (*Jud.*) – the gospel had come to Carthage through Jewish Christians. The threat of heresy is met with a general response and a statement of the essential rule of Christian faith (*praescr.*). One well-argued alternative, the dualism of Hermogenes (*Herm.*) is dissected, analysed and refuted. The public behaviour of Christians is rigorously directed away from attendance at games (*spect.*), frequency of marriage (*ux.*) and fine clothing (*cult.*). Prayer (*or.*) and baptism (*bapt.*) explain matters of devotion and worship. Patience (*pat.*) is a private virtue while penitence (*paen.*) has both private and public consequences.

During his middle period (207–8) when signs of Montanist[28] influence begin to appear, substantial works are directed against heretical dualism. The work *Against Marcion* (*Marc.*)[29] owes its present form to this period, but builds on earlier work. Valentinians are attacked both in the short work which bears their name

---

[26] Quentin Skinner, *The return of grand theory to the human sciences* (Cambridge, 1985), 12.

[27] On the chronology of Tertullian's works, I accept the argument and conclusions of R. Braun, *Deus Christianorum*, 563–77.

[28] See below, ch. 10.   [29] See below, ch. 5.

(*Val.*) and in the anti-docetic works which defend the flesh (*carn.*, *res.*). Chastity (*cast.*) and modest dress (*virg.*) continue the ascetic strain of ethics while the hostility of the state to Christians is further considered (*cor.*, *scorp.*) and a particular oppressor is challenged (*Scap.*). Idolatry is condemned as false and the source of all evil (*idol.*) and the nature of the soul is examined (*an.*).

During the final period of his writing (213–22), Tertullian is plainly at odds with catholic, 'psychic' (unspiritual)[30] Christianity. Rigorous ethical demands are expressed in the rejection of flight during persecution (*fug.*) and remarriage (*mon.*), and the commendation of fasting (*iei.*) and modesty (*pud.*). His attack on Praxeas defends the distinction of persons within the trinity and the distinction of substances within the incarnate Christ (*Prax.*). Yet the chains of secular culture retain their subordinate place below the 'better philosophy' (*pall.*).

Tertullian's one central idea (the economy of salvation perfected in Christ) runs from his *apologeticum* to the better philosophy (*pall.*) and his theology of trinity and incarnation (*Prax.*). This provides internal unity to his thought, within all complexity. It is the constant factor. Montanism is the result, not the cause, of Tertullian's concern for the perfection of the divine economy.

Tertullian has two external controls on the complexities of apologetic and theology: brevity and paradox. Brevity had been claimed as a Christian virtue from the beginning (1 Tim. 1.3f.). Justin (*1 apol.* 14) took the brevity of Christ's sayings as proof he was not a sophist, and Irenaeus contrasted the short word of the gospel with the long-winded law. Sextus (*sent.* 430) linked brevity with the knowledge of God. For Tertullian, truth and brevity (*Marc.* 2.28.3), certainty and brevity (*an.* 2.7) go together. The Lord's Prayer is a compendium of the whole gospel (*or.* 9.1). Conciseness is a welcome necessity; prolixity is a bore (*virg.* 4.4). On this theme scripture, especially the Wisdom literature, and Stoic tradition coincided.[31] We have already noted some reasons for brevity. As an orator and a preacher, Tertullian leaves a lot out, so that he will not lose his

---

[30] The term is taken from Paul (1 Cor. 2.14; 15.44–6) where ψυχικός is contrasted with πνευματικός.

[31] J.-C. Fredouille, *Tertullien et la conversion de la culture antique*, 33, notes Zeno (D.L. 7.59), Cicero, Seneca (*ep.* 38), Tacitus and Marcus Aurelius (*med.* 4.51).

audience. As a Stoic and a follower of Paul, he accepts paradox as a common means of ordering truth. Indeed there is a primal paradox. 'Truth and hatred of truth come into our world together. As soon as truth appears, it is the enemy' (*ap.* 7.3).

We return to his simplicity. Tertullian was himself, not a Christian Cicero. Seneca is often one of us (*saepe noster*); we are never his. A Christian builds his faith on his own foundation, not that of another (*an.* 26.1). Christ was not mistaken when he solemnly entrusted the proclamation of his gospel to simple fishermen instead of skilful sophists (*an.* 3.3). As his follower, Tertullian rejoices in the mere name of Christian and the message of the little fishes: 'Jesus Christ, son of God, saviour'. A simple criterion governs the Christian's logic. Confronted by exuberance of words and ideas, he applies a constant criterion of truth. In contrast, Marcion loves uncertainty, and prefers it to the certainty of the rule of faith. 'Now if to your plea, which itself remains uncertain, there be applied further proofs derived from uncertainties, we shall be caught up in such a chain of questions, which depend on our discussion of these equally uncertain proofs and whose uncertainty will endanger faith, so that we shall slide into those insoluble questions which the apostle dislikes' (*Marc.* 1.9.7). In opposition Tertullian insists 'I shall therefore insist, with complete confidence that he is no God who is today uncertain, because until now he has been unknown; because as soon as it is agreed that God exists, from this very fact it follows that he never has been unknown, and therefore never uncertain' (*Marc.* 1.9.10).

DIVINE UNICITY[32]

The first question of early Christian theology was: is there one God, good and true, who is creator of this world of sin and evil? For Tertullian, God's own simple unity is ultimate. 'God is not God if he be not one' (*Marc.* 1.3.1). He holds the universe in his hand like a bird's nest. Heaven is his throne and earth is his footstool (*Marc.* 2.25.2). However, because he is found through faith in Jesus, he does not conform to ultimate Neoplatonic simplicity. We shall see

---

[32] This word, popular among French theologians, is useful to express Tertullian's claim concerning the unity and uniqueness of God.

that, for Tertullian as for other second-century theologians, the way to one God is through the son and the spirit.[33]

Marcion is equally convinced about God's unicity, which he places above the duality of creation and redemption, and claims: 'One single work is sufficient for our god; he has liberated man by his supreme and most excellent goodness, which is of greater value than all destructive insects' (*Marc.* 1.17.1).[34] But Marcion, says Tertullian, is a great muddler and his higher god has produced nothing which might give ground for believing in his existence. How can he be superior when he can show no work to compare with, for example, the human being produced by the inferior god? The question 'does this god exist?' is answered from what he has done and the question 'what is this god like?' is determined by the quality of his work. Marcion's uncreative god does not pass the first test, so the second does not apply.

In the alleged interests of unity, Marcion multiplies. He may begin from two gods, but he finishes with many more and his account is far from simple.

So you have three substances of deity in the higher regions, and in the lower regions four. When to these are added their own Christs – one who has appeared in the time of Tiberius, another who is promised by the creator – Marcion is obviously being robbed by those persons who assume that he postulates two gods, when he implies that there are nine, even if he does not know it. (*Marc.* 1.15.6)

Here Tertullian is drawing his own polemical conclusions from Marcion's views and does not help his case; but there is more than caricature because, once mediators are introduced, multiplication sets in.[35]

There are also historical confusions for Marcion. His god turned up at his destined time, because of certain astrological complexities, which Marcionites enjoy, even if the stars were made by the lesser god; for the greater god may have been held back by the

---

[33] Clement of Alexandria solved this problem with his thematic statement that negative theology must pass through the μέγεθος τοῦ χριστοῦ (*strom.* 5.11.71). See also G. L. Prestige's account of Tertullian's 'organic monotheism', *God in patristic thought*, 98f.

[34] Which, for Marcion, deny the perfect goodness of their maker.

[35] See below, ch. 5 for the problem of polemic and ch. 9 for a discussion of Valentinianism and the bureaucratic fallacy.

rising moon, or some witchery, or by the position of Saturn or Mars (*Marc.* 1.18.1). Whatever the delay, he glided down in the fifteenth year of Tiberius, to be a saving spirit. Yet the pest-laden wind of his salvation did not begin to blow until some year in the reign of Antoninus Pius. This delay implies difference and confusion. For from Tiberius to Antoninus Pius, 115 years and $6\frac{1}{2}$ months elapsed; the god whom Marcion then introduced cannot be the god whom Christ revealed, for the interim between Christ and Marcion rules out identity.

Beyond this confusion lie Marcion's great dichotomies – the antitheses of law and gospel, creation and salvation – which run from beginning to end (*Marc.* 1.19.4). Marcion's god could not have been revealed by Christ who came before Marcion introduced the division between two gods. Yet Marcion claims that he restored a rule of faith which had been corrupted, over all those intervening years; Tertullian wonders at the patience of Christ who waited so long for Marcion to deliver him (*Marc.* 1.20.1).

This argument suggests again the cost of simplicity and the apparent naïveté of Tertullian in the interests of apologetic. By itself, the argument has no force whatever. Marcion claimed that he was a reformer who went back to the original gospel and apostle.[36] However, Tertullian makes the argument respectable by referring to Paul (in Galatians) who was not commending another god and another Christ, but attributing the annulment of the old dispensation to the creator himself who (through Isaiah and Jeremiah) had declared the intention that he would do something new and make a new covenant. Later, by exact examination of the prophets (*Marc.* 3), Luke's Gospel (*Marc.* 4) and Paul (*Marc.* 5), he shows that the evidence for Marcion's primitive gospel is not to be found.[37] Tertullian further states that the first Christians were certain about God the creator and about his Christ, while they argued about almost everything else, and that certainty continues in all apostolic churches. This argument is sound, since Marcionites could not point to a particular ancient church which followed their teaching (*Marc.* 1.21.3).

[36] Tertullian's argument is used today, at a popular level, by Orthodox against Roman Catholics and by Roman Catholics against Protestants.
[37] This is an example of Tertullian's Trick: omitting steps which he mentions elsewhere.

Divine simplicity has no vulgar fractions. God is eternal, rational and perfect; his salvation is universal, whereas Marcion's God leaves out Jews and Christians because they belong to the creator. More importantly, because he saves only souls and not bodies, the strange god never provides more than a 'semi-salvation'. Surely a god of perfect goodness could save the whole of man? 'Wholly damned by the creator, he should have been wholly restored by the god of sovereign goodness' (*Marc.* 1.24.4). Marcion's god cannot do anything to protect his believers from the malignant power of the creator, as it works through everything from thunder, war and plague to creeping, crawling insects. 'Just how do you think you are emancipated from his kingdom when his flies still creep over your face? ... You profess a God who is purely and simply good; however you cannot prove the perfect goodness of him who does not perfectly set you free' (*Marc.* 1.24.7).

There are now perverse and muddled objections made against the almighty God, lord and founder of the universe,[38] who 'has been known from the beginning, has never hidden himself, has shone in constant splendor, even before Romulus and long before Tiberius' (*Marc.* 2.2.1) The riches of his wisdom and knowledge are deep, his judgements are unsearchable and his ways past finding out (Rom. 11.34); therefore his simplicity will not be evident to the natural man, who cannot receive the things of the spirit. 'And so God is supremely great just when man thinks he is small, God is supremely best just when man thinks him not good, he is especially one when man thinks there are two gods or more' (*Marc.* 2.2.6). Innocence and understanding have gone, for man 'has lost the grace of paradise, and that intimacy with God, by which, had he obeyed, he would have known all the things of God' (*Marc.* 2.2.6).

Indeed, simplicity marked creation, for all came from and was marked by the one goodness of God (*Marc.* 2.4.6). The gift of freedom was part of this goodness and it was never revoked. Otherwise Marcion would protest 'What sort of lord is this ineffective, instable, faithless being who rescinds his own decisions?' (*Marc.* 2.7.3) None of these negative epithets should ever be applied to the unmixed goodness of God.

---

[38] 'deus omnipotens, dominus et conditor universitatis'.

The same simplicity marks his providence which dispenses light and darkness, good and evil. But how can this fail to compromise his simple goodness? Because the evil which he dispenses is a punishment for sin and therefore good (*Marc.* 2.14.3).

Is there a simple gospel? Such simplicity may be hard to see; but it is there to be found, as indeed in the different Gospels of the apostles, John and Matthew, and of the apostolic men, Luke and Mark. All follow the same rule of one creator God and his Christ, born of a virgin, fulfilling law and prophets. 'It does not matter if there be some variation in the arrangement of their narratives, provided that there is agreement in the substance of the faith' (*Marc.* 4.2.2). Marcion's mutilated Gospel subverts the substance of the gospel. It bears no name, for he stopped short of inventing a title. No written work should be recognized if it cannot hold its head erect, offer some consistency and promise some credibility by naming a title and an author.

Truth is to be distinguished by its simplicity, with which proud men fuss and fiddle, so mixing it with falsehood that nothing certain remains. 'When they had found a simple and straightforward God, they began to disagree about him, not as he had been revealed to them, but in order to debate about his properties, his nature, his place' (*ap.* 47.5). Some say he is physical, others incorporeal, some that he is made of atoms, others that he consists of numbers. Some claim he governs the world, perhaps from inside or perhaps from outside, others declare that he is idle. Such confusion is not primitive but contrived, not ancient wisdom but modern muddle. There is nothing as old as the truth of the scriptures which philosophers have perverted in every possible way.

Yet Christians wear the cloak of the philosopher, because of its simplicity and because they have found the better philosophy (*pall.* 6). The toga may offer higher status in the community; but it is an elaborate thing of many folds (*pall.* 1.1). While everything changes, not all change is good. Primitive simplicity is challenged by luxury. It was a bad day when Alexander, on fire with his triumph over the Persians, exchanged his armour for a pair of puffed-up, Persian trousers, made of silk. When philosophers move into purple, what is to stop them from wearing golden slippers (*pall.* 4.7)? What could be less philosophical than that?

The change to the philosopher's cloak is justified by its simplicity as a garment, in contrast to the many folds of the toga which are a cumbersome nuisance (*pall.* 5.1). The cloak is the most convenient garment and saves time in dressing (*pall.* 5.3). Further, it designates independence and freedom from the duties of forum, elections, senate, platforms and every other part of public life. It wears out no seats, attacks no laws, argues no pleas, is worn by no judge, soldier or king. 'I have seceded from the community. My sole business is with myself and my one care is not to care.' When accused of laziness, it replies, 'No one is born for another, and he dies for himself alone' (*pall.* 5.4). Simplicity of detachment is achieved because the philosophers' cloak has become Christian and found the better philosophy (*pall.* 6.2) in Jesus Christ, son of God and saviour. So the law of change is justified. We cannot avoid change; we should ensure that it is change to the good.[39]

PERFECTION IN DISHONOUR: 'JESUS CHRIST, SON OF GOD, SAVIOUR'

The answer to the question about one God, good and true, was: 'Yes there is one God, if he not only created the world, but also acted to renew it in Jesus Christ.' God's utter disgrace was the pledge of mankind's salvation. God came to man's level, so that man might reach God's level. God became small that man might become great (*Marc.* 2.27.7).

Simplicity was not empty. All was summed up in Christ. Following Paul, Tertullian (*pud.* 14 et passim) knew nothing but Christ and him crucified. This was the sole hope (*unica spes*) of the world, the necessary dishonour (*necessarium dedecus*) of faith (*carn.* 5.3). In a word, God is one God, when the son hands over the kingdom to the father.

Behind the fish ('Jesus Christ, son of God, saviour')[40] lay the even simpler confession of Jesus as Messiah or Christ (Matt. 27.17, 22; John 1.41; Acts 9.22; 1 John 5.1). When the gospel moved from its

---

[39] This is the point where Tertullian and Stoics differ markedly from Alexandrians and Platonists.

[40] See F. J. Dölger, ΙΧΘΥΣ der heilige Fisch in den antiken Religionen und im Christentum (Münster, 1922).

Jewish context into the Greek world, this title meant less and 'Christ' became a surname for Jesus. The basic confession then became 'Jesus Christ is Lord' (parallel to the 'Emperor is Lord' of the imperial cult)[41] or 'Jesus Christ is son of God'. Christians had their own answer to pagan and Jewish acclamations, such as 'one is Zeus-Serapis', 'great is Diana of the Ephesians', or even 'Hear O Israel...'. This simple formula was used as a confession of faith at baptism, being expanded first into a twofold faith in father and son, then into a threefold faith in father, son and spirit, and receiving various supplements. The simplicity of the fish remained. There was one lord, one faith, one baptism.

'Jesus Christ, son of God, saviour' points to the economy of salvation and the recapitulation of all things in Christ, who is Christus Victor.[42] Recapitulation is chiefly linked with Irenaeus;[43] but it also dominates the New Testament and the theology of Ignatius, Justin, Clement of Alexandria, Tertullian and Athanasius. It includes three sets of motifs: Christ corrects and perfects all that is; as Christus Victor he is the climax of the economy of saving history; and as the perfection of being, goodness and truth, he gives life to the dying, righteousness to sinners and truth to those in error.

Tertullian describes the work of salvation as continuous with creation.[44] The human race is summed up, 'that is to refer back to

---

[41] *mart. Pol.* 8.2.

[42] Because the concept of salvation easily becomes too subjective, 'victor' is often to be preferred as a translation of σωτήρ (*TWNT* VII, 1,005–24). In the Old Testament, salvation points to the rescue of those oppressed by military power or injustice; because of human limitations, God emerges as the ultimate deliverer. In the New Testament, the same notion of rescue is found in God's relation to the whole human race. In the classical world, saviours could be gods, men who helped or healed, philosophers, statesmen or rulers. Hadrian is frequently celebrated as the saviour of a town or a person. On a wider scale, the emperor brought in, as saviour, the golden age. Philo gives the title of saviour to God who delivers his people, preserves the world, and liberates the soul from passion (*sobr.* 55; *immut.* 129; *somn.* 1.112; *leg. all.* 11.105).

The message of the angels to the shepherds (Luke 2.10f.) links the titles 'saviour' and 'lord'. In the Fourth Gospel, the son is seen as the saviour of the world (John 3.17; cf. 1 John. 4.14). In the New Testament, the title of 'saviour' is found less frequently than the verb 'save' and the noun 'salvation'. This may be a reaction against Jewish expectations of a national deliverer (*TWNT* VII, 1,021). The Pastoral Epistles find the title important for the rejection of heretical claims.

[43] G. Aulen, *Christus Victor* (London, 1953), 32–51.

[44] A. Viciano, *Cristo salvador y liberador del hombre* (Pamplona, 1986), 269–350.

the beginning or to revise from the beginning' (*Marc.* 5.17.1), reformed (*Marc.* 3.9.5) and restored (*pat.* 15.1).[45] Redemption through a ransom paid (*fug.* 12.2f.) leads to liberty (*carn.* 14.3).[46] Christ as mediator (*sequester, res.* 51.2) is clothed with humanity (*Prax.* 12.3) and reconciles (*Marc.* 5.19.5) man to God.[47] The sacrifice of Christ, the paschal lamb, is offered by the great high priest (*Jud.* 14.8). His voluntary death is a propitiation but not a vicarious satisfaction for sin.[48] As teacher, Christ brings illumination through saving discipline (*ap.* 47.11; *pat.* 12.4) and a better philosophy (*pall.* 6.2).[49] As divine physician, he heals sinners (*scorp.* 5.8).[50] By his descent to hell, he has restored (*an.* 55.1f.) patriarchs and prophets.

Finally, by the trophy of the cross, he has triumphed over death, the last enemy (*Marc.* 4.20.5). His victory is not that of the warrior Messiah for whom the Jews had looked (*Jud.* 9.1–20), but is the spiritual overthrow of the armies of wickedness (*Marc.* 4.20–4). This salvation was also a new creation (*iei.* 14.2; *Marc.* 5.12.6).[51]

The saving victory of Jesus began as his fulfilment of Jewish prophecies, within the saving history or οἰκονομία. Why did the gospel come so late in human history? The answer lay in the plan of God's saving economy or dispensation which prepared the way for and found its climax in the victory of Christ who overthrew the powers of darkness. For apocalyptic dwelt on cosmic triumph as well as on fulfilment of prophetic hope. Jesus reigned as the son of God over all created things and every power in heaven and on earth. Devils fled in fear before his name.

To Jews, therefore, Tertullian's answer is direct. There is only one question: whether Christ, announced by the prophets as the object of universal faith, has, or has not, come (*Jud.* 7.1). The proof is plain in the rapid, universal spread of the gospel.[52] It is evident that[53] no gate or city is closed to him, his sound is gone out into all the earth, gates of brass are opened and he reigns over all.

But Christ's name reaches out everywhere, is believed everywhere, is worshipped by all the nations we have listed, rules everywhere, is

---

[45] *Ibid.*, 118–23.　　[46] *Ibid.*, 126–9.　　[47] *Ibid.*, 129–33.　　[48] *Ibid.*, 133–8 and 318–20.
[49] *Ibid.*, 138–40.　　[50] *Ibid.*, 141–3.　　[51] *Ibid.*, 341–50.
[52] 'Die Kirchengeschichte ist eine Siegesgeschichte des Christenthums'. G. Leonhardi, *Die apologetischen Grundgedanken Tertullians* (Leipzig, 1882), 7. It was indeed the universal character of Christianity which brought it into conflict with the state.
[53] Tertullian misquotes Isa. 45.1, reading *Kurios* for Cyrus.

everywhere adored, is bestowed equally everywhere upon all; in his presence no king receives more favour, no barbarian receives less joy; no dignities or families merit special distinction; to all he is equal, to all king, to all judge, to all 'God and lord'. Nor might you hesitate to believe what we assert, since you see it actually happening. (*Jud.* 7.9–8.1).

Christ is the bull who, in fulfilment of Joseph's blessing,[54] tosses the nations to the ends of the earth, on the horns of his cross, which was also foretold in the outstretched hands of Moses (Exod. 17.8–16). How else can we explain the peculiar position of Moses, as he sat with arms outstretched, rather than kneeling or prostrate on the earth, unless it be that the name of Jesus was his theme? Jesus would one day engage the devil in single combat and conquer by the sign of the cross (*Jud.* 10.1). He is the God who reigns from the tree,[55] who came once in humility and will come again with glory (*Jud.* 10.12). Death reigned from Adam to Christ who concluded the rule of death by dying on the tree of the cross. The government is on his shoulder. No other king rules in this way. 'But only the new king of the new ages, Christ Jesus, has carried on his shoulder the dominion and majesty of his new glory, which is the cross' (*Marc.* 3.19.3).

The victory of Christ is strongly affirmed in demilitarized military terms. For he who straps his sword on his thigh is fairer than the children of men and grace pours from his lips. He who so rides in majesty, rides in meekness and righteousness, which are not the 'proper business of battles' (Ps. 45.2–4). His strange warfare of the word invades every nation, bringing all to faith, and ruling by his victory over death (*Marc.* 3.14.6).

Christ conquers as a human being, when his obedience triumphs over the same devil before whom Adam fell (*Marc.* 2.8.3). This second conflict was all the more painful to the devil because he had won the first contest, and was all the sweeter to the man who, by a victory, recovered his salvation, a more glorious paradise and the fruit of the tree of life (*Marc.* 2.10.6).

---

[54] Deut. 33.17. Moses gives this blessing to Joseph.

[55] Ps. 96.10 is often so quoted in early Christian writing; no adequate reason has been found for the reading. See E. F. Osborn, *Justin Martyr* (Tübingen, 1973), 103–5, and J. H. Charlesworth, Christian and Jewish self-definition in light of the Christian additions to the Apocryphal writings, in E. P. Sanders *et al.* (eds.), *Jewish and Christian self-definition*, vol. II, *Aspects of Judaism in the Graeco-Roman period* (London, 1981), 27–55.

'O Christ even in your novelties you are old!' (*Marc.* 4.21.5)
Incidents in the mission of the disciples (the feeding of the multitude,
the confession of Peter, being ashamed of Christ) show him to be the
Christ of the creator (*Marc.* 4.21.5). All Christ's words and deeds,
even his resurrection, point back to the prophets (*Marc.* 4.43.9). All
that Christ did was part of a continuous saving economy, which God
began immediately after the fall of Adam. His goodness now took
the form of justice, severity and even, as the Marcionites claim,
cruelty. 'Thus God's goodness was prior and according to nature,
his severity came later and for a reason. The one was innate, the
other accidental; the one his own, the other adapted; the one freely
flowing, the other admitted as an expedient' (*Marc.* 2.11.2). There is
unbroken continuity in God's goodness which, since the fall, has had
an opposition with which to contend. Spontaneous goodness is
replaced by justice which is the agent (*procuratio*) of goodness.
Goodness needed a new means to contend with its adversary and
fear of punishment was the only effective way (*Marc.* 2.13.2).

While he reforms rather than destroys, and restores rather than
abolishes (*Marc.* 2.29.3), there is change and correction. In the place
of an eye for an eye and a tooth for a tooth, he offers a cheek for a
cheek, with the difference that it is the second cheek of the victim
rather than the cheek of the aggressor which is struck (*Marc.* 4.16.4);
this kind of imaginative paradox is typical of Tertullian. This
brilliant example is emblematic of the recapitulation which both
fulfils and corrects.

Recapitulation is both retrospective and prospective, both
fulfilment of the past and promise of the future. Because of his
preoccupation with Marcion, Tertullian seems more concerned
with fulfilment than with promise. Furthermore, the miracle of
new life through baptism did not do as much as he hoped. Clement
of Alexandria and Irenaeus celebrate more vividly the present
glory of new life in Christ. In this difference some have seen the
contrast between Greek and Latin Christianity.[56] Yet the disciples
of the new covenant receive a new way to pray from the new grace
of a renewing God (*or.* 1) and Christians believe in one God in a new
way (*Prax.* 3).[57]

[56] See Daniélou, *Latin Christianity*, 341.
[57] And as for Novalis, Easter is 'ein Weltverjüngungsfest'.

The economy would not have been complete until he, to whom it had all been directed, had come. The mass of fulfilled prophecy is too great for anyone to deny. In him we find the sure mercies of David. It is he, not David, who is a witness, prince and commander to the nations, and on whom all nations now call (*Marc.* 3.20.10). His new word is decisive and brief,[58] a compendium which offers relief from the burdensome details of the law. Isaiah foretold new things and Jeremiah a new covenant (*Marc.* 4.1.6). Finally, to those who, in the face of all this evidence, deny the kingdom of Christ, there remains the second coming which will not be in humility, but in power and glory (*Marc.* 3.7.8).

Marcion is wasting his complicated time when he tries to separate the strange, simple goodness of Christ from the alleged evil of the creator (*Marc.* 1.2.3). The first Christians disagreed about almost everything else; but they did not waver from undivided faith in the creator and his Christ (*Marc.* 1.21.3). Even Marcion allows Christ to appear on the mountain with Moses and Elijah, the first who formed God's people and established the old covenant, the second who reformed God's people and consummated[59] the new covenant (*Marc.* 4.22.1). 'He, who made, is best able to remake,[60] seeing that it is a far greater work to make than to remake, to give a beginning than to give it back again' (*res.* 11.10). The wonder of the gospel should not obscure the marvel of creation.

PROBLEMS OF RECAPITULATION

The summing up of all things in Christ, who is Christus Victor, shaped the theology of the first three centuries. It has persisted since then, in varying form, whether it be in the Eucharist of eastern and western churches or in hymns like *Vexilla regis prodeunt* and *Ein' feste Burg* or in the Easter liturgy of every tradition. Its place in the Latin Mass, in the Greek *Christos Niketes* and in the Lutheran tradition[61] is equally secure. It found its strongest statement in

[58] See The short word, in Osborn, *Beginning of Christian philosophy*, 206–40.
[59] Elijah is an eschatological figure who came as John the Baptist.
[60] As so often, Augustine takes up Tertullian's ideas, 'qui fecit, refecit'. *Ep.* 231.6. He discards Tertullian's exaggeration of creation's superiority over recreation. Tertullian reverses the priority in *Prax.*
[61] Aulen, *Christus Victor*.

Athanasius' *De Incarnatione* and its difficulties are most apparent in the conclusion of this work.

For as when the sun is up darkness no longer prevails, but if there is any left anywhere it is driven away; so now, when the Divine Manifestation of the Word of God is come, the darkness of the idols prevails no longer, but every part of the whole earth is everywhere illuminated by his teaching . . . and men, looking to the true God, the Word of the Father, abandon idols, and themselves come to a clear knowledge of the true God.

Now this is the proof that Christ is God, the Word and Power of God. For, human things ceasing, and the Word of Christ remaining, it is plain to all that the things which are ceasing are temporary, but that He who remains is God and the true Son of God, the Only-begotten Word. (*de inc.* 55, Bindley trans.)

The triumphal claims of this passage concerning the destruction of evil do not fit reality then or now. There does not appear to have been a change of government. Indeed, from the beginning there were difficulties with recapitulation. Death, despite the sting of martyrdom, may have been destroyed; but sin was still clearly present. Christians were not displaying the climax of divine and human history, for mediocrity spread widely in the early church. Laodiceans were neither hot nor cold, but drastically indigestible (Rev. 3.15f.).[62] Tertullian speaks of *mediocritas nostra* (*paen.* 6.1) and develops a doctrine of original sin.[63]

From such disappointment, two types of perfectionism emerged – apocalyptic and Gnostic. Irenaeus and Tertullian both viewed with sympathy the New Prophecy of the followers of Montanus. Clement of Alexandria gave critical recognition to some elements of Valentinianism. Irenaeus had wonderful millenarian expectations. If all was summed up in Christ, what remained had to be sensational – a thousand branches on every vine and a thousand grapes on every twig. Lions normally eat only the best of animal steaks.[64] Yet in the last days, says Irenaeus, we know from the scriptures that lions will eat straw. They cannot

---

[62] Today it is claimed that 'unambitious mediocrity is of course part of the Anglo-Saxon tradition' (Iris Murdoch, *The sovereignty of good* (London, 1970), 50), and the arguments against enthusiasm in National Socialism and Islamic Fundamentalism are overwhelming.

[63] See below, ch. 8.

[64] They would not be interested in the contemporary Cheeseburger.

eat the lambs with whom they lie down. If the straw is so good as to be attractive to lions, we shall truly feast on what is provided for us.

The perfectionist movement known as Gnosticism was not confined to Christianity. The desire to surpass (*supergredi*) others is always widespread; to the question 'What must I do to be saved?' is added the question 'What must I do to be a better Jew or Christian, than my neighbour?' Gnosticism is a complex movement. Tertullian saw that its final strength and weakness lay in its claim to surpass reason. Like all theosophy, Gnosticism presents philosophy without argument, which is like opera without music, Shakespeare without words and ballet without movement. Complex argument can be replaced by pretentious narrative. The Gnostic reply is always that his critic is shallow (not profound) or even intellectually and morally depraved.[65] The relevance of Gnosticism for Tertullian is first, its reaction against mediocrity in favour of perfection and second, its movement from argument to story. Unlike Clement of Alexandria, he neither appreciated its abstract tendency nor offered a higher competitive gnosis.

Perfectionism had emerged as a problem very early in Christian history. The Letter to the Ephesians affirmed strongly that all has been summed up in Christ and that the church is the eschatological miracle which rises from earth to heaven. There is no way in which this miracle can be surpassed. The believer must simply hold to the one faith within the one body, walk in the light and stand firm in the whole armour of God.

Apologists claimed evidence for finality in the moral excellence of Christian lives and in the spread of the gospel. Such moral excellence was the ground for Justin's conversion, and Tertullian made much of it. He pointed to the chastity and integrity of Christians, the courage of the martyrs and the mutual love of the community. This claim caused his discontent with the church universal. He remained within the community of the church at Carthage;[66] but he certainly expressed dissent. When his bishop offered absolution for the sins of adultery and fornication, Tertullian was outraged, because this controverted his claim that

---

[65] The issue is more complex. See the discussion on Valentinianism, ch. 9, below.
[66] See David Rankin, *Tertullian and the church* (Cambridge, 1995), 41–51.

Christians were eschatological paragons of virtue. Tertullian wrote off the majority of Christians as psychics or carnal, in contrast to the spiritual Christians of whom he was one.

The spread of the gospel was a second proof of recapitulation. We are of yesterday, Tertullian said, but we fill the forums and the towns. We are in every country, growing from seed which is the blood of martyrs. The world, too, is a better place; marshes are drained and roads are better.[67] Theodicy could point to a future consummation in Christ's return and to the present and visible fruits of his triumph. When Christians faced persecution the latter were precious signs. Even persecution, said Justin, showed that the demons (or pagan gods) were fearful. It was different when Christians had gained political power. Christians soon realized that they were not at the *eschaton*.

PERFECTION IN GOD

In a Christian empire theodicy ceased to be the first question, until Augustine faced the end of empire in his *City of God*, and explained why Christians could not expect to win any but the final and decisive test.

While recapitulation of all things in Christ, which dominated the theology of Tertullian, Irenaeus and the early Athanasius, gave way in the fourth century, to christology and trinity, the questions could never be held apart. The first question and answer were 'Is there one God?' and 'Only if the creator has acted to redeem the world in Christ.' The second question 'How can one God be both father and son?' is necessary if God is to be credible. The divine economy has to be within God; it cannot be the detachable plan of a changeable being. The economy of the mystery had been hidden from all ages *in* the God who made all things (*Eph.* 3.9).

Christology moved to the centre. How could God be both father and son? Recapitulation might remove distinctions in God. Tertullian spoke of the entire dishonour of his God; but he attacked the monarchianism of Praxeas for crucifying the father, and proposed a doctrine of trinity. The christological debates were

---

[67] To 'disseminate' with Post-modernists, the camels are running on time.

inevitable. Before they finished, recapitulation no longer had to do with history and Christus Victor, but with the trinity which summed up the divine being.

This was not, as some have thought, a mistake. The history of the councils of the fourth century is no more elevating than the history of councils in any century: 'After Constantine, there is not much that is not humiliating – the long period of dogmatic squabbling while the Empire was falling to pieces; the destruction or loss of most of the irreplaceable treasures of antiquity; the progressive barbarisation of Europe; we need not follow the melancholy record.'[68] Arius did miss the point of the whole early tradition, that faith in one God is only possible if that God redeems the world which he first made; but his lack of perception sparked off a genuine advance. For faith in divine redemption can never rely on fulfilled prophecy, external plan or natural evidences, but only on the being of God.

This profound move is apparent in the theology of Gregory Nazianzus.[69] After the fall of Adam, God corrected and sustained, in diverse ways, the fallen race (*orat.* 38.13.36.325). When it became clear that a stronger medicine was needed, the incarnation provided the peak of God's saving work. The key to salvation is that Christ is God (*orat.* 33.16f.36.236). God is father, son and holy spirit. The full deity of the son must be preserved (*orat.* 33.17.36.236). In the incarnation there is condescension (*orat.* 37.2.36.284f.) and recapitulation (*orat.* 2.23f..35.284f.). God sums up and contains all (*orat.* 38.7.36.317). 'A few drops of blood recreate the whole world and draw men together into a unity' (*orat.* 45.29.36.664). The new Adam is a suffering God (*orat.* 30.1.36.36.104) who overcomes human sin. For Gregory, even where the economy is given pre-eminence, the summing up which is its centre is the triune God. Indeed it is recapitulation which makes God one and perfects human knowledge of the divine.

Tertullian anticipates this move from recapitulation to incarnation and trinity. Christus Victor reflected the prophetic apocalyptic

---

[68] W. R. Inge, *The Platonic tradition in English religious thought* (London, 1926), 111.

[69] See E. F. Osborn, Theology and economy in Gregory the Theologian, in H. C. Brennecke, E. L. Grasmück and C. Markschies (eds.), *Logos, FS for L. Abramowski* (Berlin, 1993), 361–83.

tradition. ἰχθύς declared the Johannine mystery of the word made flesh. This was for Tertullian, the *unica spes*, the *necessarium dedecus*, the *sacramentum oikonomiae*. In the end, the mass of prophetic fulfilment is replaced by this one claim, and by faith in the triune God.

Simplicity and recapitulation, which dominated early Christian theology, including that of Tertullian, found their place in one God, father, son and spirit. Tertullian's ideas persist into the fourth century and indeed into the twentieth century, where a metaphysical poem ends:

> A condition of complete simplicity
> (Costing not less than everything)
> And all shall be well and
> All manner of thing shall be well
> When the tongues of flame are in-folded
> Into the crowned knot of fire
> And the fire and the rose are one.[70]

[70] T. S. Eliot, *Four Quartets* (London, 1944), 44. Note also p. 33:

> Here the impossible union
> Of spheres of existence is actual,
> Here the past and future
> Are conquered, and reconciled.

CHAPTER 2

The puzzle: Athens and Jerusalem

Before a detailed study of Tertullian's arguments may proceed, it is wise to consider his reputation as the enemy of argument and the apostle of unreason.[1] There are two famous passages where Tertullian seems to reject argument and reason: 'What has Athens to do with Jerusalem?' (*praescr.* 7.9) and 'it is credible because inept ... certain because impossible' (*carn.* 5.4). The first is a puzzle because in the Stoic Tertullian Athens has a lot to do with Jerusalem; the second is a paradox because credibility and ineptness, certainty and impossibility are opposites. These two claims have become slogans in fideist alternatives to the Enlightenment where they have each acquired a meaning which is foreign to Tertullian. Analysis of Tertullian's text will show that both puzzle and paradox make good sense, and that Tertullian's explicit claim to follow the discipline of reason (*disciplina rationis*) and his demand 'here again I must have reasons' are amply justified. The first may be called 'the puzzle' and the second 'the paradox'. Tertullian has countless paradoxes but this one is celebrated.

One by one the common opinions concerning Tertullian have fallen. Barnes[2] has shown the improbability of his being the jurist Tertullian, the son of a centurion, or a priest. Hallonsten[3] has shown that his accounts of satisfaction and merit do not anticipate later legalism. Rankin has challenged the view that he was a schismatic.[4] It is equally necessary to show that Tertullian was not a

---

[1] This will involve examination of his critics as well as of his text.
[2] T. D. Barnes, *Tertullian, A historical and literary study.*
[3] G. Hallonsten, *Satisfactio bei Tertullian* (Malmö, 1984), and *Meritum bei Tertullian* (Malmö, 1985).
[4] Rankin, *Tertullian and the church.*

fideist.[5] Not only did he never say, '*credo quia absurdum*', but he never meant anything like it and never abandoned the claims of Athens upon Jerusalem. This may be achieved by a simple analysis of what he said. Only to the extent that a hearer connects the truth conditions of an uttered sentence with those of many others with which the speaker connects them, and largely agrees with the speaker about whether those truth conditions are satisfied, will he understand what the speaker says.[6]

Tertullian's question,[7] 'What has Athens to do with Jerusalem?', looks like a rejection of Greek rationalism in favour of unreasoning faith. Yet Tertullian always asks for reasons. Marcion should investigate the origins of his one apostle Paul; for he, Tertullian, also follows Paul as a new disciple. 'For the time being my only belief is that nothing should be rashly believed' (*Marc.* 5.1.1).[8] The most recent perpetrator of the misunderstanding[9] avoids analysis and explicitly interprets Tertullian in terms of thirteenth-century theology and the first Vatican Council. A more puzzling conclusion[10] accepts C. G. Jung's analysis of Tertullian as a paradigm case of *sacrificium intellectus*, 'vollbrachte Selbstverstümmelung' (total and self-inflicted intellectual castration). Tertullian hates dialectic, we are told, but uses it from beginning to end of his work; this can only be explained psychologically. He could not renounce

---

[5] In support of J.-C. Fredouille and others.

[6] I owe this statement of analytic principle to Alan Donagan and Donald Davidson. Donagan (Can anybody in a Post-Christian culture rationally believe the Nicene Creed?) adds 'For the most part, contemporaries speaking or writing the same language do connect sentences in the same ways and do agree about the truth.' T. Flint (ed.), *Christian philosophy* (Notre Dame, 1989), 92–117 (96).

[7] In imitation of Paul, 2 Cor. 6.14–16; 1 Cor. 1.18–25.

[8] To believe any one without examining his origin is certainly rash belief. The only grounds for accepting the Benjamite Paul are found, not in the Gospels, but (in the creator's scriptures) in the blessing of Jacob, in Saul and David, and in Jesus who came from the line of David and Benjamin (*Marc.* 5.1.).

[9] N. Kretzmann, Faith Seeks, Understanding Finds, in Flint, *Christian Philosophy*, 1–36, and also, Reason in mystery, in G. Vesey (ed.), *The Philosophy in Christianity* (Cambridge, 1990), 15–39.

[10] A. Labhardt, Tertullien et la philosophie ou la recherche d'une 'position pure'. He quotes C. G. Jung, *Psychologische Typen* (Zurich, 1941), 24: 'Die im sacrificium intellectus vollbrachte Selbstverstümmelung Tertullians führte ihn zur rückhaltlosen Anerkennung der inneren irrationalen Tatsache, der wirklichen Grundlage seines Glaubens... Mit dem sacrificium intellectus fielen für ihn Philosophie und Wissenschaft, konsequenterweise auch die Gnosis.' Labhardt insists that we should not reject Jung because of the problematic nature of his discipline.

his intellectual formation; philosophy remains both his seducer and his enemy. Tertullian deserves something better than anachronistic psychoanalysis.

Tertullian is the most improbable fideist; no one has argued so irrepressibly. We are fortunate to have him as a Christian representative of the Second Sophistic, where argument could be vigorous and offensive. Diogenes told Plato, according to one story, that he could see a table and a cup but could not see tableness and cupness. 'That is reasonable', said Plato, 'for you have eyes to see the table and cup; but you do not have a mind (νοῦν οὐκ ἔχεις) with which to see tableness and cupness.'[11] Tertullian said much the same about Marcion who claimed Christ had no human body. One thing is clear for Tertullian: it would be harder to find a man born without a body than to find one, like Marcion, born without heart and brains (Marc. 4.10.16). This kind of invective, which may amuse modern readers, can make it harder for them to follow Tertullian's intricate argument; within the tradition which Plato and Tertullian helped to form, invective is today seen as a substitute for argument.

As a Stoic, Tertullian, like Seneca, revelled in the reproof of others.[12] Seneca wrote, 'I can harangue against vice without end' (*Ep.* 51.13). Tertullian saw, but rarely admitted, the strengths of his opponents, because his readers would have been confused by compromise, *brevitas* was the secret of good Stoic style, and meekness (ἐπιείκεια) was suspect to Stoics because it implied that one could treat equal offences differently.[13]

A. FOUR SOLUTIONS TO THE PUZZLE

(i) Psychoanalysis of a puzzled mind

The psychological explanation[14] is reached only after investigation. Tertullian's conflict is not unique. Most early Christian writers compromised with their classical heritage. They thought in one way and lived in another. They both rejected and accepted

[11] Diogenes Laertius, *The lives of the philosophers*, 6.53.
[12] See J. M. Rist, Seneca and Stoic orthodoxy, *ANRW*, Teil II, Band 36, Teilband 3 (1989), 1,993–2,012 (2,012). [13] *Ibid.*, 2,007.
[14] Note further discussion of this point in ch. 3.

philosophy. Tertullian is important because he tried to hold to a 'position pure'[15] which consistently denied anything beyond the content of revelation. There are three passages which crystallize his ideas (*ap.* 46–50; *praescr.* 7–9; *an.* 1–3).

While most attention has been given to the *apologeticum* and the *de praescriptione*, the fullest treatment is found at the beginning of *de anima*. Tertullian begins with the claim that there is no truth outside God (*an.* 1.4) and that it is therefore safer to be ignorant than to inquire beyond the limits of revelation (*an.* 1.6).[16] Here he anticipates Augustine's condemnation of the vain curiosity which masquerades as knowledge (*conf.* 10.35.55) and follows Paul's warning against philosophy (Col. 2.8). The *de praescriptione* similarly forbids curiosity because of the sufficiency and perfection of faith (*praescr.* 7, 9, 13). Philosophers cannot control their curiosity; their motive is always wrong.

The method of philosophers is also to be rejected. For it is concerned with appearance rather than reality, with words rather than realities. Through rhetorical skill philosophers are able to build or demolish what they will, being more concerned to talk than to teach (*an.* 2.2). Dialectic has the same duplicity, which casts doubt on its integrity (*praescr.* 7.6). Yet Tertullian makes more use of dialectic than do other early Christian writers.

Tertullian admits that philosophers sometimes say the same things as are found in scriptures. He uses the Stoic argument from common consent to prove that there is a God. In spite of these coincidental similarities, philosophy brings more confusion than clarity, because it is marked by disagreement: 'nevertheless you may find more disagreement than agreement among philosophers' (*an.* 2.4f.).[17] Philosophers hold some true opinions; but they derive them from a different source and apply them in a different way. Truth is harmed when it is linked with false origins or false results.

On the one hand, philosophers take opinions which they share with Christians and join them with their own arguments which contradict the rule of faith. On the other hand, they defend their distinctive opinions with arguments which Christians would accept

---

[15] See Labhardt, fn. 10 above.
[16] 'Quis enim revelabit quod deus texit?'
[17] 'tamen plus diversitatis invenias inter philosophos quam societatis'.

as valid and consistent. This means that truth does not have a chance and it is therefore necessary to separate common opinions from philosophers' arguments and to separate common arguments from philosophers' opinions.

Therefore Tertullian does not reject or accept philosophy as a whole. He knows his philosophers better than do most Greek fathers.[18] The points where philosophy has hit on the truth may be used to convince educated pagans that the gospel is true. Some Christians, whose works Tertullian has before him, have studied ancient writers and shown that there is nothing new or outrageous in Christianity; but pagans are not honest enough to accept such testimony (*test.* 1.2). Tertullian does not hide his sympathy for Seneca (*an.* 20.1) nor his genuine regret that all heretics have seasoned their works with Plato (*an.* 23.5).[19] Yet Christian artisans readily find the creator God whom Plato declared to be so difficult of discovery and description (*ap.* 46.9).

In contrast to simple Christianity, philosophy is aligned with sophistry (*ap.* 46.18). This is further linked with magic (*Marc.* 1.1.5, and *praescr.* 41.5), Valentinian fantasy (*Val.* 24.1) and rhetoric (*res.* 5.1). The reference to Christianity as the better philosophy (*pall.* 6.2) may be seen as the unfortunate consequence of a metaphor and a concession to secular usage.[20]

The proposed solution[21] of the puzzle is that Tertullian is the classic example of *sacrificium intellectus* as described by C. G. Jung.[22] As a believer, he rejected philosophy; but his own training in philosophy and rhetoric could never be discarded.[23]

---

[18] For details see Labhardt, Position pure, 174, who refers to M. Pohlenz, *Die Stoa* (Göttingen, 1948), vol. I, 437. Tertullian does not possess the penetration of Clement's knowledge of Plato.

[19] 'doleo bona fide Platonem omnium haereticorum condimentum factum.'

[20] Labhardt, Position pure, 176f. This is not a cause for embarrassment with Tertullian. Everyone uses words in different senses; all that matters is that the context of the argument should make the specific sense evident.

[21] By Labhardt, *ibid.*, 177–80.

[22] Jung, *Psychologischen Typen*, 22ff., cited in Labhardt, Position pure, 180.

[23] The psychological interpretation drew a quick response. It was condemned as simplistic and unbalanced (F. Refoulé, Tertullien et la philosophie, *RevSR*, 30 (1956), 42–5), and regret was expressed for the passing of older benign interpretations (e.g. G. Schelowsky, *Der Apologet Tertullianus in seinem Verhältnis zu der griechisch-römischen Philosophie* (Leipzig, 1901); J. Lortz, *Tertullian als Apologet*, 2 vols. (Münster, 1927, 1928), vol. I, ch. 7). These had claimed that Tertullian's quarrel was with philosophers rather than with philosophy.

(ii) Cultural history

A more extensive account comes from cultural history. It begins from the bewildering mass of secondary material, which derives from Tertullian's appeal for different modern groups: philologists, theologians and historians.[24] Puzzlement is enhanced by the different concerns of these three groups: one sticking to isolated texts and ignoring connections, the next bothered by apologetic concerns, the last driven to simplification within the wider range of general history.[25] From New Testament times, Christians began, at conversion, with a renunciation of their former ways, and the pagan world accepted this rejection long after Christians tried to modify it. Before Constantine[26] there were already Christians who, like Tertullian, were highly cultured but opposed to the pagan world. The tension between faith and culture must not be lessened[27] by minimizing Tertullian's learning or placing him on the analyst's couch; his polemic against classical culture is not merely rhetorical but theological.[28]

Ancient Paideia was a way of education and culture, an attitude to fundamental problems. Its anthropocentric rationality[29] clashed head on with the Christian faith. Tertullian's antithesis between Athens and Jerusalem demonstrates this clash;[30] but his writings show technical dependence on classical Paideia[31]and he is proud of his cultural strengths (*an.* 21.5f.).[32] While his many citations serve different purposes, when taken together they show a positive attitude to culture: in the *apologeticum* alone, Tertullian cites thirty different authors. Tertullian's literary formation begins from the richer heritage of Carthage rather than Rome and goes on to

---

[24] Not to mention, as we have seen, psychologists.

[25] H. Steiner, *Das Verhältnis Tertullians zur antiken Paideia* (St Ottilien, 1989), 1. Philosophers and historians of ideas should be added. This plurality of interested groups is a fundamental problem of patristics.

[26] When the opposition changed without disappearing.

[27] 'Das schillernde Phänomen Tertullian umfassend abzuhandeln, seiner komplizierten Denkweise eindeutig auf die Spur zu kommen – diese Aufgabe dürfte wohl morgen so wenig wie heute zu bewältigen sein.' Steiner, *Paideia*, 4.

[28] *Ibid.*, 37.

[29] 'Man is the measure of all things.'

[30] *Ibid.*, 43. See also P. Stockmeier, *Glaube und Kultur* (Düsseldorf, 1983), 131.

[31] For an example see analysis of the *apologeticum*, Steiner, *Paideia*, 49.

[32] *Ibid.*, 92.

include Silver Age writers like Pliny, Tacitus and Seneca. Still further, Homer and Herodotus are fundamental, while his extensive knowledge of Plato's writings is seen as a late growth from his controversy with Gnostics.[33] Some writers he knows only from anthologies; many of his references are allusions rather than citations. In the *apologeticum* and *ad nationes*, the mass of citations is for the benefit of his readers.[34] His corpus of citations goes well beyond the requirement of style and exceeds that of any other early Christian writer. He is reluctant to acknowledge his debts, especially his supreme debt to Cicero; but unacknowledged citation was a common convention of his time. His debt to Paideia was far more profound than has been recognized.[35]

Tertullian held the Roman state in high regard, as the classical tradition required. It troubled him that, as a Christian, he had to qualify this evaluation.[36] To the historian, Tertullian's occasional rejection of philosophy is outweighed by his positive general attitude. His 'better philosophy' (*melior philosophia*) is not a rhetorical flourish but a theme found elsewhere in his accounts of philosophers as 'authors and teachers of wisdom' (*sapientiae auctores* (*ap.* 19.3), *sapientiae professores* (*Marc.* 1.13.3)), who possess an amazing wisdom (*mira sapientia, nat.* 2.2.1).[37] Christianity remained the better philosophy, partly because it could point to an historical manifestation of the truth to which earlier development was subordinate.[38] Tertullian's description of Justin as 'philosopher and martyr' is not antithetical but complementary.[39]

In the end, the historian cannot harmonize all that Tertullian

---

[33] This is hard to reconcile with the fact that he gives Valentinians no philosophical standing.

[34] *Ibid.*, 111–15.

[35] *Ibid.*, 130.

[36] *Ibid.*, 172. This issue will be dealt with more fully below, ch. 4.

[37] Deep down, it is suggested, Tertullian looks for a co-operation between philosophy and faith. His historical circumstances made it impossible for him either to seek or to comment openly on such a joint venture. *Ibid.*, 205; cf. Fredouille, *Conversion*, 352.

[38] M. B. Stritzky, Aspekte geschichtlichen Denkens bei Tertullian, *JAC*, Supp. 10 (1983), 261, makes much of the difference between Platonic and Christian views of history. Steiner (*Paideia*, 205) thinks this antithesis might be overworked; but my judgement is that it points to the chief answer of the puzzle, which is found in the *oikonomia*.

[39] Steiner, *Paideia*, 206. He would not place Justin together with Miltiades, Irenaeus and Proculus if he had any reservations about his philosophy. Noeldechen took the opposite view.

wrote on culture, for all was not written at the same time and even in one work, the *apologeticum*, Tertullian can speak both positively and negatively of Socrates. Perhaps there is no plain answer to the relation between a complicated man and a complicated culture; but at least he cannot be represented as the radical opponent of that culture.[40]

(iii) Tertullian as philosopher

An older account[41] looks at the philosophy behind the puzzle and the paradox. After scripture and tradition, Tertullian places nature as the third source of knowledge. Reason is natural and comes from the God who is himself essential reason. Unreason comes from the devil and is against nature (*an.* 16.2). Reason finds God in the natural order of the world (*Marc.* 1.13.1 and 1.18.2).

On the evidence of reason and nature, Tertullian attacks the ancient philosophies for their presumption (*ap.* 21.4; *spect.* 28.4). Philosophers first took and falsified elements of revealed truth (*ap.* 46.7); then curiosity led them on to things which God had not revealed (*an.* 2.7; *ap.* 47.3; *nat.* 1.4.2). Further, they perverted the testimony of nature (*praescr.* 7.2; *an.* 1.5) and then cut loose from it (*an.* 2.2). The lives of philosophers (*ap.* 46f.) and their sole concern for glory (*ap.* 46.18) call for criticism. Even Socrates was possessed by a wicked demon (*an.* 1.4 and 39.3). There can be no common ground between such worldly wisdom and faith in Christ (*praescr.* 7.12). To make things worse, heretics have used philosophy to falsify the gospel (*ap.* 47.9; *Marc.* 1.13.3). The Gnostics derive from Plato and Marcion from the Stoics. Philosophers are the patriarchs of heresy (*an.* 3.1; *Herm.* 8.3). Finally, Tertullian must not be divorced from his setting in which paganism and Christianity were diametrically opposed. Such a setting explains Tertullian's immoderate language and intolerance.[42]

There is a more favourable view of philosophy: just as by good luck, ships, in a storm, find a harbour and men in total darkness

[40] *Ibid.*, 269–71.
[41] G. Rauch, *Der Einfluss der stoischen Philosophie auf die Lehrbildung Tertullians* (Halle, 1890).
[42] J. Neander spoke of the 'grossartige Einseitigkeit seines Wesens'. *Antignostikus. Geist des Tertullianus und Einleitung in dessen Schriften*, 2nd edn (Berlin, 1849), 4.

find a door, so philosophers stumble on the truth (*an.* 2.1). There is also a deeper principle at work. God rationally ordered nature (*paen.* 1.2) and gave reason that nature might be understood (*cor.* 4.1). The partial successes of pagan philosophy derive from these causes (*an.* 2.1). In man and in nature there are points where philosophy and faith join. All that is true in philosophy is the historically conditioned development of the true reason which is revealed in the gospel (*paen.* 1; *test.* 5.7).[43] Tertullian constantly uses the Stoic terms: body, spirit, substance, nature and word.[44] As a result, his concepts of being, soul, knowledge, God and goodness bear clear marks of Stoic influence.[45] The same reason which is applied to natural questions must also be applied to the intelligent exploration of God. Because Tertullian sees the need for rational theological inquiry, he has been placed among the first philosophical Christians.[46]

(iv) Clarity through disjunction

More and more work reveals the extent to which Tertullian is marked by classical culture.[47] He is a Stoic in logic as in ethics and metaphysics. Philosophy points the way to God (*Marc.* 2.27.6; *virg.* 11.6), immortality (*test.* 4.1–8) and even resurrection (*test.* 4.9–11). Philosophers and Christians agree on many points (*ap.* 14.7). Seneca, 'often one of us', Presocratics and even Lucretius are cited with approval. Christianity is the 'better philosophy' (*pall.* 6.2). Tertullian condemns the curiosity of heretics but commends Hadrian as an 'explorer of all curiosities' (*ap.* 5.7). His own curiosity goes beyond elementary inquiry (*res.* 2.11), is insatiable and ever-present.

---

[43] Rauch, *Einfluss*, 15f. Rauch claims this point as original to Tertullian; but the similarity with Justin is obvious. For Justin, there were seeds of logos in everyone, especially in the prophets and Socrates; the whole logos came in Christ.

[44] *corpus, spiritus, substantia, natura* and *sermo. Ibid.*, 18. For a fuller account see M. Spanneut, *Le stoïcisme des pères de l'église* (Paris, 1957).

[45] Rauch, *Einfluss*, 19–55.

[46] H. Ritter, *Geschichte der Philosophie*, 12 vols. (Hamburg, 1829–53), v, 579. Cited Rauch, *Einfluss*, 16.

[47] The major recent work, which broke new ground, is by J.-C. Fredouille, *Tertullien et la conversion de la culture antique*. It is enhanced by the more recent work of H. Steiner, discussed above.

There are initial objections against taking the Athens-Jerusalem formula literally. Twenty-six imitations of 2 Cor. 6:14–16[48] point to a still wider love of antithesis.[49] Nevertheless the puzzle remains.[50] Tertullian's hostility to philosophy begins at a superficial level, where he attacks the personal deficiencies of philosophers and follows the satirical tradition of Aristophanes, Horace, Petronius and especially Lucian. He goes on to more serious objections against philosophers: their mutual contradictions, inconsistent behaviour and dialectical display. The first criticism had been answered by Posidonius who claimed that disagreement is a part of life, not just a part of philosophy; to avoid it one would have to give up life as well as philosophy.[51] The second criticism – inconsistency between life and thought – is stated or answered in Cicero, Seneca, Plutarch and the many anecdotes of Diogenes Laertius. Lastly, the sterile verbosity of *dialectici* is derided by Seneca,[52] and Lucian contrasts the practice of justice, wisdom and courage with verbal gyration and aporetic argument (*Hermotimos* 79). Tertullian adapted all these standard criticisms to his own circumstances. Disputation with heretics prompted his objections to dialectic and his call for simplicity (*cult.* 2.11.2) is a protection against their eloquence.

Disjunction becomes a stylistic *tic* in the writings of Tertullian. He wants to simplify what others have confused. He resists (*ap.* 46.18) the reduction of Christianity to one among many kinds of philosophy.[53] He fights (*praescr.* 7.9) on the uncertain front between orthodoxy and heresy, selects the improper use of philosophy by heretics as the chief source of confusion and recommends, in this context, the renunciation of philosophy. Simplicity is his concern and disjunction his method.

---

[48] Here Paul puts the rhetorical question: what common ground has light with darkness, Christ with Belial, believer with infidel, God's temple with idols?

[49] Note also the Semitic Hellenistic formula τί ἐμοὶ καὶ σοί (John 2.4).

[50] Fredouille, *ibid.*, 301–57.

[51] Diogenes Laertius, *Lives*, 7.129.

[52] *Ep.* 45.5–13, 48.4–12, 49.5–12, where Euripides, *Phoenissae* 469, is cited: 'veritatis simplex oratio est'.

[53] Using five neologisms to stress his point.

(v) Common ground

All four solutions recognize the depth of the puzzle.[54] The first confesses that a rational solution is not to be found and falls back on Tertullian's psychology. The second establishes the claims of classical culture on Tertullian, shows that the problem is theological rather than psychological, but retires with a tribute to Tertullian's personal complexity and the confused world to which he belonged. The third solution makes Tertullian a philosopher in his own right, so that it is proper for him to handle insoluble problems. The final solution shows that disjunction is Tertullian's way of clarifying things. This is the best of the four solutions; but I think there is another important element.

B. THE PERFECT AND THE IMPERFECT

An analysis of the puzzle, in the context of *de praescriptione*, falls easily under three headings: faith as criterion, summing up in perfection and the discipline of reason. The solution of the puzzle lies in the perfection of Christ; when the perfect is come, that which is in part, like philosophy, must be done away. The puzzle is not peculiar to Tertullian. Justin says negative things about philosophy in his account of his pre-Christian pilgrimage; yet all have the spermatic logos and Socrates and Heraclitus are Christians before Christ. Clement sees philosophy as a tutor to bring the Greeks to Christ, but the individual schools of philosophy have torn the body of truth apart. Clement and Tertullian use philosophy openly and attack fideism frequently.

(i) The rule of faith

Much Hellenistic philosophy is directed against the infinite regress of Sceptics who deny the possibility of knowledge. What Tertullian dislikes about Gnostics and sceptical Sophists is their endless

---

[54] E. I. Kouri, *Tertullian und die römische Antike* (Helsinki, 1982), sets out contrasts and contradictions in Tertullian and his interpreters. He suggests that Tertullian did compromise in his use of pagan culture. See also the article of J.-C. Fredouille, Tertullien, in *Dictionnaire des philosophes* (Paris, 1984), II, 2,485–8. Stoicism provides Tertullian with his categories of thought and these will be definitive for the West.

wandering. Christian philosophizing began in the second century with epistemology. Clement used Epicurean and Stoic epistemology to combat the Platonist rejection of faith. Epicurean anticipation (πρόληψις) was the substance of things hoped for, Stoic assent (συγκατάθεσις) was Christian piety (θεοσέβεια), perception (αἴσθησις) was perceived with a Christian new eye and ear, the bible was the voice of God which called with the power of Sirens' voices. Platonists, who denigrated faith (πίστις) in favour of knowledge (ἐπιστήμη), had to acknowledge that they could not have knowledge (ἐπιστήμη) of their first principles for there was nothing higher from which such principles might be inferred.[55]

Clement's sixth argument for faith is attributed by Cicero to Zeno (*Acad.* 1.41f.) in an extended form which sets out these claims:

1. Assent is a voluntary act.
2. Only those sensible presentations, which possess clarity and are cognitive presentations, are worthy of faith (*fides*).
3. Cognitive sensation is knowledge (*scientia*), irremoveable by reasoning. All other sensation is ignorance (*inscientia*).
4. The move to knowledge from ignorance is comprehension, and it alone is credible (*Acad.* 1.42).
5. Hence Zeno granted *fides* also to the senses, because a grasp achieved by sense was true and *fidelis*, because it let go nothing which was capable of being its object, and because nature had given a canon (or criterion) and a first principle of itself.
6. Antiochus of Ascalon accepted this as an indication that the Stoics developed rather than rejected the tradition of Plato and Aristotle.

Clement's summary of the argument is brief and he wrongly (because of Antiochus) attributes it to Aristotle: the judgement concerning the truth of a presentation decides whether it is faithful and this verdict is reached by faith, using faith's own criterion. Everything begins from the rule of faith as the Stoic/Platonic criterion of truth.[56]

The criterion, canon (or rule), of truth is the central point at

[55] See E. F. Osborn, Arguments for faith in Clement of Alexandria, *VC*, 48 (1994), 1–24.
[56] See the excellent discussions in: P. Huby and G. Neal (eds.), *The criterion of truth, FS George Kerferd* (Liverpool, 1989) and G. Striker, Κριτηρίον τῆς ἀληθείας, *NAWG: Phil. hist. Klasse* (1974), 47–110.

which Tertullian assimilates Greek philosophy into Christian theology.[57] From Antiochus to Alcinous, dogmatic Platonism began its fight against Scepticism with the Stoic teaching of the criterion and certainty.[58] Antiochus found certainty in the cognitive impressions which he identified (contrary to Stoic materialism) with the ideas of Plato.[59] Alcinous expounded the criterion as the first topic of his dialectic (*did.* 4): he distinguished the faculty which judges, the object of judgement and the judgement made. Both the faculty and the judgement could be seen as the criterion. The objects judged are intellectual for the senses cannot reach beyond opinion.

Clement's account of the rule or criterion became the most important of his arguments for faith. Tertullian used it in his pretended ban on philosophy, as he adhered to Stoic logic and argued vigorously. For him inquiry is only possible when we follow our criterion, the rule of faith, which Christ taught and we confess (*praescr.* 13). We may seek and find as long as we wish if we hold on to the rule. 'To know nothing against the rule is to know everything' (*praescr.* 14.5). The expansion of the rule of faith from 'Jesus Christ is lord' later achieves a double aspect: it is the total content of revealed truth and also a list of articles of faith. As it is correlative to faith, truth, doctrine, teaching, instruction and pledge,[60] difficulties were bound to arise from such a wide range of meanings.[61]

(ii) Summing up all things in Christ

Tertullian's rule (*praescr.* 13) declares that all is corrected and perfected in Christ:

(a) that there is only one God, and that he is not other than the creator of this world who produced all things out of nothing through his word,

[57] See E. F. Osborn, Reason and the rule of faith, in R. Williams (ed.), *The making of Orthodoxy, FS H. Chadwick* (Cambridge, 1989), 40–61. Clement speaks of the canon of the church which includes the confession of the essential articles of faith (*strom.* 7. 15. 90).
[58] See discussion in J. M. Dillon, *The Middle Platonists* (London, 1977), 63–9 and 273–6.
[59] *Ibid.*, 93.
[60] *fides, veritas, doctrina, disciplina, institutio* and *sacramentum*.
[61] G. G. Blum, Der Begriff des Apostolischen im theologischen Denken Tertullians, *Kerygma und Dogma*, 9 (1963), 102–21. The development of magisterial *potestas* was one answer to the problems. See David Rankin, Tertullian's use of the word *potestas*, *JRH*, 19.1 (1995), 1–9.

whom he sent forth first of all, (b) that this word is called his son and under the name of God was seen in different ways by the patriarchs, heard at all times in the prophets, (c) at last brought down by the spirit and power of the father into the virgin Mary, he was made flesh in her womb, and being born of her went forth as Jesus Christ; from then on he preached the new law and new promise of the kingdom of heaven, worked miracles; (d) having been crucified, he rose again the third day; taken up into the heavens he sat at the right hand of the father; he sent in his place, the power of the Holy Spirit to lead believers; he will come with glory to take the saints to their enjoyment of everlasting life and of the heavenly promises, and to condemn the wicked to everlasting fire, after they have both been raised to life with their flesh restored.

This rule came from Christ, and only heretics will question it.

Here the perfection of the son of God implies that his power, presence, truth and reality are universal. There is nothing which can be added to him. The son of God completes creation, restores what had fallen away, redeems what was lost.[62] In modern terms, just as the universe has been 'fine-tuned'[63] to produce humanity, so humanity has been 'fine-tuned' to produce Jesus Christ.

For Tertullian as for Irenaeus[64] recapitulation consists of three groups of concepts. First there are totality, perfection and correction, secondly, history and Christus Victor, and thirdly the divine activity in being, goodness and truth. The many combinations and permutations of these eight concepts preclude the possibility of comprehension without analysis.[65]

Recapitulation comes as the climax of history, of the economy which runs from the Alpha to the Omega, and which declares the triumph of Christus Victor.[66] In God's universe, sin must be

---

[62] In this way, Irenaeus challenges the claims of Gnostics to go beyond Jesus and his gospel. There is nothing left to be done after the totality of Christ. Answers to Marcion and to the Jews are also included: Jesus brings creation to its perfection and sums up the old dispensation.

[63] To use John Polkinghorne's good phrase.

[64] In Irenaeus the following themes are found in the *adversus haereses*: history (3.9, 3.11.8, 3.12.5), Christus Victor (3.23.1, 5.21.3); totality of being (3.21.10, 4.6.7), goodness (4.12.5, 4.13.3), truth (3. *pref.* and 1); perfection of being (4.19, 20, 5.1.1), goodness (4.38.2, 3, 5.16.2), truth (3.18.7, 2.27); correction of being (5.12.6, 5.14), goodness (3.20.2, 4.4.3), truth (3.16.6–8).

[65] For an extended analysis of this complex idea, see my *The emergence of Christian theology* (Cambridge, 1993), 142–72 and 299–306; also, The logic of recapitulation, in E. Romero-Pose (ed.), *Pléroma, FS, A. Orbe* (Santiago de Compostela, 1990), 321–35.

[66] This theme has already been discussed in detail in ch. 1.

corrected by going back to the first transgression, reversing it and then bringing everything to the proper and perfect end which God intended. Perfection is the goal for any world made by God. Tertullian's rule of faith covers these three points. Totality (all things were created by God through his word who was heard at all times in the prophets), correction (Jesus preached a new law and a new promise) and perfection[67] (the son and word was at the last brought down into the Virgin Mary, was crucified, risen and ascended to the right hand of the father, whence he will return to take his saints to the heavenly fulfilment of all the promises) enable the son to finish the work which the father has given him to do. All must be corrected and perfected in recapitulation. In Tertullian's puzzle, perfection has priority; in his paradox, we shall see that correction is the theme.

(iii) Discipline of reason

The rejection of Athens occurs within an extended argument against heresies; second-century Christian writers commonly talk and argue about truth in the context of heresy.[68] To learn what they thought about truth and reason, we have to read their disputation with heresy.

(1) Heretics are no surprise (*praescr.* 1.1);[69] we were told to expect them (Matt. 7.15 and 24.4, 11, 24; 1 Thess. 3.1–3 and 2 Pet. 22.1).

(2) Heresy is like a fever which simply exists and does harm because that is the reason for its existence (*praescr.* 2.1). A heresy may topple the weak man but it cannot stand against strong faith. Humans are prone to be toppled. If heresy claims the odd

---

[67] Some scholars find it difficult to combine the notions of correction and perfection, e.g. C.R. Smith writes 'recapitulation is not a definition of *Heilsgeschichte* as the task of restoring conditions before the fall, but rather an insistence on the essential harmony of the true soteriological task, that of bringing humanity from its Edenic state of infancy to the true maturity of God-likeness' (Chiliasm and recapitulation in the theology of Irenaeus, *VC*, 48 (1994), 329). However, Irenaeus speaks both of the fall and restoration of Adam (*haer.* 5.12.4–6) and of his rise from infancy (*haer.* 4.38.3f.). While mankind has fallen in Adam, God's grace turns the racial catastrophe into part of the process of redemption.

[68] This is not what a twentieth-century reader would expect or enjoy. For an extended study of Tertullian's approach to heresy, see P. A. Gramaglia, Il linguaggio eresiologico in Tertulliano, L'approchio cattolico all'eresia, *Aug.*, 25 (1985), 667–710.

[69] We follow the argument of the *de praescriptione haereticorum*.

bishop, deacon, widow or even martyr, that does not discredit the rule of faith, for the rule tests and is not tested by persons (*praescr.* 3.4).

(3) Since we have been warned about heresy and apostasy, we must prove all things and hold fast to what is good (*praescr.* 4.1).

(4) Philosophy is the material of the world's wisdom which interprets God's nature and dispensation with too much speed and not enough thought (*praescr.* 7). Behind the scenes, the ultimate cause of heresy is philosophy. Valentinus' aeons and forms come from Plato, Marcion's tranquil God is a Stoic, the Epicureans produced a soul which is mortal, for Zeno God was made of matter, and for Heraclitus God was fire. Heretics and philosophers forever argue about and propose successive answers for the same questions: the origin and purpose of evil, the source of man and the manner of his origin ('unde malum et quare? et unde homo et quomodo?') (*praescr.* 7.5).

Tertullian's objections against his philosophers concentrate on their inconsistency and interminability. Dialectics build up and then pull down. They are evasive, wildly conjectural, harsh in argument, troublesome, infinitely retractable and inconclusive. They produce endless genealogies (1 Tim. 1.4) by means of the bureaucratic fallacy which introduces p to relate x and y, then q to relate x and p, then r to relate p to y, useless questions (Titus 3.9), cancerous words (2 Tim. 2.17) and vain deceit (Col. 2.8).

(5) This is why there must be separation between Athens and Jerusalem, academy and church, heretics and Christians (*praescr.* 7.9). The porch of Solomon, where Christian preaching began is marked by simplicity of heart (Wisd. 1.1). There can be no Stoic, Platonic and dialectical Christianity, no precious curiosity after possession of Christ Jesus, no inquiry after the gospel has been believed. *nihil ultra credere* is the final verdict.

'Seek and you will find' (*praescr.* 8.2) means that there is a proper curiosity in contrast to the nit-picking scrupulosity of heretics. The command was spoken at the beginning of Christ's ministry[70] when there was still doubt as to who he was. There is

---

[70] This claim is interesting because historical exegesis was unusual in Tertullian's day.

one definite thing taught by Christ, which should be sought. We should seek in order to find, find in order to believe. Seeking must continue until the fullness of Christ is reached (*praescr.* 9.5).[71]

(6) We should follow the discipline of reason, which shows that the command has three parts: matter, time and limit. These point to the three questions and their answers: what must we seek? (Christ's teaching), when must we seek? (until Christ's teaching is found), and how long must we seek? (until what is found is believed) (*praescr.* 10.1f.). The only purpose of seeking is to find and the only purpose of finding is to believe ('finis quaerendi, statio credendi') (*praescr.* 10.7).

(7) Heretics should not be allowed to argue from the scripture which does not belong to them (*praescr.* 15.4). This is the main 'prescription' or restraining argument aimed at excluding heretics. Argument over scripture produces a belly-ache or a headache ('nisi plane ut aut stomachi quis ineat eversionem aut cerebri') (*praescr.* 16.2). Heretics mutilate the text of scripture or, worse still, pervert its meaning by logical error, which combines and selects irrationally, plays on ambiguity and gets nowhere, until critical questions are asked (*praescr.* 17.1–5). The discipline of reason asks these critical questions: 'Among whom belongs that very faith which the scriptures possess? From what original source, through whom, when, and to whom, has been handed down that discipline by which Christians are made?' Where there is true Christian discipline and faith, we shall find true scripture, true exposition and all Christian traditions (*praescr.* 19.2).[72]

Where there is a fear of God, there is the beginning of wisdom and *gravitas honesta*, while diligence and carefulness are matched by an ordered ministry and community and by a church which is united and belongs to God. So the discipline of reason leads to truth and preparation for judgement (*praescr.*

---

[71] 'No one should be ashamed of progress; for even in Christ knowledge goes through different stages' (*pud.* 1.11–12).

[72] Tertullian is today criticized because, after hanging so much on historical succession, in the end, he puts his own conscience before tradition. See Munier, La tradition apostolique chez Tertullien, 192.

43.5). The same gospel is the rule which runs from Alpha to Omega and never changes. The judge whom all must face is not going to withdraw his original doctrines in order to spare those who must stand before him.

Tertullian closes by saying that this treatise is a preface and a general refutation of all heresies, without using scriptural argument on points of detail.[73] It makes formal objections which are clear, just and necessary ('certis et iustis et necessariis praescriptionibus') (*praescr.* 44.13). It is a logical defence which claims a criterion of divine truth. Cicero had mocked the Epicurean rule because it must have fallen from heaven, if its pretentious claims were to be respected (*de finibus* 1.19.61ff.). Christians claimed that their rule and gospel had come from heaven and that the incarnate logos included rather than precluded the discipline of reason. There was no excuse which might justify the evasion of persistent thought. Jerusalem does not need Athens because it has included and gone beyond it.

Following the chosen criterion of truth, Clement of Alexandria was able to select, from different schools, the right kind of philosophy to form an eclectic whole which he called 'philosophy'. Further, if by philosophy is meant the practice of argument, as when Clement claims the necessity of philosophy because one would have to argue to prove it superfluous, then all second-century Christian thinkers (even Tatian) were disciples of Athens. Indeed, Christian theology came into existence and European thought began, because of the practice of argument, which was learnt from Athens and used according to the rule of faith or canon of truth.

C. FINALITY OF CHRIST AS A SOLUTION TO THE PUZZLE

There is no place for curiosity after Christ and there is no need for inquiry after the gospel. In the centre of his argument stands the

---

[73] The link of scripture with church tradition here is interesting. Tertullian's historical claim that certain churches possess undefiled faith is linked with his claim for apostolic succession of office (see Telfer, below, p. 181). It is historically less secure than the *caput fidei* which he finds in the critical centre of scripture (see below, p. 153). Argument with heretics about the centre and limits of scripture gave him a headache or belly-ache (*praescr.* 16.2), however, and he was not in a position to discover the historical weakness of any form of historical succession; he therefore used the rule which he had received.

claim of Tertullian for the perfection of Christ. Like Justin, who saw seeds of logos in all human beings (especially in philosophers and prophets) so that Socrates was a Christian before Christ, Tertullian believed that the whole logos had come in Christ. He could encourage philosophers to move on to perfection in Christ. To suggest that anything should be added to Christ was to deny the criterion of the gospel.

For Tertullian there are three stages in the development towards the Christian gospel: natural religion, philosophy and Judaism. These may all be recognized; the chief error is to take one of them as the final stage.[74] The perfection of Christ is the climax of a history which includes Greek philosophy. After the rule there is no need for philosophy because it has been summed up in Christ. Summing up means totality and perfection. There is difficulty with using philosophers who came after Christ. Tertullian meets this problem by saying that Seneca is *saepe noster*, one of us. We are never his. The same problem had existed with Judaizers who wanted to add the practice of the Law to the gospel. Paul explains to the Galatians that they have reversed the order of things; law precedes gospel, flesh precedes spirit, the *paidagogos* precedes freedom. To improve on the gospel is to deny it.

We see here that the key idea is not hammered repetitively (Irenaeus had done that); rather, it stays in the background and dominates the argument. It is stated negatively at the beginning. What indeed has Athens to do with Jerusalem, what concord is there between the Academy and the church, what between heretics and Christians? 'Let them beware who put forward a Stoic, Platonic, dialectical form of Christianity. For us there is no need of curiosity after Christ, no need of inquiry after the Gospel. When we have believed we have no desire to add to our faith. For this is our primary faith that there is nothing further which we ought to believe' (*praescr.* 7.11–13). It emerges obliquely at the end of the *de praescriptione haereticorum*, where sarcasm portrays Christ as saying, 'I once gave the gospel and the doctrine of the said rule to my apostles; but afterwards it was my pleasure to make considerable changes in it!' (*praescr.* 44.8)

[74] See P. Monceaux, *Histoire littéraire de l'Afrique chrétienne*, vol. 1, *Tertullien et les origines* (Paris, 1901), 338.

The final perfection of Christ solves each confrontation which Tertullian presents.[75] He points Romans and Jews to Christ 'born for the salvation of all' (*ap.* 21.17). Against the Valentinians, Christ is no mere angel, but the 'one bearer of salvation' (*carn.* 14.3) who came not just to be seen (*carn.* 12.6), but to save, and to save not a few but all. His flesh is the 'hinge on which salvation hangs' (*res.* 8.2). Against Marcion, the incarnation offers final redemption through the real flesh of Christ (*carn.* 5.10; *Marc.* 2.27.7). Against the Monarchians, the climax of salvation is the coming of the son from the father into the world (*Prax.* 2.1). The father did not spare the son but delivered him up for us all (*Prax.* 30.3; Rom. 8.32 and Isa. 53.6). The son, not the father, is made a curse for us (*Prax.* 29.3; Gal. 3.13). Yet it is the one God the father who did everything which was done by the son (*Prax.* 16.7). The 'final end' is in the hands of the son who will deliver the kingdom to the father, that God may be all in all (*Prax.* 4.2; 1 Cor. 15.24ff.). The perfection of Jesus Christ as son of God and saviour was the secret of simplicity, the rule of faith and the canon of truth.

Tertullian's acceptance of the concept of rule or criterion of truth leaves him open to some of the objections, ancient and modern, against this concept. It should be noted, however, that the most influential modern apology for Christian faith[76] takes Tertullian's view of faith as rational choice, and that he and his pagan predecessors were concerned to limit faith to make room for reason. Literalist unease over different verbal forms of the rule may be removed by the distinction between sense and reference.[77]

His move also elucidates the tiresome problem of whether he and Clement should be called 'philosophers' today; there is no doubt that they philosophized or argued. Both took the Christian rule of faith and the scriptures which that rule summarized as their criterion of truth. This was a philosophical move in that philosophers at that time worked with a canon of some kind. It was a strikingly different kind of canon, however, so that it created a new

---

[75] Viciano, *Cristo Salvador*, 235–67.

[76] Hans Küng's book, *Existiert Gott?* [*Does God exist?*] (München, 1978; London, 1980) sold hundreds of thousands of copies in five languages.

[77] Frege's distinction between *Sinn* and *Bedeutung* points to the way in which 2 times 4, 2 times 2 times 2, 8 times 1 all refer to 8.

language. The contrast between perception as the criterion of truth and scripture or rule as criterion of truth could hardly be greater. Tertullian, we shall see, breaks down that paradigm shift when he speaks of the scriptures as presenting a cognitive impression which compels belief.[78] Further, the use of literature in the ancient world, where poetry served as an encyclopedia of ethics, politics, history and technology, a vast storehouse of wisdom and knowledge,[79] made the use of the bible less shocking. However, the move is violent and the first centuries of Christian thought present the assimilation of this strange body of truth into philosophy, so that by Augustine the difference between philosophy and theology no longer makes sense. When Clement and Tertullian speak of a Christian philosophy, their speech is metaphorical; when we come to Augustine the metaphor has died to become part of the language.[80]

Finally, Tertullian's theme derives from scripture. The warning against philosophy and vain deceit according to the tradition of men (Col. 2.8) is justified by the claim, 'For in Christ the perfection of the godhead dwells embodied and you have been brought to perfection in him, who is the head of every first-principle and power' (Col. 2.9, 10).[81] It is remarkable that Tertullian does not quote this text. While he quotes Col. 2.8 (*praescr.* 7.7), he puts the substance of Colossians 2.9 and 10 into his own words in the antithesis between Athens and Jerusalem (*praescr.* 7.12). This shows that he is thinking and not merely citing, using scripture as a criterion not as an oracle. In a similar way the words of Clement (*strom.* 7.1.1) claim to draw their life and breath from the meaning (νοῦν), not the letter (λέξιν), of scripture. Therefore Tertullian is able to add to the disjunction of Colossians the economy of salvation which he finds in Ephesians and Galatians. What has Athens to do with Jerusalem? Everything, provided you travel (economy class) by way of Ephesus and disembark at Jerusalem.

---

[78] See below, ch. 4. Clement went further and found the world of forms in scripture; for Albinus dialectic and the forms provided the criterion of truth.

[79] E. A. Havelock, *Preface to Plato* (Oxford, 1963), 27.

[80] Donald Davidson has shown the appropriateness of this way of talking about metaphor. 'What metaphors mean', in *Inquiries into truth and interpretation* (Oxford, 1984), 245–64.

[81] ὅτι ἐν αὐτῷ κατοικεῖ πᾶν τὸ πλήρωμα τῆς Θεότητος σωματικῶς. Καὶ ἐστὲ ἐν αὐτῷ πεπληρωμένοι, ὅς ἐστιν ἡ κεφαλὴ πάσης ἀρχῆς καὶ ἐξουσίας

CHAPTER 3

The paradox: credible because inept

My books, at this epoch [wrote a modern novelist] if they did not actually serve to irritate the disorder, partook, it will be perceived, largely, in their imaginative and inconsequential nature, of the characteristic qualities of the disorder itself. I well remember, among others, ... Tertullian's 'De Carne Christi' ... in which the unintelligible sentence, 'Mortuus est Dei filius; credibile est quia ineptum est; et sepultus resurrexit; certum est quia impossibile est [The son of God has died: this is believable because it is silly; buried he has risen again: this is certain because it is impossible] ... ' occupied my undivided time, for many weeks of laborious and fruitless investigation.[1]

Others have been less fortunate, because their fruitful investigations produced clear, but false, results which have encouraged irrational piety.

Tertullian is famous for his paradox (*carn.* 5.4),[2] which is commonly misquoted and seen as the archetype of irrational faith.[3] Yet his most assiduous modern editor and translator writes, 'This is one of the most lucid sections of Tertullian's work, in which his Latin flows with unwonted ease and perspicuity.'[4] Is this claim, asks another, 'unconscious humour'?[5] Some writers take the passage by itself and find irrationalism, while others look at the context and

---

[1] Edgar Allan Poe, Berenicë – A tale, in *The unabridged Edgar Allan Poe*, ed. T. Mossman (Philadelphia, 1983), 158.

[2] The paradox has two epistemological forms: credibility and certainty. The ethical form (*non pudet quia pudendum*) will be considered when we look at Tertullian's ethics.

[3] Cf. F. W. Farrar, *History of interpretation* (London, 1886), 180, who writes of Tertullian: 'he adopted the paradox *Credo quia absurdum est*, and the wild conclusion that the more repugnant to sound reason a statement was, it ought so much the more to be deemed worthy of God'.

[4] E. Evans, *Tertullian's treatise on the incarnation* (London, 1956), 107.

[5] Fredouille, *Conversion*, 326: Evans 'ignore tout des remous soulevés par ce "paradoxe"'.

48

find rational argument. A refrain of the treatise is 'But here again I demand reasons' (*carn.* 10.1).

Tertullian's paradox is a cruel test for sorting out those who analyse arguments from those who do not. Most error is caused by the attempt to use the paradox in settings where it does not belong.[6] Tertullian wrote that:

X. (1) He is not ashamed of the crucifixion of God's son because it is necessarily shameful.

(2) The death of God's son must be believed because it is inept.

(3) His burial and resurrection is certain because it is impossible.

Y. All this can only be true if he had flesh which could die, be buried and rise again.

Z. Christ had two substances: divine and human, two states, two natures. This may be proved: 'The powers of the spirit proved him to be God, his sufferings proved his human flesh.' Therefore 'Why halve Christ with a lie? He was wholly the truth' (i.e. both God and man) (*carn.* 5.4–8).

What have scholars made of the paradox? One group has interpreted it as irrational; the other has seen it as rational.

A. IRRATIONALIST INTERPRETATIONS

We shall look first at the main irrationalist interpretations: psychological, empiricist and medievalist.

(i) Neurotic fideism

Because of his psychological problem,[7] Tertullian opposes the one irrational truth of the gospel to the many rational accounts[8] and makes ineptitude the test for credibility (*carn.* 5). His exclusive fideism must not be qualified.[9] This is Tertullian's 'position pure' in

---

[6] Rational reconstruction and historical reconstruction must proceed separately; both are necessary. R. Rorty, The historiography of philosophy: four genres, in R. Rorty, J. B. Schneewind and Quentin Skinner *Philosophy in history* (Cambridge, 1984), 49–75 (49).

[7] Discussed in ch. 2.

[8] Labhardt, *Position pure*, 177. Labhardt accuses Gilson of minimizing the rigour of Tertullian; but solving a paradox is understanding, not weakening, its claim.

[9] *Ibid.*, 'Paradoxe choquant pour l'esprit qui raisonne, mais que le contexte interdit absolument d'atténuer.'

which he is able to settle questions by citation of scripture without any argument.[10] In contrast to Clement, there is no trace of a Christian philosophy.[11]

Tertullian's exclusive fideism is linked with his environment in two ways. First, he was opposed to Gnosticism which falsely affected a philosophical position and showed the dangers of possible confusion. Secondly, in the West, philosophy never had the priority which it held in the East. Cicero was an orator and politician first and only a philosopher second insofar as an orator needed some philosophy. Tertullian could more easily link philosophy with rhetoric and sophistic.[12]

At his conversion Tertullian sacrificed his fundamental drive towards rationality. He became a 'man of feeling', with his faith fixed on that irreducible irrationality of the incarnation, which the paradox declares. However, it is one thing to renounce one's past and another to be free from it. Tertullian's rationality was too deeply ingrained and he could not resist its claims.[13] The conflict is evident in the exaggerated claims of the paradox. The weakness of this interpretation is that Tertullian does not universalize the paradox. He finds a credible ineptitude in the incarnation and not elsewhere.

(ii) God-talk and world-talk

The empiricist account gives due weight to the several components of the argument. Against Marcion's rejection of a real incarnation Tertullian argues: God can do anything except what he does not wish to do; God can become incarnate without a change in his essential nature; and the shame of incarnation is necessary.

How do paradoxes work? The strength of paradox is that an objector is like someone who has missed the point of a joke and looks foolish. Whatever the dangers of this way of talking, Tertullian's paradox should be taken seriously as a striking

---

[10] But Tertullian does argue, avoids mechanical citation (see above p. 47) and dislikes exegetical debate.

[11] Labhardt, *Position pure*, 178, This opinion depends on a particular definition of philosophy, which could not claim wide acceptance today, and on a neglect of Tertullian's Stoicism.

[12] *Ibid.*, 179.   [13] *Ibid.*, 180.

formulation of an essential Christian belief.[14] In the *Tractatus Logico-Philosophicus* (6.432), the early Wittgenstein drew a sharp line between language about God and language about the world. '*How* the world is, is completely indifferent for what is higher. God does not reveal himself *in* the world.' This raises problems for religious language when the incarnation points to an intersection of God-talk and world-talk, when 'it has to be said not only that a certain person was crucified, but that that person was the Son of God'.[15] This leads to a clear discussion of the problems which face any analysis of religious language and of the special difficulties which face a defence of the incarnation of a changeless God.[16]

These are genuine problems, but they are not the problems which Tertullian faced, and they do not offer an accurate analysis of what he said. First, he was concerned to refute someone who claimed that a human body and crucifixion were inconsistent with a divine person and that therefore a simulated body must be preferred. Tertullian replied that an unreal body would not be a real incarnation and that the shame of the incarnation was a test of its reality.[17] He is further concerned that present denial of the shameful cross will lead to final rejection by Christ, and to denial of the salvation of mankind, besides which there is nothing more appropriate for God. God's dishonour is necessary for man's safety.

Secondly, it is wrong to claim as a corollary: 'because it is inept it is not credible'.[18] Tertullian does not universalize his claim for ineptitude; it is the test of a true incarnation. There would be no paradox if ineptitude were not normally a pointer to falsehood.

[14] Bernard Williams, Tertullian's paradox, in A. Flew and A. MacIntyre (eds.), *New essays in philosophical theology* (London, 1955), 187–211 (192).

[15] *Ibid.*, 203.

[16] *Ibid.*, 207. 'But this is to counter one's opponent's move by smashing up the chessboard.' On the contrary, we shall see that Tertullian makes a clever move.

[17] His critics may ask whether, in choosing between a realist and docetic christology, Tertullian leaves a place for those who deny any mode of incarnation. This was prejudged by his Heraclitean thought-world; cf. Clement, *paed.* 3.1.2. ὀρθῶς ἄρα εἶπεν Ἡράκλειτος "ἄνθρωποι θεοί, θεοὶ ἄνθρωποι. λόγος γὰρ ωὑτός" μυστήριον ἐμφανές. Θεὸς ἐν ἀνθρώπῳ, καὶ ὁ ἄνθρωπος θεός.

[18] Williams, Tertullian's paradox, 211. He admits that he is not concerned with an analysis of Tertullian's paradox but with certain consequences and the general question of verifiability. He would need to do a proper analysis if he wished to make this claim.

(iii) Mystery and reason

A medievalist account is not concerned to analyze Tertullian's argument, but to examine the general question of theological mystery and to correct the exuberance of Reformed philosophical theology in contemporary North America. The writer is quite explicit about taking Tertullian's claims out of their context: 'I do not know, where, if anywhere, Tertullian said "credo quia absurdum" as he is so often said to have said.' The nearest thing, which he can find, is the paradox of *de carne Christi* 5.4.[19]

The discussion concerns the relation of reason to mystery. The archetypes are taken from a thousand years before the medieval debate. Tertullian and Augustine both discuss the relation between authority, faith, reason and understanding. The contrast, it is claimed, could not be greater. For the latter accepted and the former denied 'the application of reasoning to religious truth'.[20] It is unfortunate for this interpretation that Augustine's claim that human reason has an affinity with God,[21] quoted in support of the contrast, appeared earlier in Tertullian (*an.* 16.1) who seems to have provided Augustine with some of his best lines.[22]

Tertullian's joining of philosophy and heresy (*praescr.* 7 and *ap.* 46.8) presents no difficulty: 'I think it is clear that what he is really repudiating, even in passages of that sort, is the very idea of a *Christian philosophy.*'[23] Along with the link with heresy, there was a more important reason for rejecting philosophy: essential Christian doctrines were inaccessible to reason and must be accepted 'as certain on the basis of divine authority alone, or perhaps on no basis at all'.[24]

These doctrines are treated, we are told, as divine 'mysteries'.

---

[19] N. Kretzmann, Faith Seeks, Understanding Finds: Augustine's Charter for Christian Philosophy, in Thomas Flint (ed.), *Christian Philosophy* (Notre Dame, 1989), 1–36 (4).

[20] Kretzmann, *ibid.*, Tertullian 'viewed the project of a Christian philosophy as at best a waste of time'.

[21] *Ep.* 120.1.3. Also quoted by Kretzmann, Reason in mystery, in G. Vesey (ed.), *The philosophy in Christianity* (Cambridge, 1989), 20. This opinion, which is commonly attributed to Augustine, is already firmly established in Justin, Clement of Alexandria and Tertullian.

[22] 'Qui fecit, refecit' has already been noted. Another is 'tam antiqua et tam nova'. *conf.* 10.27.

[23] Kretzmann, Faith seeks, 4. With great respect, surely there is more than one *idea* of a Christian philosophy, and not merely different attempts to do the same thing?

[24] *Ibid.*, 5.

Under the theme of 'Reason in Mystery', the rejection of classical foundationalism by Reformed epistemology is seen as a challenge to the usefulness of Aquinas and medieval philosophy.[25] Tertullian's wholesale 'repudiation' of philosophy is contrasted with the views of Peter Lombard, Aquinas and Bonaventure. All of which might well be in order if it were not tied to Tertullian as a type. Bonaventure's claim for the consummation of the innate light of reason by the infused light of revelation is remarkably close to the position of Tertullian.[26]

The first and third irrationalist interpretations of the paradox depend on a doxographical (one word – one meaning) approach while the second presents a useful but incomplete analysis. The third position uses Tertullian to fight a contemporary battle about medieval usefulness.

B. RATIONALIST INTERPRETATIONS

(i) Improbability and certitude

A brief note[27] shows a parallel between Tertullian's paradox and Aristotle (*Rhetoric* 2.23; 1400a5), where it is argued that if incredible events are claimed to have occurred, they, or something similar, must have happened to make the claim possible. Such incredible events are all the more likely to be true, because what we believe is either (a) actual fact or (b) probability. If we believe something improbable (not-b) then it must be actual fact (a).

Incredible things would not be believed if they were not true or nearly true. An object of belief is either a fact or a probability; 'if, therefore, a thing that *is* believed is improbable and incredible, it must be true, since it is certainly not believed because it is at all probable or credible'.[28] The examples, given by Androcles of Pitthus, when he claimed that the laws need a law to set them right, are that fish need salt and olive-cakes need oil.

[25] A. Plantinga, Reason and belief in God, in A. Plantinga and N. Wolterstorff, (eds.), *Faith and Rationality*, (Notre Dame, 1983), 16–93 (48, 63–93). Cited by Kretzmann, Reason in mystery, 18.

[26] Kretzmann, Reason in mystery, 38. See Tertullian's account of faith as recognition, below, ch. 4.

[27] James Moffatt, Aristotle and Tertullian, *JThS*, 17 (1916), 170f.

[28] *Rhetoric*, 2.23.1400a. Translation W. Rhys Roberts, *The complete works of Aristotle: the revised Oxford translation*, ed. Jonathan Barnes (Princeton, 1984), 2,231.

This is not as good an argument as that offered by Tertullian. The enthymeme (syllogism with one premiss unstated) was presented by Aristotle as a commonplace, and Aristotle was taken into the Stoic tradition, as Cicero (*Acad.* 1.41f.) declares. It is sufficient to note the parallel and its evidence that Tertullian was not the first to infer certainty from improbability and that the assumption of irrationalism is groundless.

(ii) Context, scripture and particularity

Another rationalist interpretation of the paradox begins with the exegesis of scripture. The author recognizes, while other interpreters ignore, that the major source of Tertullian and his contemporary Christians is always the New Testament. He rejects the irrationalist interpretation of the paradox on three grounds: it neglects the context of the argument, it ignores the two basic texts of scripture (1 Cor. 1 and 2; Mark 8.38 with Luke 9.26 and Matt. 10.32), and confuses a particular case with a universal rule.[29]

The writer acknowledges the wide range of interpretations, from provocative rationalism to absolute irrationalism: one account rightly reminds us that a rational Tertullian is speaking to heretics who need to be recalled to the rule of faith,[30] while another discerns the superior certainty of faith and rightly doubts whether even an individualist like Tertullian would place the criterion of truth in absurdity.[31]

Tertullian begins with God's folly and shame. The 'stupidities which belong to the abuse and suffering of God'[32] are the foolish things of the world which, according to Paul, God has chosen to confound the wise. This divine shame is linked to the words of Jesus, 'He who is ashamed of me, of him shall I be ashamed'; human advantage lies in accepting the disgrace of God. What is unworthy of God (*indignum deo*; cf. *inconveniens* (*carn.* 3.26)) is whatever could

---

[29] V. Décarie, Le paradoxe de Tertullien, *VC* (1960), 29–31. See also Viciano, *Cristo salvador*, 249f.

[30] A. d'Alès, *La théologie de Tertullien* (Paris, 1905), 34f.

[31] E. Gilson, *La philosophie au Moyen-Age* (Paris, 1952), 97f. In addition to the three antirationalist positions which we have discussed, Décarie mentions G. J. de Vries, *Bijdrage tot de psychologie van Tertullianus* (Utrecht, 1929).

[32] 'stulta quae pertinent ad contumelias et passiones dei'.

cause the disciple to be confounded and to disown his lord. The causes *(materiae)* of such confounding – crucifixion, death, burial and resurrection – are twice identified. Good impudence confesses what is unworthy of God and felicitous stupidity acknowledges the foolishness of God. What is, for the worldly, morally and intellectually inappropriate *(impudens, stultus)* is good and profitable in the presence of God. The particular case of crucifixion is credible and inept. So the alleged 'antirationalism' of Tertullian (like that of Paul in 1 Corinthians) is simply a rationalism which takes account of a wider, eschatological range of factors. It proves, against Marcion, the possibility of the incarnation *(carn.* 3) because neither the natural humiliations of life in the flesh *(carn.* 4) nor the painful humiliations of the cross are unworthy of God *(carn.* 5).

Credo quia absurdum misquotes and misrepresents Tertullian's logic and exegesis. Logically, it isolates a proposition from the context which gives it meaning, alters it, and then generalizes from the particular irrationality of the crucifixion to the universal rejection of reason. Exegetically, it neglects the two scriptural sources which, for Tertullian, represent the word of God. It represents a neat example of the doxographical dangers which threaten all study of the early fathers – failure to analyze the argument within which a proposition occurs and failure to examine the exegetical basis of a theology which is always meant to be based on the bible.

(iii) Paradox, scripture and syllogism

The third rationalist interpretation of the paradox[33] begins by a consideration of the wider context (especially *ap.* 17.1–3). There is an initial paradox: God's great power both places him beyond our understanding and enables him to bridge, from his side, the gap which is for us unbridgeable.[34] We cannot see God, but we cannot deny the evidence of his works. His transcendence and intelligibility are inseparable. Tertullian here opposes the irrationalism of the unknown God of the Gnostics with the rationalism of the Christian God who is creator of the world. But the paradox is clear. Three

---

[33] Fredouille, *Conversion*, 326–37.
[34] 'ita eum vis magnitudinis et notum hominibus obicit et ignotum'.

times Tertullian states the antinomy of intelligibility and transcendence, three times he resolves it.

In his reply to the Jews (*Jud.* 9.7f.), he shows how the sign promised by Isaiah has to be outrageous to be seen as divine ('a virgin mother deserves to be believed'). The simplicity of baptism (*bapt.* 2.1–3)[35] is joined to divine omnipotence, at once a biblical (Job 42; Matt. 19.26; Luke 1.37) and a Stoic[36] principle. Against Marcion (*Marc.* 2.2.4–6 and 2.27.1) he exploits the Pauline paradox of the folly and the wisdom of the cross: Marcion, for all his protestations of Pauline loyalty, does not respect Paul's claim that God's wisdom and power are foolishness and weakness to the world. 'So when God is small, by human standards he is especially great, when he is not good by human standards he is especially good, when he seems two or more to man, he is especially one' (*Marc.* 2.2.6). The humility of incarnation seems unworthy of God; but the incarnation is necessary for salvation, and nothing is more worthy of God than human salvation (*Marc.* 2.27.1).

When we consider the Stoic widespread use of paradox and Tertullian's frequent return to the Pauline scandal of the cross, the famous *credibile quia ineptum* ceases to be outrageous. Rather than a cynical rejection of reason, the paradox points to the syllogism:[37]

1. The divinely true scriptures have in different ways announced the foolishness of the cross.
2. This folly implies incarnation and crucifixion.
3. Therefore the incarnation and the crucifixion are necessary and true.

All three rationalist interpretations emphasize context and argument. An analysis of the argument which surrounds the paradox provides the only firm basis for interpretation.

C. TERTULLIAN'S ARGUMENT

(i) Marcion disproved

Marcion denies the flesh and nativity of Christ. Certainly the creator's prophet talks of a virgin birth; but this is not relevant

---

[35] See ch. 1, above.   [36] Cicero, *de natura deorum*, 3.92.
[37] Fredouille, *Conversion*, 334.

because Marcion's creator never knows what he is talking about. Christ comes suddenly, without the proofs of his flesh which the birth provides, and indeed birth is either impossible or inappropriate for God. Nothing, replies Tertullian, is impossible for God, except what he does not will. Further, since God willed to appear as a man, he must have willed to be a man, because he would never have willed to seem what he was not.[38] According to Marcion, others could have wrongly supposed him to be a man; but Christ would not have exhibited himself as that which he knew he was not.

(ii) God's unique transcendence

God is sovereign and unique, the supreme greatness, established in all eternity. The most high God is beyond comparison (*Marc.* 1.4.1), is independent of time and has no beginning or end (*Marc.* 1.8.3). God is unique in knowledge, revelation, origin and sinlessness. The knowledge of God is given by him alone, since only God can reveal what God had formerly hidden (*an.* 1.6). He is the only being who is unmade, unborn and unchangeable (*an.* 21.7). Nothing is equal with God; his nature differs from the condition of all things (*carn.* 3.5). Unlike all other things, he can change without losing the existence which he previously had. Even angels can change into human bodily form and remain angels. Anything angels can do, God can do better.

(iii) Correction through opposites

God loves and redeems what he has made. While nature is an object of reverence to others, Marcion, who hates all humans including himself, spits on it in contempt.

Recapitulation occurs because God loves and therefore redeems and renews his creature. While in *de praescriptione haereticorum* Tertullian looked chiefly to the unsurpassable *perfection* of Christ, in *de carne Christi* Tertullian declares the miracle of divine *correction* and salvation.

---

[38] God is not in danger of losing his state and condition; he cannot change if changing means an end to something, for God has no end.

Our birth he renews from death by a heavenly regeneration;
he restores our flesh from every sickness which afflicts it;
he cleanses the stain from the flesh of the leper;
he gives light again to it when it is blind;
he restores strength to it when it is paralysed;
he exorcizes flesh possessed by demons;
he gives life again to flesh which is dead. (*carn.* 4.4)

(iv) Folly and wisdom

As Paul says, in paradox, God has chosen the foolish things of his humiliation to confound the wise. Tertullian demands a re-assessment of the foolish things which include conversion to worship of the true God, rejection of error, and moral progress in righteousness, chastity, mercy, patience and innocence. They are true wisdom.

The rejection of Christ's birth means rejection of his cross and sufferings; yet Paul is clear that Christ and him crucified constitute the whole content of faith.

Indeed our only hope is the necessary dishonour of our faith. Whatever is unworthy of God is to our gain. Tertullian is not ashamed of the crucifixion of God's son because it is inescapably shameful. The death of God's son is an essential belief because it is inept. His burial and resurrection are certain because they are impossible.

The point of the argument is plain. If God, who is wholly other, is joined to mortal man in a way which is not inept, then either God is no longer God or man is no longer man, and there is no true incarnation. Truth on this issue can only be achieved by ineptitude. Tertullian does not universalize his claim; most ineptitude is false. This argument is put into paradox, to imitate Paul and to make it more striking and provocative. Paradoxes are useful because they are wonderful and against common opinion.[39]

(v) Two natures

The correction of our need could only take place if Christ had flesh which could die, be buried and rise again. Therefore he had two

---

[39] Cicero, *Paradoxa Stoicorum*, 4.

substances: divine and human, two states, two natures. This may be proved: 'The powers of the spirit of God proved him to be God, his sufferings proved his human flesh.' Therefore 'Why halve Christ with a lie? He was wholly the truth' (*carn.* 5.7f.). He chose to be born rather than to pretend in any way. Birth and death are correlates and Christ's death proves that he was once born. To die a human death he had to have human flesh; mortal flesh has to be preceded by birth.

Here we have in a nutshell the development of early christology.[40] The contrasts between the second and the fourth century should be evident. We should not begin by looking for fourth-century controversies in the second century; but we have seen how a concern with divine economy and recapitulation moves into trinity and christology. Recapitulation points to the need for two natures if God is to renew man. Similarly Tertullian writes against Praxeas that simple people must recognize that the one God can only be understood in terms of his economy (*Prax.* 3.1). The trinity is unintelligible apart from economy and recapitulation. God is one in a new way: by the son and spirit. If there were no recapitulation, there would be no way of knowing the trinity. The striking thing in Tertullian is the clarity with which, from the beginning of his theology, the move is made from the primitive acclamation 'Jesus Christ, son of God, saviour' to a threefold rule of faith. Recent theology recognizes that trinitarian theology depends not on the scattered formulae found in the New Testament but on the ever-present proclamation of the cross. 'What God did on the cross is the most concise statement of the trinity.'[41]

(vi) Correction as final clue to paradox

Christ taught the new way of life, preached the kingdom of God and healed the sick. Here the 'exchange formulae' (*Tauschformeln*), beloved of Irenaeus, point to newness and correction. The most striking source is prophetic hope which gives 'beauty for ashes, the oil of joy for mourning, the garment of praise for the spirit of

---

[40] See below, ch. 6.
[41] B. Steffen, *Das Dogma vom Kreuz* (1922), 152, cited in E. Jüngel, *Gott als Geheimnis der Welt* (Tübingen, 1977), 481.

heaviness' (Isa. 61.5). For Tertullian the ineptitude of the change is important.[42]

With Irenaeus, the idea of balance, exchange, symmetry or fitness is used to argue the necessity of the incarnation. 'Because of his infinite love, he became what we are, to make us what he is' (*haer. pref.* 5). A *Tauschformel*[43] describes an exchange between properties or people. The father witnesses to the son and the son announces the father (*haer.* 3.6.2). Through obedience, Jesus destroys disobedience (*haer.* 3.18.3); he had to become human among humans, to be visible and tangible, if he were to unite humanity and God (*dem.* 6). Tertullian goes further when he insists that the two sides of a balance must be opposite if a just balance is to be achieved; what was *aptum* for Irenaeus is both *aptum* and *ineptum* for Tertullian.

The passages, which Apelles and Marcion use against Christ's human flesh, prove his birth and flesh, when they are interpreted 'according to the truth of the whole and uncorrupted gospel' (*carn.* 8.1).

Some tried to take him from his great work, so he says, 'Who are my mother and brothers?' This was an appropriate question for Christ 'who was preaching and revealing God, fulfilling the law and the prophets, dispelling the dark gloom of the long preceding age' (*carn.* 7.11), when others wanted to take him from this work of correction and fulfilment. He did not deny his birth and family (as the Marcionites claim) but gave them second place to his mission. He requires us and all his disciples to do the same. Again when he did not deny his mother's womb and breasts, but declared the greater blessing of the word of God, he was concerned with the priority of the gospel.

The sufferings of Christ prove that his flesh was not a celestial substance. No one would have dared to lay a finger on his body, let alone spit on it, if it had not borne the signs of physical weakness.

---

[42] For Irenaeus, the whole history of salvation is *aptum*, joining beginning to end. That is why it took so long. For Tertullian the *aptum* of the dispensation is achieved by balancing what is inept.

[43] See A. Bengsch, *Heilsgeschichte und Heilswissen, Eine Untersuchung zur Struktur und Entfaltung des theologischen Denkens im Werk 'Adversus Haereses' des hl. Irenäus von Lyons* (Leipzig, 1957), 157f.

His hunger, tears, trembling and spilt blood point to the earthiness of his incarnation.[44]

What did he want to correct? He came to destroy sin done by the flesh, not the flesh which sinned, 'not the substance but the flaw' (*carn.* 16). The flesh of Christ resembled sinful flesh in its nature, but not in the corruption which it had received from Adam.[45]

Why must Christ be born of a virgin? A full statement of recapitulation follows to show how correction involves both continuity and newness (*carn.* 17). He who was to consecrate a new order of birth must be born in a new way, as Isaiah predicted: 'a virgin shall conceive ... Emmanuel'. In this new nativity, man is born in God and God is born in man. He takes flesh of ancient stock without ancient seed, to reform it with new spiritual seed and to cleanse it from ancient stains.

The parallel is clear. A virgin (like untouched earth) is the medium of the new dispensation of divine nativity. The Second Adam, as Paul says, is a life-giving spirit out of the ground, i.e. out of unstained flesh. God regained his image and likeness in the same way as he had been robbed by the devil.

While the word which snared virgin Eve crept into her ear to bring death, the Word enters the virgin's soul to bring life. The feminine gender which brought ruin now brings salvation. Eve believed the serpent; Mary believed the angel. Eve bore a devil who murdered his brother; Mary bore one who was to bring salvation to Israel, his brother and his murderer. God sent down his word as the good brother, to blot out memory of the evil brother. It was necessary that, to save man, Christ should come in that flesh in which man had lived since his condemnation (*carn.* 17.4–6).

Only the Spirit was needed to assume flesh of man, because the seed of man was unnecessary for one who had the seed of God. As God the Spirit he is born of God; being generated in the flesh as man, he is born of the flesh of man (*carn.* 18.7). (God, the beginning, is joined to flesh which is the end, when the word becomes flesh.)

---

[44] Other explanations are rejected because their proponents cannot produce good reasons for turning Christ's flesh into soul, or his soul into flesh. Christ took a soul in order to redeem both souls and bodies of mankind. He came to save men not angels.

[45] Those who deny the human flesh of Christ because he did not have a human father, should remember that Adam received his flesh without a human father.

This account of flesh and virgin birth is invaluable because it shows the numerous truth conditions with which Tertullian connects the incarnation. Those truth conditions enable us to understand what he says.[46]   We return to our summary of the paradox.[47]

X. 1. Tertullian is not ashamed of the crucifixion of God's son because it is necessarily shameful.
   2. The death of God's son must be believed because it is inept.
   3. His burial and resurrection is certain because it is impossible.
Y. All this can only be true if he had flesh which could die, be buried and rise again.
Z. Christ had two substances: divine and human, two states, two natures. This may be proved: 'The powers of the Spirit proved him to be God, his sufferings proved his human flesh.'
   Therefore 'Why halve Christ with a lie? He was wholly the truth.'

The paradox may be analysed:

God is wholly other, and differs from man and from all else. If he is joined to man in a way which is not shameful, inept and impossible, then either God is no longer God or man is no longer man. If God is joined to man in a way which is shameful, inept and impossible, then God is truly God and man is truly man.

Recapitulation is, for Irenaeus, the joining of the end to the beginning, the joining of man to God (*haer.* 4.20.4). For the Fourth Gospel, that word who was in the beginning (John 1.1) becomes flesh (John 1.14) which was God's final creation. When he follows the way of human life to the end on the cross, recapitulation is complete, for the end has been joined to the beginning and he can say, 'It is finished.' For Tertullian, 'Just as Alpha rolls on to Omega and then Omega rolls back to Alpha, so he might show in himself the way from the beginning to the end, and the way from the end to the beginning' (*mon.* 5.2).

Alpha is not Omega and Omega is not Alpha. Therefore Alpha/Omega will be Alpha/not-Alpha, which is inept. Beta/Omega or Alpha/Psi would modify the ineptitude by moving the terms closer together, but would not be true because Beta is not God (Alpha) and Psi is not man (Omega). What is at

---

[46] The resurrection of the flesh and the virgin birth were both rationally acceptable to Tertullian's audience.
[47] See above p.49.

issue here is not whether God somehow became man, but whether he did it in a way which is apt and therefore untrue, or in a way which is inept and therefore true. The paradox requires that ineptitude commonly implies falsehood but does not imply falsehood in this special case.

D. SUPPORTING ARGUMENTS

There are supporting arguments for the analysis which has been put forward. They make the popular picture of Tertullian as an apostle of unreason even less probable.

(i) Tertullian claims to follow the discipline of reason against Marcion who, he says, is brainless. While many rationalists say things which are not rational, they neither intend to do so nor do they confess their departure from reason. Tertullian's paradoxes here are to be understood together with all his other cryptic sayings. 'Blood is seed' is an equally enigmatic but perfectly reasonable and evangelical (John 12.24) claim. For Tertullian almost anything worth saying can be expressed in a paradox.

(ii) This was both a personal habit and part of his Stoicism. Cicero had set out six paradoxes:

those doctrines which the Stoics scarcely succeed in proving in the retirement of the schools of philosophy. These doctrines are surprising and they run counter to universal opinion – the Stoics actually call them *paradoxa*; so I wanted to try whether it is possible for them to be brought into the light of common daily life and expounded in a form to win acceptance, or whether learning has one style of discourse and ordinary life another; and I wrote with the greater pleasure because the doctrines styled *paradoxa* by the Stoics appear to me to be in the highest degree Socratic, and far and away the truest.[48]

The six paradoxes[49] are:
1. Only what is morally good is noble.
2. Possession of virtue is sufficient for happiness.
3. Transgressions are equal and right actions are equal.
4. Every foolish man is mad.
5. Only the wise man is free and every foolish man is a slave.

---

[48] *Paradoxa Stoicorum*, 4.   [49] *Ibid.*, 6–52.

6. The wise man alone is rich.

These are in no way a denial of reason; they are truths which derive from Socrates and which persist into Stoicism because they are most true.

(iii) Today, fideism is most commonly linked with that rejection of the Enlightenment proposed by Dialectical Theology. Whereas the Enlightenment opposed faith and reason and enthroned the latter, Barth, or at least some Barthians, accepted the opposition but deposed reason. Barth's evaluation of Tertullian is therefore interesting. He sees him as having understood the distinctive Christian claims and yet having failed to modify his apologetic appropriately. Tertullian is not a true believer. All the apologists present a sorry picture of competition with the existing religions, a competition which they regrettably won. 'How strangely did a man like Tertullian see the danger which threatened at this point, and at the same time never really see it at all, but actually help t o increase it.'[50]

(iv) Against irrationalist interpretation stands Tertullian's an-thropology which finds the divine image in human rationality, his opposition to Marcion's irrational god and his Stoic priority for all that is according to nature.

[50] K. Barth, *Church dogmatics*, I.2 (Edinburgh, 1956), 333f. Barth's condemnation of Tertullian is strange. Was Tertullian to stand by while his fellow believers were persecuted for following a depraved superstition, without offering any defence against the charge?

CHAPTER 4

Strife of opposites and faith as recognition

The *apologeticum* is a defence of Christians in face of persecution by Roman authorities. As elsewhere in early Christian literature, the virtues of Christians are set out, their blameless lives are extolled and the demonic origin of persecution exposed. However, as with Justin's *Apology*, there are general principles and themes which give coherence and intensity to the long list of details.

The first general principle is that the world is governed by the strife of opposites – of light with darkness, of good with evil. Following this axiom, three points are made. First, within universal conflict, justice or reason must balance all things, suppress evil and encourage good. Secondly, God is present from beginning to end, from first to last. His economy runs without faltering from creation through all his dealings with mankind, until the coming of the man Jesus in whom all is brought to perfection. Thereafter Jesus is present in the varied virtues of the church and in the seed of the martyrs, so that nothing lies outside his rule which is to be plainly declared in his final judgement. The third theme is the persistence of the cross. The worship of Christ as God comes from those who are tortured and afflicted. Out of the depth of their suffering, they proclaim salvation and out of their seed the gospel grows.

To these three themes (balance of justice, divine economy and seed of suffering), Tertullian adds a note of confidence. Since God gave Christians as his gift to the world (*ap.* 40.13), there has been a change. Their innocence has tempered injustice in the world and their prayers have prevailed upon God for good. In summer drought, pagan anxiety produces pagan panic. However Christians 'parched with fastings and pinched with every sort of self-restraint, separated from all bread which is necessary to life,

65

wallowing in sack-cloth and ashes, importune heaven with re-proach, touch the heart of God. When we have wrested mercy from him, Jupiter gets the honour!' (*ap.* 40.15). Pagan violence is dangerous since it is directed against Christians who mitigate injustice and disaster. Christians are not merely one half of the dialectic between good and evil. They are also part of the reason or justice which preserves the balance of opposites, the *logos spermatikos*, the seed of the cross. The incarnation gave Tertullian a strong sense of God's involvement in events.

A. THE STRIFE OF OPPOSITES

(i) *The balance of justice*

In the strife between good and evil, hatred for the Christian name springs from ignorance which always hates the wrong thing. Nature has stamped on every evil the qualities of fear and shame: evil hides itself and does not offer a defence. In contrast, Christian faith overcomes fear, shame, false denial, regret and despair.[1] A Christian confesses his faith and even gives thanks for his condemnation (*ap.* 1.12).

The goodness of Christians is confirmed by contrasting the treatment of real criminals who must answer accusations with that of Christians who are not allowed to answer the charges brought against them. When Pliny (the Younger), says Tertullian, examined Christian behaviour, he found entirely blameless lives. Yet Trajan instructed him not to seek out Christians but to punish them if they were brought to trial. There is no logic here: Christians are not to be sought out because they are innocent, yet when they face judgement, they are automatically punished as criminals (*ap.* 2.9). In all this, the strife between good and evil goes on; but Roman justice does not discern the realities of the conflict. This blindness spreads throughout the community so that it is commonly assumed that a good or wise man will not become a Christian (*ap.* 3.1). When a Christian chooses virtue and goodness, hatred blinds his fellows to a recognition of his improvement.

Now follows a refutation of those charges against Christians,

---

[1] There remain a higher fear and shame, to be discussed below, ch. 11.

which culminate in the law which forbids them to exist ('non licet esse vos'); but a law should both be just and also exhibit justice to those who must obey it. Justice must be done and must appear to have been done. A law which cannot pass this test is an evil thing (*ap.* 4.13). The goodness of Christians is confirmed by the wicked-ness of those who, like Nero, have persecuted them (*ap.* 5). In the violence of Nero against Christians, it is easy to see on which side good and evil are placed.

Such confusion of good and evil is due to rumour (*fama*) which is always swift and false (*ap.* 7.8; cf. Virgil, *Aeneid* 4.174). Indeed the charges of infanticide and cannibalism which are levelled against Christians may be proved against their accusers (*ap.* 9). No sense can be made of the punishment of Christians simply for their failure to worship the gods. Pagan practice (*ap.* 14) and pagan fantasy about Christian worship (*ap.* 16) are equally irrational. Magic and deceit (*ap.* 23) pervert the course of justice, while pagan festivals dishonour modesty (*ap.* 35). The enemies of Rome do wrong against their fellows as well as against the emperor, while Christians refrain from wrong-doing at every point (*ap.* 36). Christians are enemies of human error, not enemies of humankind (*ap.* 37.8). There is no evil in the rules and practice of the Christian community which expels sinners, dispenses charity for others and displays mutual love (*ap.* 39). Christian innocence goes beyond public acts to inner attitudes, for their God searches all hearts and nothing can be hidden from his judgement (*ap.* 45); yet it collects blame for every catastrophe (*ap.* 40.2).

Tertullian's central idea is that the universe is made of opposites which must be harmonized and held together by reason. The persecution of Christians destroys this harmony and is therefore fundamentally wrong and due to demonic perversion. The balance of ethical opposites is necessary and anticipates God's final justice which will restore all things. The persecution of Christians undermines the moral fabric of the world. Tertullian's claim is strengthened by an insistence that the justice of the world is always proleptic and imperfect, whereas the final justice of God initiates the eschaton now.

Having refuted the main accusations against Christians, Tertul-lian moves to minor charges (*ap.* 39–48). Christian lives are marked by exuberance in life and prayer, a 'violence pleasing to God', and hold a common profession, discipline and hope. Christians meet to offer fervent and united prayer to God, praying for all in authority and for peace and the postponement of the End. Together they read their divine Scriptures and stir up faith and hope. Judgement of wrong-doers is duly pondered and members are solemnly expelled. Those who judge are certain that God is watching them. Money, collected once a month on a voluntary basis, is spent, not on orgies but on the poor, on destitute children, on old people who are shut in and on survivors of shipwrecks. Those banished to mines, islands or prison for their faith become the *alumni* of their confession (*ap.* 39.1–6).

This practice of excessive charity burns a brand on Christians so that their neighbours say, 'See how they love one another!' Yet this brotherhood is not exclusive, but joins Christians to pagans 'by law of nature, our common mother' ('iure naturae matris unius') even if the latter are hardly human because they fail as brothers. How much more fittingly (*quanto dignius fratres*) are they called brothers who recognize one God as their father, have drunk one spirit and have burst from one womb of ignorance to the one light of truth.

Fraternity is made stronger because Christians share their material possessions. Unlike Socrates or Cato, they do not share their wives, refusing to imitate Attic wisdom or Roman gravity in this respect. The Christian love-feast contrasts with pagan orgies, for it is a religious office, free from all immodesty. Prayer is followed by a chaste and frugal meal, hands are washed and lights are brought. Each stands to sing a hymn, either from scripture or from his own composition and this means he *has* to be sober. Such a gathering of pious and chaste people is not a faction but a solemn assembly (*ap.* 39).

The real factions (*ap.* 40.1f.) are found among those who blame Christians for every disaster, with shouts of 'Christians to the lion!' This is absurd. There were plenty of calamities before Christians appeared, because sin always had to be punished. 'The human race has always deserved ill of God' (*ap.* 40.10). Men did not work on their limited natural knowledge of God but invented other gods to fill his place. They wilfully ignored Jesus, the righteous teacher. If they had sought and obeyed God, then God's grace would have replaced his wrath. Their ingratitude brought suffering. By contrast, Christian fasting, penitence and prayer check wickedness and hold back disaster (*ap.* 40.14).

Christian enthusiasm plunges into life in the world which their God has created. As sailors, soldiers, farmers, traders and craftsmen, Christians play a full and useful role in society. It is true that, like some others, they do not pay money to the temples; but they give much more to beggars in the street. They meet their other taxes, because they will not defraud their natural brothers (*ap.* 42). Of course, it must be admitted that Christians are not much good to pimps, poisoners and soothsayers; but their prayers to the true God protect their persecutors (*ap.* 43). Further, it is a loss to the commonwealth when the truly good people are killed off (*ap.* 44.1).

Christian perfection comes again to the fore. Only Christians keep clear of crime; this is a necessity not a contingency. Those, who are taught goodness by God himself, have perfect knowledge through their perfect teacher. Other ethical views are human opinions, carry human authority and are narrow in scope. Which are the larger claims: 'do not kill!' or 'do not be angry!', 'do not commit adultery!' or 'do not lust!'? The Christian incentive to virtue is equally enlarged. Other punishments cease at death. The Christian fears eternal punishment from a divine judge, before whom he can never hide (*ap.* 45).

The climax of Tertullian's argument combines Johannine dualism, where death brings life, and Paul's account of God who raises the dead and creates from nothing with a Heraclitean and Stoic belief in the ultimacy of opposites. Resurrection simply repeats creation. We who once did not exist were made; when we have ceased to exist, we shall be made all over again (*ap.* 48.5f.). Creation from nothing implies resurrection from death. Light and darkness alternate, as the seasons return in their order. All things are preserved by perishing and all things are remade out of death. For the divine logos or reason made the universe from opposites (*ap.* 48.11).

That same reason which constructed the universe out of diversity, so that all things from their antithetical substances agree in a unity – empty and solid, animate and inanimate, comprehensible and incomprehensible, light and darkness, even life and death – has also so disposed the whole course of existence according to a distinctive plan, so that the first part of it, which we inhabit, reckoned from the creation, flows on to its end in the age of time; and the following part, to which we look, extends into boundless eternity.'[2]

When, however, the end comes, the temporal form of the world will pass away (*ap.* 48.12). All men shall be raised, judged and sent either to eternal life with God or to eternal punishment in fire. Like the mountains which burn but remain, the wicked will endure in fire. The opposites, justly ordered, go on forever.

This view of the changing world is older than the Platonism which took charge of early Christian thought. Thales described the world as a cycle of watery change and insisted that all things are full of gods (*PP* 85, 91; Aristotle, *Met.* A3.983b6, *de anima* A5.411a7). Anaximander said that all things came from and returned into the Indefinite, 'making reparation and satisfaction to one another'. Instead of one material substance the 'oppositions in the substratum, which was a boundless body, were separated out' (*PP* 101: Simplicius, *in Phys.* 24, 13). Air, water and fire oppose one another so that if 'any one of them were boundless, the others would by now have ceased to be' (*PP* 105: Aristotle, *Physics* 5.204b22). As the elements fought with one another, they must make reparation at an appointed time for trespassing over their limits.

Anaximenes believed that all things came from air, which was invisible when even and visible when disturbed by cold, heat, moisture or motion. In constant change and motion, it became fire, wind, cloud, water, earth and finally stone (*PP* 141: Hippolytus, *Ref.* 1.7.1).

For Xenophanes, as early Christian writers rejoiced to hear (*PP* 170: Clem. Alex., *strom.* 5.109.1), there is one god who sees, thinks and hears all (*PP* 172: Sextus, *adv. math.* 9.144), being immoveable and ruling by his mind (*PP* 171: Simplicius, *in Phys.* 23.11 and 23.20). He unifies the opposites in himself, while man is born of earth and water (*PP* 181: Simplicius, *in Phys.* 189.1D) and earth is gradually

---

[2] Quae ratio universitatem ex diversitate composuit, ut omnia ex aemulis substantiis sub unitate constarent, ex vacuo et solido, ex animali et inanimali, ex comprehensibili et incomprehensibili, ex luce et tenebris, ex ipsa vita et morte, eadem aevum quoque ita distincta condicione conseruit, ut prima haec pars ab exordio rerum, temporali aetate ad finem defluat, sequens vero, quam exspectamus, in infinitam aeternitatem propagetur. (*ap.* 48.11)

dissolved by the moisture of the sea, in a process of universal change (*PP* 184: Hippolytus, *Ref.* 1.14.5).

Heraclitus gives the most striking account of opposites and of the sovereign logos which must be the goal of knowledge and guide to life (*PP* 194f.: Sextus, *adv.math.* 7.132–3, *PP* 196: Hippolytus, *Ref.* 9.9.1). The union of opposites may be inherent or successive. First, 'There are opposites which inhere in or are simultaneously produced by a single subject.'[3] The same sea water is good for fish and harmful to humans (*PP* 199: Hippolytus, *Ref.* 9.10.5). The path up and the path down is the same (*PP* 200: Hippolytus, *Ref.* 9.10.4). Only disease, hunger and tiredness can show the goodness of health, fullness and rest (*PP* 201: Stobaeus, *Ecl.* 3.1.177).

Second, there are successive opposites which are 'different stages in a single invariable process'.[4] Between life and death, waking and sleeping, youth and age, there is change and interchange. Things are brought together and held apart, are whole and not whole, are in and out of tune.[5] God indeed is both day and night (*PP* 204: Hippolytus, *Ref.* 9.10.8). From the balance of opposites comes a deep unity. Hidden harmonies are stronger than those which are apparent (*PP* 207: Hippolytus, *Ref.* 9.9.5). Nature prefers concealment (*PP* 208: Themistius, *or.* 5.p.69D). War which governs all things (*PP* 211: Origen, *Cels.* 6.42) is universal father and king (*PP* 212: Hippolytus, *Ref.* 9.9.4). Yet there is continuity, like that of a river; he who tries to step into the same river, steps into different waters which scatter and gather, join and flow away, come near and depart (*PP* 214: Arius Didymus *apud Eusebium Praeparatio Evangelica* 15.20 and Plutarch, *de E apud Delphos* 18.392B). Fire is the stuff of all things. 'This world-order (the same for all) was made by no god or man; but it was ever, is and shall be an ever-living fire, with measures of its kindling and measures of its going out' (*PP* 217: Clem. Alex., *strom.* 5.104.1). Fire, sea and earth mutually change and balance one another (*PP* 218: Clem. Alex., *strom.* 5.104.3). As money and goods are exchanged, so it is with fire and all things (*PP* 219: Plutarch, *de E* 8.388D). The thunderbolt which guides all things is purest heavenly fire (*PP* 220: Hippolytus, *Ref.* 9.10.6). The sun is new every day (*PP* 225: Aristotle, *Meteor.* B2.355a13) and is

---

[3] *PP*, 189.   [4] *Ibid.*

[5] ἐκ πάντων ἓν καὶ ἐξ ἑνὸς πάντα (*PP* 203: [Aristotle], *de mundo* 5.396b20).

governed by measure which justice enforces (*PP* 226: Plutarch, *de exil.* 2.604A). To know how 'all things are steered through all' (*PP* 227: Diogenes Laertius, *Lives* 9.1) is the sole wisdom and is found only in a god who resembles and differs from Zeus (*PP* 228: Clem. Alex., *strom.* 5.115.1). In a changing world, self-knowledge (*PP* 246: Plutarch, *adv. Colotem*, 20.1118C), restraint (*PP* 248: Diogenes Laertius, *Lives* 9.2) and dependence on divine law (*PP* 249: Diogenes Laertius, *Lives* 9.2) provide the way of understanding (*PP* 250: Stobaeus, *Ecl.* 3.1.179).

Stoicism took the harmony of opposites as the fundamental feature of nature under the control of reason. It is to the *Hymn* of Cleanthes that we owe the clearest statement of Heraclitean strife, moderated by divine reason. 'But you know how to make things crooked straight and to order things disorderly. You love things unloved. For you have so welded into one all things good and bad, that they share in a single everlasting reason' (LongSedley, 54 I, *SVF*, 1.537). According to Chrysippus, those who object to providence because of the existence of troubles and evils are foolish. Good and evil 'must necessarily exist in opposition to each other and supported by a kind of opposed interdependence'. Indeed opposites are 'tied to each other in polar opposition, as Plato said. Remove one and you remove the other.'[6] Infirmities of the body, like the thinness of the skull were necessary for rationality. Virtue was born through nature's plan (*per consilium naturae*) and vices were born by relation of opposition (*per adfinitatem contrariam*) (Gellius 7.1.1–13; *SVF*, 2.1669, 70; LongSedley, 54Q). Three hundred years later, closer to the time of Tertullian, Epictetus wrote, 'Zeus has ordained that there be summer and winter, plenty and poverty, virtue and vice and all such opposites for the sake of the harmony of the whole' (*Diss.* 1, 12, 165).[7]

Seneca explained the movements of heavenly bodies (*nat. quaest.* 7.27): 'What then can we say? Is not the universe itself, if you look at it, composed of contrasts (*ex diversis compositus*)?' Despite their

---

[6] This will not satisfy Lactantius as an explanation of evils. The Stoics are wrong when they 'reply most clumsily that among plants and animals there are many whose usefulnesss has up to now gone unnoticed; but that this will be discovered in the course of time' (*de ira dei* 13.9f.; *SVF* 2.1172; LongSedley, 54R).

[7] See A. A. Long, *Hellenistic philosophy* (London, 1974), 181, and also H. Lloyd-Jones, *The justice of Zeus* (London, 1971).

affinity, Leo produces scorching heat and Aquarius brings frozen ice; they are both of the same external condition but their effect and nature are different. The rise of Aries is sudden and that of Libra is slow. The elements are opposites (*contraria inter se*): heavy and light, hot and cold, wet and dry. The world is a harmony of discords ('tota haec mundi concordia ex discordibus constat'). The same kinds of heavenly bodies may take up their positions once a year or once every thirty years. Nature prefers variety to uniformity ('non ad unam natura formam opus suum praestat, sed ipsa varietate se iactat'), producing things large and small, fast and slow, strong and weak, violent and moderate, individual and communal. The power of nature is evident in the freak phenomena which do not fit the normal pattern.

The world of Seneca's plays exhibits the conflict of *furor* and *ratio* against a Stoic background. Seneca's description of the forum (*ira*, 2.81–91) is reminiscent of a school of gladiators. 'They are a collection of wild animals or worse; but if the wise man gets angry with them, he will always be angry. Anger, in fact, is out of place.'[8]

For Philo Judaeus (*Quaest. Gen.* 2.55), nature depends on the changing pattern of seedtime and harvest, cold and heat, summer and spring, day and night. Each variation is necessary for the safety and growth of an individual species or plant. Nature is like a harmony of different notes, some high some low; indeed the universe is composed of opposites. Unless we preserve nature's order of cold and warm, wet and dry, all things on earth will die.

As usual, Philo finds a deeper meaning in the relevant verse (Gen. 8.22 (LXX)). Seed and harvest are beginning and end, which are both causes of salvation. Beginning needs end and end needs beginning. Philo interprets cold and heat as fear and anger, day and night as reason and folly. All of which shows the presence of opposites in man as in the cosmos.

So Heraclitean opposites persist in Hellenistic and Roman thought.

Just as language may be riddling, ambiguous, paradoxical, so in the world opposites coexist, unity is a product of diversity, harmony a consequence of strife . . . the world is a unity of opposites, a harmony of opposing forces

---

[8] Cited by Rist, Stoic orthodoxy.

which can be signified by such statements as 'God is day night, winter summer, war peace' (fr. 67 DK); 'The road up and down is one and the same' (fr. 60 DK).[9]

(ii) The divine economy

To moderate the strife of opposites, God is present from the beginning of all things to their end. There is no room for new gods. The world, whether it had a beginning or not, was 'surely found to have been once for all arranged and equipped and ordered in its present structure entirely under the guidance of reason. That (God) could not be imperfect, which has perfected all things' (*ap.* 11.5). From the beginning, righteous and spirit-filled messengers came into the world to spread the knowledge of God as creator, law-giver and judge (*ap.* 18.1–3). Prophecy shows the continuity of all time and the power of God's sovereignty over past, present and future (*ap.* 20). Fulfilled prophecy confirms faith in past and present, and such faith may reasonably be projected into the future (*ap.* 20.3f.). The unity of divine history (*ap.* 21)from creation to the coming of Christ saw the rejection of the Jews and a new dispensation. The son of God came to reform and illuminate the world, to enlighten and lead the human race. The divine word, of whom the philosophers had also spoken, constructed the universe and preserved its rational order.

After the son (word/reason) came the spirit, within the same divine dispensation, and through him God's people have spread throughout the world. 'We are but of yesterday, yet we have filled all that is yours: cities, islands, fortresses, country towns, meeting-places, even camps, tribes, companies, palace, senate, forum; we have left you only your temples' (*ap.* 37.4). Without Christians the empire would be empty and Romans would be panic-stricken in their solitude and the 'death-like stupefaction of the world' (*ap.* 37.7). Fortunately, Christians do not compete in the race for fame and position. For them the world is a single commonwealth; to declare them an illegal association is absurd (*ap.* 38.1).

As the providence of God runs on, he deals impartially with all

---

[9] Long, *Hellenistic philosophy*, 146.

the human race. God's plan moves inexorably to final judgement and the end of the world (*ap.* 41.2f.). In the meantime, Christians play their public role within the world which their God has made (*ap.* 42), following the pattern of that divine justice which passed from Moses to the Romans (*ap.* 45).

In his concluding paragraphs Tertullian pleads that, however foolish Christian claims may seem, they are necessary for the defence of virtue which flourishes under threat of punishment and promise of eternal bliss. Such foolish things are useful. 'It is therefore never expedient to declare as false or to hold as foolish what it is expedient to regard as true.'[10] If it be nonsense, it should be met with ridicule rather than with sword and fire. Such punishment is futile, for the Christian (like the Stoic sage) cannot be harmed against his will. He will choose condemnation rather than apostasy and thereby achieve his desire (*ap.* 49.6).

'Therefore, in dying, we conquer' (*ap.* 50.3).[11] Tertullian ends triumphantly in the face of opposites. Roman rulers, whose injustice confirms Christian innocence, win favour through killing Christians, but Christians increase in number. 'The blood of Christians is seed' (*ap.* 50.13). Their courage inspires more people than do the words of Cicero and Seneca. Stubbornness conquers strife. 'Mastery belongs to that very obstinacy which you consider disgraceful' (*ap.* 50.15).[12] A witness of such obstinacy will be moved to inquire about its doctrines, become convinced[13] and himself go on to martyrdom, winning forgiveness for all his sins. Paradox has the last word. When condemned by earthly rulers, Christians are acquitted by God.[14]

(iii) The triumph of the cross

For Tertullian, as for Justin,[15] the cross has a persistent place. Pagans treat Christians as they treat their idols! They place them

---

[10] 'itaque non expedit falsa dici, nec inepta haberi, quae expedit vera praesumi' (*ap.* 49.2).

[11] 'ergo vincimus, cum occidimur'.

[12] 'Ipsa illa obstinatio quam exprobatis, magistra est'.

[13] Justin tells how he followed this sequence.

[14] 'Ut est aemulatio divinae rei et humanae, cum damnamur a vobis, a Deo absolvimur' (*ap.* 50.16).

[15] For whom the cosmic cross was known to Plato and there are crosses everywhere.

on a cross or stake, they tear their sides with claws and axes or they throw them into the fire. Christians are condemned to the very mines whence the pagan gods draw their material substance (*ap.* 12.3–5). The Christian cross is an unmutilated and complete god, and the legionary standards in a Roman camp are but decorated crosses (*ap.* 16.8). The effectiveness of Christian expansion goes back to the cruelty of Nero which sowed the blood of Christians as seed (*ap.* 21.25). Torn and bleeding, Christians confess under torture: 'We worship God through Christ' (*ap.* 21.28).

The Christian faces martyrdom as a soldier faces war. Where the man, who complained about battle, 'fights with all his strength and rejoices when he conquers in battle ... our battle is that we are summoned before tribunals to fight there for the truth at the risk of our lives' (*ap.* 50.2). The prize is victory, the glory of pleasing God and gaining life eternal, even if before Roman eyes Christians may seem to be desperate and reckless men.[16] Governors execute Christians to gain popularity with the mob; yet 'we spring up in greater numbers the more we are mown down by you; the blood of Christians is seed' (*ap.* 50.13). Here Tertullian again points back to Justin, for whom a seed of logos is in every human being and Christians participate in the reality, the logos who sows the seed. Christians are themselves seed, and a cause in the nature of things (Justin, *2 apol.* 7.1).[17] Both Justin and Tertullian point back to the theme of the Fourth Gospel, where a grain of wheat must fall into the ground to die and bear much fruit (John 12.24). The law of creation and the law of redemption are one law; here again Heraclitus is useful.

Tertullian's account of conflict between good and evil, the divine economy of a God who is first and last, and the persistent seed of the cross, all point to a unifying ethic and metaphysic which needs to be kept in mind if his argument is to be understood. Christians are not accidental victims; they are part of God's total plan, for divine reason established the world and came

---

[16] Yet their actions continue the tradition of Mucius, Empedocles, Dido, Regulus and Anaxarchus who was able to joke about his cruel death (*ap.* 50).

[17] From such ground springs that which forever renews the earth
Though it is forever denied.
   T. S. Eliot, *Murder in the cathedral* (London, 1935), 87.

in Christ, 'that original firstborn word, attended by power and reason, sustained by the spirit' (*ap.* 21). They are God's gift to the world, moderating calamities (*ap.* 40.13) and looking to the final judgement which is delayed (*ap.* 41.3). Fearful of God and his searching judgement, they alone achieve righteousness (*ap.* 45), and when the conflict of the world is finally resolved, the true worshippers of God will be forever with him, while others pass into eternal fire.

B. RECOGNIZING THE WELL-KNOWN GOD

Tertullian's second general principle in the *apologeticum* is that Christian faith is the recognition of a God who is universally known. We have already seen in his puzzle (ch. 2) and paradox (ch. 3) how Tertullian's apparent contradictions point to decisive elements in a coherent pattern of thought. This is equally true in the *apologeticum*, where he claims that the soul is naturally Christian (*ap.* 17.6) and yet that Christians are made, not born (*ap.* 18.4). This looks like a straight contradiction, for what is naturally Christian must be born that way. How then do men know God?

Christians do not worship the Roman gods who are merely glorified men, have created nothing and are guilty of wicked crimes. Those who follow pagan deities insult them, multiply them and trade in them. The gods are cheated in rites of worship, ridiculed in literature, laughed at in theatres. Their temples are polluted by their own followers and not by the Christians who stay outside. Christians do not worship the head of an ass, but pagans worship many kinds of animals.

What God, then, do Christians worship? Tertullian's statement is concise. God is he who by his word, wisdom and power, created the cosmos from nothing for the glory of his majesty (*ap.* 17.1). The elements of bodies and spirits are ordered by his wisdom. Paradoxically, he is invisible but can be seen, incomprehensible but made known through grace, beyond highest thought but conceivable by the human mind. For whatever the senses or the mind grasp is inferior to the faculty which apprehends, so a human mind cannot grasp God who is known to himself alone. The power of his greatness makes him known and unknown. Man's supreme fault is a refusal to recognize or recollect the God whom he cannot fail to know.

Tertullian uses proofs of God's existence, when other apologists had considered them unnecessary.[18] After all, Christians were regarded as stupid atheists not stupid theists. Proof of God, for Tertullian, shows common ground with Stoics. First, God may be proved from his works by which we are preserved, sustained, and covered with delight and wonder. Secondly, God is proved by the testimony of the soul which is naturally Christian and which declares spontaneously, 'Great God! Good God!', as it looks up to skies where God dwells and whence he descended (*ap.* 17.5f.). Mankind's universal awareness of gods is yet another Stoic theme.

From nature we move to the account of God in scripture which tells of his first messengers who, from their righteousness, were worthy to know and to declare him. By the creator's spirit, they declared him as the true Prometheus who orders the seasons and their courses. They gave further proofs of God from his chastisement of sinners, his laws and his future and final judgement. Once, like his present readers, Tertullian laughed at all this; but he and others have changed by deliberate choice. 'We come from among you; Christians are made, not born' ('de vestris sumus: fiunt, non nascuntur Christiani') (*ap.* 18.4). The ancient authority of these writings (*ap.* 19.2) is increased by the way (attractive to Stoics) in which their prophecies are confirmed by natural disasters, human depravity, regularity of seasons interspersed with catastrophes, the exalting of the humble and the putting down of the proud (*ap.* 20.2).

Antiquity, it is objected, cannot be claimed when the Christians have rejected so many of the ancient ways of the Jews. Are they simply hiding under the protection of a distinguished religion which is sanctioned by the law? Most people, replies Tertullian, know something of Christ but regard him simply as a man; a few statements about his divinity are therefore required ('necesse est igitur pauca[19] de Christo ut Deo' (*ap.* 21.3). Tertullian begins from

---

[18] Clement thought such proofs unnecessary and impious.

[19] This word is wrongly taken to indicate a limited interest in christology, by J. Lortz, *Das Christentum als Monotheismus in den Apologeten des zweiten Jahrhunderts*, in A. M. Koeniger (ed.), *Beiträge zur Geschichte des christlichen Altertums und der Byzantinischen Literatur, FS A. Ehrhard* (Bonn, 1922), 301–27.

the failure of the Jews to do what God required and the prophecy of
a new and faithful people who would receive a wider grace and a
nobler discipline. God's son came to renew and enlighten. He was
the ruler and master of this grace and discipline, the illuminator
and guide of the human race (*ap.* 21.7). How was he born? Neither
the shameful pedigrees of the pagan gods nor the normal mode of
human procreation can apply to him.

His work was appropriate to his substance as word, reason and
power of God. Zeno and Cleanthes spoke of him in terms of
creator, fate, god, mind of Jupiter, necessity and spirit of the
universe. Like them we see his unity as word, reason and power.
Proceeding from God, 'he is called "son of God" and "God" from
unity of substance for God also is spirit' (*ap.* 21.11).

As with a ray of the sun, there is extension, but no division of
substance. Spirit of spirit, God of God, he entered the womb of the
Virgin and was born as God and man. So he was expected and is
still expected by the Jews who do not believe that he has come; but
he was always to come twice, once in human form and a second
time in divine majesty. The Jews, in their blindness, did not see him
as word and power of God and assigned his miracles to magical
powers.

His death was freely chosen and his resurrection was not public
because that would have made things too easy for the wicked, 'so
that faith, being destined to a great reward, should not stand firm
without difficulty' (*ap.* 21.22). Faith was not meant to be easy. Yet
Pilate was converted, the disciples of Jesus spread over the world,
and the savagery of Nero sowed the seed of Christian blood at
Rome.

This, says Tertullian, is the way we began, how we took the
name of our sect from our founder. Consider him as a man, in and
through whom God wishes to be worshipped. Moses taught the
Jews religion; the Greeks had several teachers; Numa Pompilius
burdened the Romans with superstitions when he used religion to
tame crude savages through fear of many gods; Christ comes to
bring truth to those who are deceived by their very culture (*ipsa
urbanitas*) (*ap.* 21.30). He challenges Romans to test the truth of
Christ's divinity, by investigating its power to destroy the falsehood
of many gods.

When the Jews turned from God, they were scattered in all directions and 'wander over the world without either man or God for their king' (*ap.* 21.5). The dispensation of God continues through the coming of Christ, the son of God, to reform and enlighten the world. Faith *recognizes* God in the incarnate Christ who sends his disciples into all the world with the promise that he is with them. He has gone before them in the universal consciousness of the soul which is naturally Christian.

Tertullian's argument here expounds, with great subtlety, an epistemology of recognition or recollection. The testimony of the soul which is naturally Christian is completed in the recognition of the universal God at the climax of his dispensation in Christ. Faith recalls God as one God at different stages of his economy. Tertullian is able to write to Romans because they are human and all humans know God and should be able to recognize him in Christ.

This epistemology is clear in the chapters (*ap.* 17–21) which have just been considered. Christians worship one God who created all things by his commanding word, his ordering reason and his enabling power. The world is a cosmos, an ornament of God's majesty. The invisible God may be seen, the incomprehensible may be known by grace, the inestimable is accessible as the true and mighty God. Known only to himself, he may be found by all except those who 'refuse to *recognize* him, of whom they cannot be ignorant' (*ap.* 17.3). Despite all burdens and barriers the soul names God: 'Good God! Great God! ... O testimony of the soul which is naturally Christian!' (*ap.* 17.6).

To this natural evidence, God has added the document of scripture.[20] From the beginning, God had sent into the world messengers to make himself known as the one God who founded the universe, creating mankind and fixing the order of the world with its seasons. He appointed statutes and laws, rewards and punishments, so that at the end each would receive his deserts. The record of the prophets passed from Hebrew into Greek to provide universal access to God's truth. 'He who listens will find God: he who also takes pains to understand will be compelled to believe' (*ap.*

---

[20] The Christian bible was a very new thing in Tertullian's day.

18.9). The authority of the sacred books derives from their age which far exceeds that of other writings. It is confirmed by the course of history: 'whatever is taking place was prophesied, whatever is now seen was heard of' (*ap.* 20). The truth of scripture is confirmed as it is read. The scriptures are proved to be divine by their daily disastrous fulfilment : 'While we suffer, they are read; while we recognize them, they are proved' ('dum patimur, leguntur; dum recogniscimus, probantur' *ap.* 20.3)). The human race has always deserved the punishment of God. Its first neglect lay in not following up the partial knowledge which it had of him, inventing other gods and sinning exuberantly in ignorance of a divine judge. Had men looked for God, they would have learnt to know him and when they recognized him, they would have obeyed him and found his grace (*ap.* 40.11).

Tertullian does not separate the natural order from the divine, nor reason from faith, in his account of Christian faith as recognition.[21] In many places he talks about 'recognizing' (*recognoscere*) (*ap.* 17.3, 20.3, 39.3; *praescr.* 27.6; *Jud.* 9; *Val.* 3; *Marc.* 1.18, 3.2.4, 4.1; *nat.* 1.10.11, 1.16.13.) which may mean 'to know again, recognize, recall, investigate, examine, inspect, review' or 'describe'. When Peter had seen the miracle of the loaves and compared it with precedents in Elisha, he recognized the fulfilment in Christ and confessed, 'You are the Christ!' (*Marc.* 4.21.6) Against Marcion, Tertullian insists that God must first be known through works of nature, then recognized by the predictions of the prophets. Without the first, natural knowledge, recognition through scripture could not occur (*Marc.* 1.18.2). Most people believe in God, but only because they have evidence of his works (*Marc.* 1.12.2f.). It is proper for anyone 'to recognize as God one whom nature has already commended to him, whom he perceives daily in all his works, who is less known for one reason only, namely, that man has not thought of him as uniquely one, has given him a plurality of names and has worshipped him in other forms' (*Val.* 3.2).[22]

---

[21] A. B. Muñoz, El antifilosofismo de Tertulliano y la fe como reconocimiento, *RET*, 36 (1966), 3–28, 233–80 (234).

[22] 'quem iam illi natura commisit, quem cotidie in operibus omnibus sensit, hoc solo minus notum, quod unicum non putavit, quod in numero nominavit, quod in aliis adoravit'.

Justice would never permit Marcion's unknown God to punish
those who do not know him (2 Thess. 1.28f.), because they have
never heard his gospel. A God who is unknown by nature, but
known only through his gospel, could not punish the ignorance of
those who had no access to this unique source of knowledge. On
the other hand, the creator is known through his works which are
everywhere; knowledge of him is natural, even obligatory (*Marc.*
5.16.3).

Christ's coming was announced for several reasons. First, the
father should announce the son, not the son the father. Second,
Christ was sent and the authority of the sender must be evident,
before the one sent may be received. He who is sent receives his
commission from a sender. A son is named by his father; this is a
general rule and whatever contravenes it must be suspect. Neither
in order of recognition nor in its disposition can a copy take
precedence over an original. A sudden Christ without God, a son
without a father, an envoy without a sender would be absurd. God
works by order and arrangement and it makes good sense to
announce what has been prearranged, so that when it happens, its
divine authority may be proved. When it comes to a work of such
magnitude as the salvation of the human race through faith,
preparation by arrangement and announcement is essential for
recognition of the divine. There is no recognition (*agnitio*) without
disposition (*dispositio*). 'Faith, when informed by such a process,
might justly be required of man by God; for once recognition has
made faith possible, it is obligatory to believe what one has indeed
learned to believe from what has been predicted (*praedicatio*)' (*Marc.*
3.2.4).[23]

Tertullian's account of faith as recognition and recollection is
not an apologetic improvisation. It fits his theology of divine
unicity, the goodness and magnificence of creation, the identification of Christ as son of the father, the salvation and responsibility of
humanity. It is part of a Stoic conviction of divine providence and

[23] Muñoz, El antifilosofismo, 242. 'La creación permite reconocer al Dios de la revelación;
los profetas permiten reconocer que el mísimo Dios promete y cumple. Así la creación
desempeña con respecto a la revelación un papel análogo al de las profecías con respecto
a Cristo. En todo ello, la fe cristiana aparace siempre como un reconocimiento de algo
que ya se había conocido.'

disposition. Truth in theology may be reached from common powers (*sensibus*) provided it follows divine dispensation. The supreme God, immortality and divine judgement are all known by nature (*res.* 3.1–2). Before Moses wrote, the creator was known from his creation. The beginnings of recognition (*natales agnitionis*) do not date from the Pentateuch. The greater part of the human race, who had never heard the name of Moses, nevertheless knew his God and referred to him habitually. The knowledge of God is given to the soul from the beginning (*Marc.* 1.10.1–3). This does not mean that everything which the soul presents may be accepted. But the testimonies of the soul which are true, simple, common, natural and divine (*test.* 5.1) point to a natural knowledge of God. This knowledge precedes the coming of Christ and therefore means that faith is not merely the substance of things hoped for but the recollection of things past. 'What is our sin, I ask you, if we believe the future also, as we have already learned through two stages to believe it?' (*ap.* 20). Natural order and prophecy have already provided a past and present knowledge of God. Faith, freely chosen, is the recognition of this knowledge. It welcomes God as one already known. This explains the puzzle with which we began: how the soul is naturally Christian (*ap.* 17.6), yet Christians are made not born (*ap.* 18.4) ('testimonium animae naturaliter christianae ... fiunt non nascuntur christiani').[24]

C. TERTULLIAN AS APOLOGIST

Since Tertullian's apologetic (strife of opposites and faith as recognition) has turned out to have a more complex argument than was expected, a general evaluation is appropriate. Was Tertullian an effective apologist? This may be divided into two questions – Did he respect his Roman audience? Did he shape his message for this audience and thereby endanger the central theses of his theology?

---

[24] The same sequence of recognition or recollection applies to ethical values. Marcion was wrong because he denied the universal knowledge of the Golden Rule and the freedom of all men to follow it. 'For although good and evil are known in different forms by nature, yet life is not thereby spent under the discipline of God, who alone at last teaches men the proper liberty of their will and action in faith, as in the fear of God' (*Marc.* 4.16.5).

(i) Respect for Rome

'Why are we thought to be enemies and denied the name of Romans?' (*ap.* 36.1) An apologist cannot afford to despise his audience; he must have common ground, or points of contact. On the surface, Tertullian never shows much respect for his opponents; only the care of his argument proves that respect was there. It is remarkable that 'the mother of harlots and abominations in the earth' (Rev. 17.5), 'that great city which rules over the kings of the earth' (Rev. 17.18) should receive such sympathy from him.

All early Christian theologians believed that history had a purpose and that it was summed up in Christ. This goes for Clement of Alexandria as much as for Irenaeus. What is notable in Tertullian is that he found a place for the Roman empire in the divine purpose.[25] This meant that he could extol and share the Roman virtues of Mucius Scaevola and others, assimilating them with the ancient Spartan ideals. The heroic Roman virtues lent respect to reckless Christian desperadoes who conquer in death. Mucius Scaevola plunged his hand into fire. Empedocles jumped into Mount Etna. Tertullian also puts public-minded Christians into the life of the community and contrasts them with pale Eastern mystics who escape from the world.

Tertullian's relation to Rome has been handled impressively by many writers.[26] One recent work[27] studies the political terms which Tertullian uses. None of the terms which deny liberty is applied to the Roman empire, except when Tertullian denounces military service on religious and moral grounds (*idol.* 19; *cor.* 11). Idolatry is part of a soldier's allegiance and inconsistent with a Christian's obedience as the episode of the crown shows. Even here Tertullian's position is ambiguous for he speaks of Christian soldiers and cites them as evidence of Christian loyalty (*ap.* 42.3). The question of the votive crown which a Christian soldier refused, takes precedence over a general objection to military service. He cites the story of the *legio fulminata* (*ap.* 5.4; *Scap.* 4.1), when Christian soldiers, by their intercession, brought much-needed rain. Chris-

---

[25] As Clement of Alexandria found a place for Greek philosophy.

[26] For example, Richard Klein, *Tertullian und das römische Reich* (Heidelberg, 1968).

[27] A. Z. Ahondokpe, *La vision de Rome chez Tertullien*, 2 vols. (Lille, 1991).

tians pray for the bravery of the imperial armies (*ap.* 30.4). Tertullian quotes military precedents in Moses, Aaron and Joshua. Soldiers came to John the Baptist and received instruction from him (*idol.* 19.3). Military service nevertheless raised difficulties for Tertullian. Soldiers could be baptized (*cor.* 11.4) but those baptized should either leave the army or be on guard against committing any act against God (*cor.* 11.4). He sanctions military service, it seems, through a distinction between *bellare* and *militare* which he takes to indicate the distinction between police activity and military aggression.[28] Christian prayers reinforce the courage of Roman armies (*ap.* 30.4).

Christians do not return hatred to those who hate their name (*ap.* 2.19). Their only real enemy is the devil (*ap.* 9; *paen.* 7.7; *or.* 29.2) who is the sole source of anti-Christian enmity (*ap.* 37.4). Roman society does not lose favour when its rulers misuse their power (*ap.* 2.14).

Tertullian answers at length the charges that Christians were a subversive society (*ap.* 34). He applauds the evolution of legislation into better and juster laws, following a Stoic theme of progress.[29] Law is rational (*cor.* 4.5). As Paul (Rom. 13.1) commanded, the political order must be respected (*scorp.* 14.1; *cor.* 13.4). Criticism of abuses is appropriate: of idolatry which determines so much that happens, of political fraud (*ap.* 33, 35) and of conspiracies (*ap.* 35). Christians pray for the emperor (*ap.* 30–2), acknowledge his *maiestas* (*ap.* 33.2; *nat.* 1.17.2), rendering to Caesar what is his and denying to Caesar what belongs to God (*ap.* 32f.). There is no incompatibility between Christians and the emperor,[30] even if there have been good (friendly to Christians) and bad (hostile to Christians) emperors.

Behind his respect for Rome and the emperor lay Tertullian's positive anthropology[31] which placed humanity at the peak of creation, in anticipation of Christ (*res.* 6.3f.). Man's rationality (*an.* 17.11) makes him lord of creation,[32] and from him come the laws which, in changing situations, must always mirror what is good (*ap.*

---

[28] See J. M. Hornus, *It is not lawful for me to fight, Early Christian attitudes toward law, violence and the state* (Scottdale, Pa., and Kitchener, Ontario, 1980).
[29] Fredouille, *Conversion*, 246.
[30] J.-C. Fredouille, Tertullien et l'empire, *REA*, 29 (1984), 121.
[31] Spanneut, *Stoïcisme*, 131.
[32] *Ibid.*, 382f.

4.5). The emperor is chosen by God to enforce the law (*ap.* 32f.) and is necessary for the stability of the empire. He must preserve the peace and punish crime (*scorp.* 14.1), never forgetting that he is a fallible man before he is an emperor (*ap.* 30.1f.). In his exercise of his god-given authority, the emperor must be upheld by all (*ap.* 30–2) and Christians are called to scrupulous regard and loyalty (*ap.* 33.1), or to devotion, loyalty and fidelity to emperors (*ap.* 36.2). Pagan flattery, deceit and hypocrisy stand in contrast to Christian piety. The emperor stands supreme over the senate and in this exalted state he receives the loyalty of Christians. One final qualification always remains. Freedom of conscience is a natural right (*Scap.* 2.2) and must be respected by political authority. With that safeguard, Christians serve the state, 'in respect for justice and human dignity, and in respect for the divine laws which alone are immutable'.[33]

(ii) Selective monotheism

Did Tertullian adapt his message to his readership? Certainly he did. The variety of Tertullian's work shows how specific he was in defining his target. An apologist cannot apologize to everyone at once. The logic of apologetic is a logic of specific objection and specific rebuttal. Simplification was essential. Pagan religion was complex, despite a general similarity in purpose. Christianity with its exclusive, universal claims could only collide with it. How was the opposition to be understood? Christianity was defined in contradiction to polytheism as monotheism pure and simple.[34] Tertullian's first concern is to attack polytheism[35] and seventeen chapters of his *Apology* dwell on this point. Christians define themselves by their ban on idolatry (*idol.* 24.3).[36] Christian worship of one God ('quod colimus, deus unus est') (*ap.* 17.1) is confirmed by the testimony of the soul to one God.

This 'selective monotheism'[37] was necessary and obvious to every defender of Christian faith. Tertullian's other writings show

[33] Ahondopke, *La vision*, II, 453.
[34] Lortz, *Monotheismus*, 302. 'in einer stark vereinfachten Form', 'einfach als Monotheismus'.
[35] *Ibid.*, 307.
[36] 'lex nostra ... propria Christianorum per quam ab ethnicis agnoscimur'.
[37] 'die monotheistische Auswahl'.

that his theology went further. As an apologist 'the African genius' displayed, we are told, his superior refinement over other apologists; but like them he put a rational monotheism in the centre.[38] Did this impoverish his theology? He talks about 'deus' everywhere and the idea of God dominates his writing. It is claimed[39] that only one passage shows intensity of passion for Christ as, 'a flower of the stem of Jesse, on which the fullness of the grace of the divine spirit has come to rest – a flower incorrupt and unfading, which will last forever' (*cor.* 15.2). On the contrary, Tertullian does not need any defence at this point. Despite the demands of apologetic simplification, the centrality of Christ in the *Apology* has been noted. Similarly, the first three chapters of this book have shown that, for him, Christian simplicity was found in the perfection of Christ, to whom nothing can be added and whose divine disgrace is mankind's sole hope.

Indeed Tertullian elaborates on the life of Jesus (*ap.* 21) as he hammers the paradox of Jesus and monotheism. It is no surprise therefore that his critic concludes that Tertullian's treatment of christology as a function of monotheism was the most remarkable achievement of an eminent tactician.[40] But it was not merely a tactic. Monotheism without Christ was incomplete and therefore impossible. God could not be God unless the son delivered the kingdom to him. Only in Christ is found the very God and life eternal whereby the children of God are delivered from idols. The importance of christology for Tertullian is discoverable by analysis of his argument and not by counting words. 'Christ is spirit of spirit and God of God, as light is kindled from light ... We say before all men, and while torn and bleeding from your tortures we cry, "We worship God through Christ"' (*ap.* 21.28).

[38] Lortz, Monotheismus, 315f.
[39] *Ibid.*, 322.
[40] 'Wie Tertullian das erreicht, durch enge Verbindung des monotheistischen und christologischen Vorstellungskreises, durch Behandlung der Christologie als Function des Monotheismus, gehört zum Wundervollsten was dieser eminente Taktiker im Apologeticum (Kap. 17–21) vollbracht hat.' *Ibid.*, 309.

CHAPTER 5

Antithesis in one God: 'Against Marcion'

There were several reasons for the length and care of Tertullian's reply to Marcion.[1] Dualism was the foremost threat to emerging Christian theology. Marcion gave a negative answer to the first question of that theology: 'Is there one God good and true who is creator of this world of evil and chaos?'[2] Since Marcion produced the strongest case against one God, and supported his argument from scripture, his work required careful discussion. Deeper still, Marcion's denial went to the central contention of the common response. He denied the economy of salvation, centred on Christ, which was the theme of the early Christian answer. For Marcion, God's total disgrace could not be the sacrament of man's salvation.

Paradox was unacceptable to Marcion because it contradicted the primary pledge to simplicity which Marcion and Tertullian shared. In God there could be no change nor shadow cast by turning. All that contradicted perfect love must be denied. In this Marcion followed a common view of God. For Plato, the form of the good was above all contradiction; dialectic was the way to reach the summit where all conflict ceases and there is an everlasting loveliness that neither flowers nor fades. For Aristotle, the first cause of all, like a magnet in an armchair, needed to do nothing.

---

[1] A most useful recent work on Marcion is E. P. Meijering's *Tertullian contra Marcion, Gotteslehre in der Polemik* (Leiden, 1977). It includes a wealth of valuable detail which shows how deeply Tertullian is indebted to other Christian thinkers. Meijering covers the first two books of *adversus Marcionem*. A general treatment is that of A. von Harnack, *Marcion, Das Evangelium vom fremden Gott*, 2 Aufl. (Leipzig, 1924). A valuable review of recent study of Marcion (G. May, Marcion in contemporary views – results and open questions, *The Second Century*, 6 (1988), 129–51) recognizes Tertullian as the best source for Marcion, despite polemical distortion.

[2] Christian monotheism began as theodicy.

For the Epicureans, the chief attribute of gods was their remoteness and their lack of involvement in human affairs. Even for Paul, there was no contradiction in God whose promises were not 'yea and nay' but in Christ were all 'yea and amen' (2 Cor. 1.19–20). Only Stoicism, following Heraclitus, saw the need for paradox in God; to this opinion Tertullian readily turned.

Marcion was a serious threat because he was completely right in discerning the critical centre of Pauline theology.[3] God was, in a way which bewildered all believers, a God of mercy and love. Confirmation of this theme is found in nineteenth-century Liberal praise for and sympathy with Marcion. For Harnack, a child of the Enlightenment, had asked the critical question about the essence of Christianity and came up with an answer similar to that of Marcion. Harnack had no hesitation in disowning the Old Testament, which had been necessary for the early church and inevitable for the Reformation, but was now a part of the Protestant canon only because of the religious paralysis of its readers.[4] Marcion, of course, went further and combined theodicy with his rejection of the created world which reflected the weakness and wickedness of its maker.

The same dualism was characteristic of the Gnostics with whom Marcion has often been classed.[5] The Gnostics, indeed all heretics on Tertullian's account, began from the problem of evil ('unde malum et qua re?' (*praescr.* 7)). Their supreme God was untroubled by the chaos below him and protected, by a subordinate hierarchy, from contact with it. Yet Tertullian gives only a slender work to refute the Valentinians, because there were fundamental differences between them and Marcion. Marcion taught no higher gnosis of intermediary aeons and argued for the consistency of his view and the incoherence of incipient orthodoxy. Most important of all, Marcion argued, the *Antitheses* showed that the creator was not

---

[3] While R. J. Hoffmann (*Marcion: on the restitution of Christianity. An essay on the development of radical Paulinist theology in the second century* (Chico, 1984)) rightly separates Marcion from Gnosticism and affirms, following Harnack, the radical link with Paul, his own theory seems to have difficulties. See G. May, Ein neues Markionbild, *ThR*, 51 (1986), 404–13.

[4] Harnack, *Marcion*, 217.

[5] Unwisely, because he was a man of faith and taught no Gnosis. 'Marcion perperam gnosticus vocatur', wrote A. Hahn, cited by F. Loofs, *Leitfaden zum Studium der Dogmengeschichte*, vol. II (Halle-Saale, 1950), 83.

merely different from but opposite to the God of the gospel. Gnostics were above the need for argument, which could never reach ultimate truth. Their claim for vision could only be met by aesthetic considerations, which showed that their claims were countered.[6]

Tertullian's writing *Against Marcion* is the first extended work of Christian argument. For this reason, it presents a theology which is more systematic than most apologetic writing. Marcion produced a system and had to be answered systematically, with corollaries to cope with detail. Tertullian's first two books present his case; the remaining books deal with scriptural argument from Old Testament,[7] Gospel and Pauline texts.

To understand the intricate argument of these two books, we shall first go to their conclusion.[8] Here Tertullian says that he has shown that the creator is both good and just. Goodness and justice (*bonitas, justitia*) are the proper fullness of divine being. Marcion's move has been one of distinction or division. He separates the different qualities of the creator's works and divides Christ from the creator. The most high, the merciful bringer of salvation is other than the ruthless judge who brings ruin. For Tertullian, these opposites are compatible in one God. Take away Marcion's title (*Antitheses*) and you have a demonstration of the one God who is supremely good *and* a judge. God is good and severe to the same people, but at different times. The existence of evils points to the austerity of God; their absence points to his mercy. Christ does not annul and destroy, but rather reforms and restores the dispensation of the creator.

Tertullian sums up: 'I shall by means of these antitheses recognize in Christ my own jealous God. He did in the beginning by his own right, by a hostility which was rational and therefore good, provide beforehand for the maturity and fuller ripeness of

---

[6] Tertullian's humour and its relation to argument will be considered in ch. 9.

[7] See W. Kinzig, Καινὴ Διαθήκη, the title of the New Testament in the second and third centuries, *JThS*, 45.2 (1994), 519–44, for the claim that the title 'New Testament' for a collection of books comes from Marcion. This is well argued but cannot be supported from Tertullian's usage, where 'Old' and 'New' imply unity of origin and depend on the prophetic distinction in Jeremiah and Joel.

[8] Tertullian claims that he could have attacked Marcion more vigorously if he had thought it necessary. In view of Tertullian's propensity for argument, there is no reason to doubt this claim. Whether a stronger attack would have been more effective is doubtful.

the things which were his' (*Marc.* 2.29.4).[9] God's antitheses are reflected in his own world which consists of opposite elements regulated in perfect proportion; but the antithesis (like the economy) belongs first in God and not merely in his world.[10] The reader must hold on to this central theme through all the twists and turns of Tertullian's argument.

A. ONE GOOD AND RATIONAL GOD

(i) Why there is one God

Tertullian begins his response by asking, 'What is Marcion's rule of faith?' He believes (*Marc.* 1.2.1) in two gods, one the creator (whom no one can deny) and another god (whom no one can prove). For all his love of transcendence, Marcion is not transcendent enough. He has taken Jesus' saying about good trees and bad trees, which produce good and bad fruit, and wrongly applied a human distinction to God.[11] The bad tree is the creator who creates evil (Isa. 45.7), while the good tree is a strange new divinity of pure and unmixed benevolence. This heresy embitters the whole of faith and gives double vision to those of feeble sight. One god has been overthrown as evil, another has been fabricated on a scaffolding of goodness.

Why must there be only one God? Because 'God is not, if he be not one' (*Marc.* 1.3.1). God is the supreme greatness (*summum magnum*),[12] supreme in form, reason, strength and power and therefore unique.[13] The first objection asks why there cannot be

---

[9] Evans's translation.

[10] 'ceterum eius erit antithesis cuius est et in mundo'. What could be more Stoic and Heraclitean than this final sentence? Yet for Tertullian it goes to the centre of Christian faith in a crucified son of God. On this point E. Jüngel cites Goethe, 'nemo contra deum nisi deus ipse', *Dichtung und Wahrheit*, 4 Teil, 20 Buch, Weimarer Ausgabe, Bd. 29 (1891), 177. See Jüngel, *Gott als Geheimnis der Welt*, 498.

[11] Tertullian later applies the metaphor in the human realm. Marcion gets bad fruit from Cerdon and Apelles gets bad fruit from Marcion (*Marc.* 4.17).

[12] The other attributes of the true God 'in aeternitate constitutum, innatum, infectum, sine initio, sine fine' (*Marc.* 1.3.2) are common to early Christian literature. Cf. Irenaeus (*haer.* 2.11.1, 2.34.2, 3.8; *dem.* 5, 6). See Meijering, *Tertullian*, 15f.

[13] This argument (supreme greatness implies uniqueness) seems to be original to Tertullian. See A. Bill, *Zur Erklärung und Textkritik des ersten Buches Tertullians 'Adversus Marcionem'* (Leipzig, 1911), 10.

two highest beings, just as there are many kings with different kingdoms. If there were two, then there could be three or more; but none would be God because God is unique. The second objection quotes scripture which speaks of many gods. But these are just names, not unbegotten and unmade essences (*Marc.* 1.7.4). The antithesis between substance and name is common in the debate with Marcion (cf. *Marc.* 2.2).[14] It was widely debated whether names were natural to or imposed on things.[15]

Two corollaries follow. There can be no new God because God's true nature is independent of beginning, end and all time (*Marc.* 1.8.3). There can be no unknown God,[16] for his greatness prevents him from being unknown and his goodness makes it improper for him to be unknown (*Marc.* 1.9.4). The creator is known as the only God from paradise and Adam, not from Egypt and Moses; indeed the whole universe (especially every human being) bears witness to God (*Marc.* 1.10.1f.).[17]

(ii) Why there is one world, a harmony of opposites

Why did God make one world, with man at its centre? Everything which exists must produce something. Nothing can exist to which nothing belongs.[18] Everything belongs to the creator, so there is no room left for another god. Marcion's god should have produced at least a chickpea, in order to be credible. His lack of works shows him to be impudent because he still wants to be believed, and malicious because he has given no reason for belief.

The world, made for man, is not divine as philosophers have claimed;[19] but it is worthy of God. 'Will one tiny flower from a hedge (I do not say the meadow) one tiny shell from whatever sea (I do not say the Red Sea) one tiny wing from a moorfowl (I do not speak of a peacock), pronounce for you the meanness of the

---

[14] Meijering, *Tertullian*, 23f. See also G. C. Stead, Divine substance in Tertullian, *JThS*, 14 (1963), 46–66 (58), for other contrasts with *substantia*.

[15] Meijering, *Tertullian*, 25.

[16] One can argue from certainty to uncertainty, but not vice versa. Meijering, *Tertullian*, 31. R. D. Sider, *Ancient rhetoric and the art of Tertullian*, 50. Sider cites Quintilian, *Inst.* 5.10.8.

[17] This is a common claim of Tertullian.

[18] The philosophical origins of this claim have been disputed. See Meijering, *Tertullian*, 40.

[19] Tertullian follows inexactly Seneca, *Contra superstitiones*. See R. M. Grant, Two notes on Tertullian, *VC* 15 (1951), 113–15. Meijering, *Tertullian*, 43.

creator's skill?' (*Marc.* 1.13.5). Marcion has ridiculed the insects but he cannot imitate the skills of bee, ant, spider, silkworm or any other of God's tiny creatures.[20] The triumphant work of God is man, for whom even Marcion's highest god descended; inconsistently, the most high god uses the creator's water, oil, honey, milk, bread and wine in the worship of his people (*Marc.* 1.14.1–3).[21]

Worlds and gods should not be allowed to multiply. Marcion's higher god had a space of his own between his feet and the creator's head. Unwittingly, Marcion finished up with nine gods, of which the first four were the highest god, his christ, his space, the matter for his creation. The remaining five were the demiurge, his promised christ, his space and this world and evil (*Marc.* 1.15).

Here it is clear that Tertullian falls into the common error of polemic which distorts the views of an opponent by amalgam, generalization and arbitrary deductions.[22] A style of argument which gained him support in his own milieu, it would be counter-productive today.[23] However, it is important to note that he is justified in his general claim that once intermediaries are called in, there is always reason to add to them.[24]

Even if there be an invisible world as well as a visible world, there is no need to invent another god to explain it. The existence of the invisible world is proved from God's action on the visible world. All things come from God, who always produces opposites.[25] He makes things corporeal and incorporeal, animate and inanimate, vocal and silent, mobile and static, productive and sterile, dry and wet, hot and cold. Man mirrors this diversity with his parts which are strong and weak, beautiful and ugly, double and single, like and unlike, and with his emotions which include joy and anxiety, love

---

[20] Stoics had defended universal providence with determined argument. Cf. M. Pohlenz, *Die Stoa*, vol. 1, 100. Meijering, *Tertullian*, 44.

[21] Cf. Irenaeus, *haer.* 4.33.2 and 3.11.5.

[22] See P. Nautin, Lettres et écrivains chrétiens des IIe et IIIe siècles (Paris, 1961), 216, and C. Munier, Les conceptions hérésiologiques de Tertullien, in V. Saxer (ed.), *Ecclesia orans, Mélanges Hamman* (Rome, 1980), 257–66.

[23] See above, p. 29.

[24] The bureaucratic fallacy, as we might formulate it, in mediis rebus entia semper sunt multiplicanda, outdated Occam's razor by a millennium and a half. See Plato's Third Man argument and discussion below, ch. 9.

[25] 'sicuti tota operatio eius ex diversitatibus constat' (*Marc.* 1.16.2).

and hate, anger and calm. If the universe is made up of opposites, then visible things need invisible things to balance them, otherwise there would be no universe. The universe needs one creator with a taste for opposites (*Marc.* 1.16).

We have seen that this view of the world, first found in Heraclitus, present in Paul and Irenaeus, and repeated by Tertullian (*Marc.* 2.12.2), is the special theme of Seneca[26] and other Stoics. In such a world, we should expect a creator to command and forbid, to smite and to heal.[27] Arguments, which ignore this opposition, imprison Marcionites, so that they claim that one work is enough for one god, especially when that work is the liberation of mankind, and not the production of locusts (*Marc.* 1.17.1).

(iii) Why the same God creates and redeems

Creation proves God's existence; redemption proves his nature. The world demonstrates that he is; the gospel demonstrates what he is.[28] The folly of Marcion's two gods is seen in the dependence of the higher god on man, the creature of the lower god, in order to perform his unique work. Further, why did this god keep man in ignorance of himself? A better god simply had no right to remain hidden. A god should first be known through nature and then through doctrine, first through his works and then through official teaching (*Marc.* 1.18.2). Marcion's god provides neither kind of evidence.

Is there another God? Marcionites claim that their god is revealed in Jesus; but the break in time between Jesus and Marcion makes this implausible (*Marc.* 1.19.3). From Jesus to Paul there was peace between law and gospel, until Marcion separated them under different gods. Paul cannot be used in support of this duplication; he attacked the observance of the law which the creator had already rejected and he had nothing to do with a second god (*Marc.* 1.20.16). Christians have argued about almost

---

[26] *nat. quest.* 7.27. See above, ch. 4, and also Irenaeus, *haer.* 2.11.1 and 2.25.2. Note *De anima*, J. H. Waszink (ed.) (Amsterdam, 1947), 155f.

[27] See also *Marc.* 2.29, 4.1, 4.34, 5.11; and *pud.* 2.

[28] Here Tertullian takes over Quintilian's distinction: 'an sit ... qualis sit'. See G. C. Stead, Divine substance in Tertullian, 57f.

everything but never about God (*de deo nemo*). Every apostolic church believes in the creator; Christ revealed no other God.

(iv) Why God's goodness must be eternal and rational

How good is Marcion's God? Marcion's case depends on his god being better than the creator; this calls for precise argument. How can one evaluate the goodness of a god? It must be natural and ingenerate, so that it would come to help as soon as need occurs. Perennial and ever-flowing, it would know in advance the time for action.

Why then was Marcion's divine goodness not active from the beginning? If such a god had existed, he could not have kept his goodness hidden; if he restrains his attributes, they are not natural, for nature cannot deny itself; if it ceases to act, it ceases to exist. The first objection against Marcion's god is that since at one time he did not act, his goodness cannot be natural, and if not natural, then not eternal;[29] it lacks both past performance and future promise. Rather, the malice of Marcion's god is proved by his failure to do good when he had the power. He becomes an accessory to evil, when he permits the creator to distress the world so that the creator should be clearly blamed and he be excused, so that his own action would seem more splendid. He is like a doctor who lets his patient suffer for the sake of a larger fee and greater reputation (*Marc.* 1.22.9).

The second objection against Marcion's god is that his goodness is not rational. All divine attributes and activities should be natural and rational (*Marc.* 1.23.1, 2.6.2; *fug.* 4.1).[30] Goodness has to be rational.[31] It must love both neighbour and enemy, and not love enemy to exclusion of neighbour. The kindness which is due takes precedence over that which is not due, the latter underlining the former. Rational goodness looks to its own first and then overflows to others. Rationality cannot be attributed to a goodness which overflows without fulfilling its primary function, by creating

---

[29] Cf. Plato, *Timaeus* 41aff., and Aristotle, *de caelo* 1.282b. See Meijering, *Tertullian*, 64.

[30] Irenaeus describes God as *totus ratio* (*haer.* 2.13.3).

[31] 'exigo rationem bonitatis'. (*Marc.* 1.23.1). This is entirely Stoic. Seneca, *Ep.* 66.12: 'si ratio divina est, nullum autem bonum sine ratione est, bonum omne divinum est'.

humanity. Nothing which is in itself irregular can be rational.[32] Goodness towards strangers presupposes goodness to those to whom it is due. Without this primary goodness it is unjust, irrational, like being kind to another's slave so as to make him hostile to the master under whose roof he remains. Marcion's god breaks into a world which is not his own, stealing man from God and son from father. Marcion and his followers, with irrational presumption, use one God's water to baptize for another god, raise their hands to one God's sky to worship another god, indeed use many gifts of the one god to worship the other.[33]

God must be eternal, rational and entirely perfect.[34] Marcion's god is none of these, because he is not universal since there can be no Jewish Christians, and he does not save humans entirely since he abandons the human body. Man was made of dust and moulded by God into flesh, not spirit. The flesh, which does so much for God and is an essential part of every human being,[35] is excluded from salvation. If we rise without our flesh, then resurrection life will be inferior to this present life.[36] Nor are Marcionites fully liberated in this life, since the flesh is still with them and the creator's flies still crawl over their faces. There are all sorts of imperfections in Marcion's perfect god (*Marc.* 1.24.7).

(v) Why a good God must be just

Is simple goodness good enough for God? From the inadequate goodness of the god whose goodness is neither ingenerate nor rational nor perfect, we move to the question of whether goodness

---

[32] 'nulla res sine ordine rationalis potest vindicari' (*Marc.* 1.23.6).

[33] This argument, when analysed in greater detail has two independent strands and follows a typical pattern of Tertullian. First, Marcion's divine goodness is not rational because it neglected humanity for so long and because it ignores love of neighbour. Second, even if the first argument be rejected, this goodness is not rational because it is unjust. Use of two independent arguments is typical of Tertullian and also found in Clement of Alexandria who offers more than one account of the origin of philosophy.

[34] Stoics defined God: θεὸν εἶναι ζῷον ἀθάνατον, λογικόν, τέλειον, ἢ νοερὸν, ἐν εὐδαιμονίᾳ κακοῦ παντὸς ἀνεπίδεκτον, προνοητικὸν κόσμου τε καὶ τῶν ἐν κόσμῳ (Diogenes Laertius 7.147, in LongSedley 54A).

[35] On body as servant of soul see *an.* 40; Irenaeus, *haer.* 2.33.3; Plato, *Phaedo* 80a. Cf. Meijering, *Tertullian*, 72.

[36] See C. Moreschini, Temi e motivi della polemica antimarcionista di Tertulliano, *SCO*, 17 (1968), 157ff. Meijering, *Tertullian*, 72.

is a sufficient attribute for God. Is God a being of pure goodness, free from all other attributes, sensations and affections?[37] For Epicureans, the gods are remote, listless and imperturbable. In contrast, Christ troubled the Jews by his teaching and brought trouble on himself. Ever inconsistent, Marcion never fulfilled the transcendent Epicurean ideal.[38] His god willed and desired[39] that men be saved and he aroused the hostility of the creator. Indeed nothing ever fulfils its course without stirring up hostility and rivalry. Marcion's god had *aemulatio* and all the passions which go with it.

Plain goodness, without justice, would be free from rivalry and anger, would never act as a judge, and never exercise corrective discipline. It would have to give commands without intending to execute them and forbid sins without the intention of punishing them. This is incompatible with divine being which has to execute retribution for what it has forbidden (*Marc.* 1.26.5). This divine imperative is backed by Tertullian's famous question: 'if you do not fear God as being good, why do you not boil over into every kind of lust?' (*Marc.* 1.27.5). Marcion's reply, 'Absit!', is equally memorable.

More objections follow (*Marc.* 1.28f.). How can this god deliver us from sin and death, when he has never handed us over to sin and death? How can he regenerate what he never generated? How can he desire the salvation of men when, by forbidding marriage, he requires that they be not born? These and other inconsistencies in Marcion are important because he advocates coherence without paradox; Tertullian is justified in denying Marcion the reply that there is a paradox in these things, because Marcion requires monolithic coherence.

Book 1 of *adversus Marcionem* claims to have demolished Marcion's god by clear definitions which demand that deity be both

---

[37] Denial of divine passions was a major theme of Christian apologetic in its attack on pagan mythologies; Aristides, *apol.* 1, M. Pohlenz, *Vom Zorne Gottes* (Göttingen, 1909).

[38] For possible influence of Epicureans on Marcion see J. G. Gager, Marcion and philosophy, *VC*, 26 (1972), 53–9, and the criticism of Meijering, *Tertullian*, 75. Divine transcendence over weakness of passions is central to Epicureanism; Ratae sententiae 1, Diogenes Laertius, *Lives*, x, 139, LongSedley 23G; Lucretius, *de rerum natura*, 1.44–9; Cicero, *de natura deorum*, 1.17–45. Tertullian also links Marcion's apathetic god with Stoicism; *praescr.* 7 and 30.

[39] Epicurus denied creation because it implied will and desire. See K. A. Neuhausen, *De voluntarii notione platonica et aristotelea* (Wiesbaden, 1967), 120f. Cf. Meijering, *Tertullian*, 78.

unique and perfect, good and rational. Within the argument of this first book, we may distinguish detailed objections (which require, for example, that God exact retribution for sin) from the central Stoic arguments that God's goodness should be perfect and rational.

B. KNOWLEDGE, HUMANITY, JUSTICE AND SALVATION

(i) How humanity knows God

God was never hidden, as Marcion claimed, but shone like the sun, being proved by his works, his name and the laws of his being. Yet there were difficulties because of imperfect human vision,[40] because only the spirit of God knows God and the foolishness of God is wiser than men. God is greatest when man thinks him small, supremely good when man denies his goodness, absolutely one when man affirms his plurality (*Marc.* 2.2.6). Man rejected God, turned to material nature and disobeyed God, but did not blaspheme or accuse his maker; 'for since his own first beginning he had found him kind, and supremely good; and if he was a judge, it was Adam who made him so' (*Marc.* 2.2.7).[41]

Knowledge of God comes first from his works which are prior to man, who never knows him as other than good. From God's primary goodness came his refusal to be hidden and his plan for 'something to which he might become known as God. For what good can be compared to the knowledge and enjoyment of God?' (*Marc.* 2.3.3). Even before there was anyone to know him, God foreknew and willed that highest good. In contrast to this goodness without beginning, Marcion's god only became good in reaction to the malice of the creator.

In order for God to be known, man had first to be created and in order for man to be made, there had to be a world in which he could live. This world, for all its greatness, was to prepare man for something still greater. Towards this ultimate excellence, God appointed his *optimum ministrum*, his word, 'first and excellent fruit of

---

[40] Imperfect vision sees a second object when there is only one (*Marc.* 2.2). Plato (*Rep.* 508c) and the Platonic tradition made much of intellectual perception.

[41] Translation of Ernest Evans, Tertullian, *Adversus Marcionem*, 2 vols. (Oxford, 1972), vol. I, 91. This translation is cited generally in this chapter.

an equally excellent tree' (*Marc.* 2.4.1f.). In his turn the word produced a world whose goodness God attested and consummated by looking at it.[42] Then he continued to bless and make good things so that his entire being is commended by good speech and good action. His word neither spoke nor did any evil.[43] The world was wholly good and prophetic of greater good to come (*Marc.* 2.4.3).

(ii) How God's goodness is shown in the creation and freedom of mankind

It is hard to imagine a more optimistic account of human origin than that of Tertullian. Only God's image was worthy to have the works of God as his home. He was created by a specially effective goodness with a kind hand and a gentle word: 'Let us make man!'

It was goodness who spoke, it was goodness who formed man out of clay into that noble substance of flesh, a substance built out of one material to possess all those many attributes. It was goodness that breathed soul into him – soul not dead, but living. Goodness gave him dominion over all things, to enjoy, to govern, and even to give them names. Still more it was goodness that gave man additional delights, so that although in possession of the whole world he had his dwelling in the healthier parts of it: so early was he transferred to paradise, as he has been transferred out of the world into the church. The same goodness sought out a help for him, so that no good thing might be lacking: 'It is not good', God said, 'that the man should be alone'. He foreknew that the femininity of Mary, and subsequently of the church, would be to man's advantage.[44]

The divine goodness was active supremely in the making of man. Goodness spoke persuasively, formed nobly, breathed life, gave dominion and delights, so that no good thing was absent from the crown of God's creation. The law was given to hold man to God and raise him above the level of animals, subjecting him as rational and free to God alone, while all else was subject to him. Goodness warned of the penalty for disobedience, hoping that it would not be necessary. God's goodness is evident from his works and words, and his gracious admonitions.

---

[42] 'honorans et consignans et dispungens bonitatem operum dignatione conspectus' (*Marc.* 2.4.2).
[43] Later, even God was to be provoked by the need for evil.
[44] *Marc.* 2.4.4f.

The account of man continues with Tertullian's sustained contrapuntal logic, where the two parts represent man and God. Everything said about man agrees with a fresh claim about the goodness of God. Human freedom removes from God the blame for sin, and displays the generous outpouring of his likeness (*Marc.* 2.5f.).[45] God limits himself to allow this freedom, while retaining his long-term providence.[46] His creation disposes man towards good, while he himself is good by nature. God's faithful goodness is proved abundantly: in man's power of spontaneous goodness, in the law which enabled free obedience, in the lack of limit to freedom, in the choice which some angels made badly but which enables man to regain paradise, and in man's status as the *afflatus*[47] of God (*Marc.* 2.9). *Afflatus* is the image, *spiritus* is the divine reality.[48] The divine breath in man is not sinful in substance;[49] free will is the accidental, changeable source of sin. Free will also explains the fall of the devil who in time is to be overthrown by the man he had at first defeated (*Marc.* 2.10.6).

(iii) How divine justice responds to man's sin

Is justice good? God's goodness is innate, while his just severity is a response to a cause. Justice is linked with goodness, not with evil. Nothing good is unjust and everything just is good (*Marc.* 2.11.4). Justice and goodness work together; goodness creates that which justice arranges and discriminates. Divine justice is natural and not accidental (*Marc.* 2.12.3). When evil happened justice took over a secondary function which was that of distributing goodness according to the merits of each human being. In this, justice was always the agent of goodness. Goodness had lost its impregnability

---

[45] Philo gives a similar account of divine likeness (*immut.* 48) and it is a commonplace of early Christian literature. See Meijering, *Tertullian*, 102, and P. Courcelle, *Recherches sur les Confessions de S. Augustin* (Paris, 1968), 97ff.

[46] Albinus combines universal fate with freedom (*Epitome* 26.1) and Plotinus argues that providence requires a place for human initiative (*Enn.* 3.2.9). Meijering, *Tertullian*, 107.

[47] Tertullian owes the distinction between *afflatus* and *spiritus* to Irenaeus (*haer.* 5.12.2). The distinction is clearly made by Philo (*leg. all.* 1.42). See Waszink, *De anima*, 14 and 194f.

[48] Tertullian frequently (*pall.* 2.1; *an.* 23.5) adopts the Platonic distinction between *imago* and *veritas* where the latter always has precedence (*praescr.* 29.5).

[49] Similar argument about immanent divine substance is later used by Manichees and rebutted by Augustine, *conf.* 7.2.3. See Courcelle, *Recherches*, 72ff., Meijering, *Tertullian*, 114.

and needed the power of fear to threaten evil-doers. God is wholly good and in his omnipotence he is able to help and to hurt in the cause of good. He is both father and master, merciful and severe, to be loved and to be feared (*Marc.* 2.13).

While there is one unchanging goodness, evil (as Isa. 45.7 declares) takes two forms:[50] the sins which the devil helps humans to commit (*mala culpae*) and the punishments which God inflicts (*mala poenae*). God is present in everything which happens to humans either to bless or to blame (*Marc.* 2.14.1). This is Tertullian's most unconvincing argument. He accepts without qualification the avenging God of the Deuteronomist. Such severity is consistent with reason and justice (*Marc.* 2.15.1) and is good even when it comes in divine anger, jealousy or sternness. The divine surgeon must cut and cauterise in order to heal; indeed, for our healing, *God himself died* (*Marc.* 2.16.3).[51] Remarkably, this final proposition rescues Tertullian from disaster.

God alone is perfect and his saving history points to goodness, long-suffering, mercy, forgiveness and gentleness (*Marc.* 2.17.3). His law, which precedes all human laws,[52] is humane, for the *lex talionis* acts as a deterrent against violence (*Marc.* 2.18.1) and the details of the Law confirm this (*Marc.* 2.19–21). The spoiling of the Egyptians was just.[53] God acted like a good judge when he chose and then rejected Saul and Solomon, deciding and allotting according to the merits of each case in his providential rule of history (*Marc.* 2.23). His repentance with respect to Saul and the Ninevites showed his goodness and his justice[54] for his change of mind was regulated by changing circumstances (*Marc.* 2.24.8). His question to Adam: 'Where are you?' showed the same concerned goodness (*Marc.* 2.25.2).[55]

---

[50] This distinction, for which Tertullian is notorious, is found earlier in Irenaeus, *haer.* 4.40.1. Meijering, *Tertullian*, 125.

[51] See *Marc.* 1.26, and Meijering, *Tertullian*, 130.

[52] The priority of Moses is an important element in Christian apologetic.

[53] Cf. Philo, *Moysis*, 1.141; Irenaeus, *haer.* 4.30.2. Tertullian goes on to claim that the brazen serpent and the cherubim did not violate the second commandment because neither could be taken as a likeness of God. Even sacrifices had their place (*Marc.* 2.22).

[54] In contradiction to Marcion who took a negative Stoic definition of repentance. See M. Pohlenz, *Die Stoa*, vol. II (Göttingen, 1955), 199, also W. Maas, *Unveränderlichkeit Gottes* (München, 1974), 88f., and Meijering, *Tertullian*, 147.

[55] See Harnack, *Marcion*, 89, and Meijering, *Tertullian*, 150f.

(iv) The argument from retrospective indignity

Tertullian's argument in the first two books may be briefly assessed. Setting aside rhetorical excesses, how does he measure up besides Marcion? His arguments are uneven, and some readers have found in Marcion's favour. While the interpreter does not give prizes, there are times when it helps to enter the argument. It seems that Tertullian wins by linking the goodness of creation and the love of the cross. Yet Marcion wins on the interval between creation and cross because Tertullian's jealous God who smites and heals, kills and makes alive, humbles and exalts and creates evil and makes peace, does not reflect the love of the cross which is, for Tertullian, the world's sole hope. Of course, Marcion was extreme in his condemnation of the creator and Tertullian makes many good points for the humaneness of the law. But Tertullian's victory on the creation and the cross is also fragile. Today, the Third World population lives in a kind of hell and many have difficulty in seeing the second person of the blessed trinity nailed to a tree. Tertullian's inevitable reply – 'So much the worse for the blessed trinity!' – is convincing but controversial.

The debate between Marcion and Tertullian cannot be resolved without remainder. None will deny that Tertullian's validation of the Old Testament has been of influence in Christian thought, and few will deny its harmful effects in promoting the fear of God and the mutual destruction of humans. Can we identify the crucial weakness in his case? His chief argument for antithesis in God is the argument from divine condescension or indignity (*Marc.* 2.27). He wishes to answer objections to the creator's pettiness, weakness and indignity with one simple claim. To save humanity God had to be in touch with men. He could only communicate if he accepted human thoughts and feelings, abandoning divine majesty for human mediocrity. This condescension was unworthy of God but necessary to save humanity, which means, argues the antithetical Tertullian, that it is indeed worthy of God for whom there is nothing more worthy than the salvation of mankind. 'For if a god, indeed the higher god, did with great humility so abase the high state of his majesty to be subject to death, even the death of the cross, why should you not agree that a few pettinesses (*pusillitates*) were appropriate, being at least more tolerable than the revilings, scaffolds and graves of the Jews?' (*Marc.* 2.27.1). For the Christ who was mocked belongs to the same God whose human appearance and action are ridiculed. Indeed it was he who spoke to patriarchs and prophets and underwent the indignities which Marcion condemns, descending, interrogating, demanding and swearing.

In order to save mankind God took those human limitations, which culminated in the humiliation of the cross. The reply to Marcion is the same as that given in the defence of the flesh of Christ.[56] God's total disgrace is the secret sign and pledge of man's salvation.

In fact the whole of that which in my God is dishonourable in your sight, is the sacrament of man's salvation. God entered into converse with man, so that man might be taught how to act like God. God treated on equal terms with man so that man might be able to treat on equal terms with God. God was found to be small so that man might become very great.

While Marcion demands goodness from God, he despises these ultimate acts of divine kindness (*Marc.* 2.27.7f.).

The weakness of Tertullian's argument is that the cross might explain the more ancient condescension of God. It will not explain the barbarities of the Deuteronomic God of battles; these were as much a part of Marcion's case as were the foolish indignities.

(v) Antitheses in God

Do not the antitheses point to man's salvation rather than to God's discredit? This question brings us to Tertullian's conclusion, from which, indeed, we began. All the antitheses at which Marcion falters are paradoxes, capable of rational solution and united in one God. In contrast, it is claimed, Marcion's position has many contradictions which he does not recognize. Yet another clue to the conclusion comes when Tertullian puts forward some rival antitheses to Marcion who claimed that Tertullian's God knew no one above him. Balance that, says Tertullian, with the fact that Marcion's God knew no one beneath him. The road up is the same as the road down – Tertullian quotes from Heraclitus who is closer

---

[56] *carn.* 5; see above, ch. 3.

to him than are other ancient philosophers. There is nothing wrong with antitheses provided they are kept within one God.

Tertullian's antitheses tell us a great deal about his God. They were not simply a response to Marcion, for Tertullian found paradox and antithesis everywhere. His account of God is vulnerable when it denies all Marcion's difficulties, profound where it puts antitheses in God. If there be a God, he should stand above all human conflicts: if there be a God he should be with us in ours. Tertullian has clear convictions about God and the world. First, 'the two attributes of goodness and justice together make up the proper fullness of the divine being as omnipotent' (*Marc.* 2.29.1). Second, the world is immature[57] and embraces a conflict of opposites.[58]

C. PROPHECY FULFILLED

After the accumulated argument of Books 1 and 2, we anticipate a change of gear in Book 3 which, like Books 4 and 5, is largely concerned with scriptural evidence. However, Tertullian begins with a priceless comment and argues on the need for the kind of order which requires promise to precede fulfilment, father to precede son and the sender to precede the one sent.

(i) Is christology redundant?

Book 3 is concerned with christology and begins with an argument for its own redundancy.[59] Since the first two books have established the unicity of God who by his disgrace worked the salvation of men, the elaboration of christology is superfluous or gratuitous. Why is this comment so important? Because it offers a clue to the Christian claim that one God was credible, only if he had in Christ redeemed what he had created, perfected what he had begun and corrected

---

[57] 'Die Welt ist noch nicht fertig'. J. Moltmann, *Theologie der Hoffnung* (Munich, 1964), 312.
[58] The work *Against Marcion* provides a good training ground in the analysis of argument, where readers may change their verdict from year to year. Meijering found Marcion more original; but if Y writes a book against X he is *ipso facto* derivative. Harnack was convinced by Marcion that the Old Testament did more harm than good to Christians.
[59] The *apologeticum* finishes on the same note, showing how Christians are better off being persecuted. It is all part of Tertullian's taste for paradox, which is never a game.

what had gone wrong. This means that the relation of father to son and their relation to morals and reason was already settled by belief in one God. Christ belonged to the creator, as the apostolic rule had always asserted.

However, since truth should use every resource with utmost energy, Tertullian wants to confront Marcion at every point (*Marc.* 3.1.2). If he starts from christology, he will tackle Marcion from a new angle with a different set of arguments, so that new aspects of theology will emerge. The chief points about Marcion's Christ are that he comes suddenly, before the highest god is known, and, as no one denies, he is the one way to the knowledge of that god.

(ii) Why the father comes first

Tertullian has two main arguments here: first, there is a general rule that the original should take precedence; second, that miracles are not enough to prove an unpredicted Christ. The general rule implies that the father should declare the son before (as with Marcion) the son declares the father and that the sender should precede the one sent: God orders and arranges everything so that sudden irruptions into the world are excluded (as any Stoic knows).

A fortiori, so great a work as human salvation needs preparation. Such salvation is appropriated by faith which can only be clearly defined when its conditions are announced in advance. Salvation through faith could not come suddenly, because faith needs to be taught in advance in order to be a real option (*Marc.* 3.2.3f.).[60]

(iii) Can we make sense of miracles and metaphors?

The second argument is that Christ's miracles were not enough to prove that he was the son sent by the father. For Christ himself spoke of many false christs who would work signs and wonders to confuse God's chosen people; what if he were merely the first in a queue of wonder-workers and, like the early arrivals at the baths, simply got in first? This will not do because the creator had already worked miracles and can claim unrivalled priority. He worked the

---

[60] See preceding chapter for Tertullian's account of faith as recognition, p. 79.

same kind of miracles before Christ as he worked through Christ; so that ancient miracles, like prophecies, were a preparation (*Marc.* 3.3).

Now Tertullian digresses (*Marc.* 3.4) to demolish Marcion's Christ with a mass of intricate argument.[61] Then he turns to scripture where the decisive battle must be fought. The scriptures belong to the creator and they will prove his Christ (*Marc.* 3.5.1). Any such proof requires a critical awareness of the form of scripture. Two general principles need to be recognized so that they do not have to be argued in particular cases. First, there is the prophetic use of the perfect tense. Prophets commonly refer to future events as though they were past; for God sees whatever he has decided as already perfect. So Isaiah speaks of the crucifixion as already past. Secondly, there is widespread use of symbolic language; this must not be taken literally. In a land flowing with milk and honey, no one can squeeze cakes and confectionery from the soil. Since this is the way all scripture works we should not argue about its oblique form, but about the point at issue (*Marc.* 3.6.1).[62]

Marcionites deny that Christ was predicted in scripture and line up with Jews who, for different reasons, declare the scriptural strangeness of Christ. The Jews treated him simply as a magician who taught false doctrines rather than as someone unique. Tertullian's classification of Marcion with the Jews would have been unpleasant for the Marcionites who despised Jews as the people of the creator.

Against both parties, Tertullian quotes testimony for the two advents of Christ (*Marc.* 3.7), which, since Justin, had been central to Christian apologetic. Once again, Tertullian finds fundamental truth in paradox; nothing could have pleased him more than the contrast between the two advents. Truth is never in the middle but always at both ends. On the one hand, there is the man of sorrows (Isa. 53.3f.), the stone of stumbling (Isa. 8.14), lower than the angels (Ps. 8.5), a worm and no man, despised by the people (Ps. 22.7). On the other hand, the stumbling stone becomes the chief cornerstone, the son of man comes on the clouds of heaven to take up an everlasting kingdom (Dan. 7.13f.). He who is fairer than the

---

[61] Yet another proof that he is drawing on a substantial tradition.
[62] 'non retractetur de forma scripturae sed de statu causae' (*Marc.* 3.6.1).

children of men girds on his sword in glory and majesty (Ps. 45.2f.), one lower than the angels is crowned with glory and honour (Ps. 8.5f.), while those who pierced him will mourn their lack of perception (Zech. 12.10). Joshua (Jesus) comes first in filthy clothes which he exchanges for priestly robes and diadem (Zech. 3.4f.). The two goats of the great day of atonement point to the 'two natures of Christ' (Lev. 16.5ff.).

(iv) Why truth demands an incarnation

Marcion's chief error is his denial of a real body to Christ who for him is a phantom, lacking a body which would join him with the deceitful creator (*Marc.* 3.8). Marcion claims that, to avoid this link, Christ performs his own deception and pretends to do the physical things (meeting, touching, eating, drinking and working miracles) which his flesh appears to do. But how, objects Tertullian, can the unseen, real Christ be credible when his visible behaviour is deliberately dishonest?

Apart from a general objection to such a trickster, there is the loss of the critical centre of the Christian message, which Tertullian found in the sufferings of Christ which are the ground of faith in him. 'God's entire work is therefore subverted. Christ's death, wherein lies the whole weight and fruit of the Christian name, is denied' (*Marc.* 3.8.5). Paul asserts this death to be entirely real and to be the foundation on which rest gospel, salvation and preaching (1 Cor. 15.3–18). No flesh means no death, no return to the earth out of which flesh was taken by the law of its maker, no resurrection for Christ and therefore no resurrection for us, no faith, no preaching, no true apostolic witness, no deliverance from sin (*Marc.* 3.8.7).

Marcion has an intelligent response to this argument: angelic apparitions have a long and honoured place in the history of salvation and God has shown his fondness for phantoms. Tertullian replies, first, that Marcion is mixing his two gods and, second, that the angels had real flesh, because God is the maker of flesh and it was easier for him to use more of the same stuff, when he came to make angels. Tertullian's God who made the first flesh from dust and the universe from nothing could, at a word, produce bodies of all kinds, shapes and sizes (*Marc.* 3.9).

True (not apparent) flesh is the proper creation of a true God. Marcion's god despised the flesh; why did he respect its imitation? Only a wretched god would reveal his Christ in an alien and unworthy form. We can use unworthy things if they are our own but we cannot properly use things, however worthy, which are not our own. Why did not God use a worthier substance? God had used bush, fire and cloud, so he did not *need* either false or real flesh. But he chooses what he wills and by his choice, he makes flesh of himself (*Marc.* 3.10). If he could honour a fiction of flesh, then he heaped even greater honour on real flesh (*Marc.* 3.10.9). However, God deals in truth, not pretence, and Christ came in reality not falsehood. However disgusting Marcion may find the process of human generation, the birth and flesh of Christ were real (*Marc.* 3.11).

(v) How prophecies are fulfilled in truth

The rest of this third book is taken up with the further fulfilment of prophecy, which Marcion cannot accept. Most of the detail is familiar from Justin, but it is handled in a way which is distinctive of Tertullian. It is more argumentative, analysing the notions of 'sign' (*Marc.* 3.13) and 'dispensation' (*Marc.* 3.20). It is more triumphalist, drawing on military metaphors in the Psalms which point to Christus Victor and his two-edged sword (Ps. 45; Rev. 1.16). Above all, it is more dramatic, because the dispensation is more important, both for the fulfilment of its predictions in Christ and for the things which have come after him. 'See how all the nations since then are looking up out of the abyss of human error towards God the Creator, and towards his Christ, and deny, if you dare, that this was prophesied' (*Marc.* 3.20.2).

The sure mercies of David go beyond the Jewish nation to 'Christ who has by now taken the whole world captive by the faith of his gospel' (*Marc.* 3.20.3). In him will be found the 'holy and faithful things' of David. He, not David, is testimony, prince and commander to the nations; for those who have not known him now invoke his name and fly to him. Such events are present, not future. 'You cannot claim that an event lies in the future, when you see it now happening' (*Marc.* 3.20.10).

Tertullian must also answer the refinement of Marcion that there were to be two Christs, one to unite the Jews and the other to bring all men together. His answer is that the universal Christ was already here before Cerdo and Marcion made the distinction, and that Isaiah (2.2f.) foretold the coming of the nations to the mountain of the Lord. 'This way must be the gospel of the new law, and of the new word in Christ, no longer in Moses (*Marc.* 3.21.3). The apostles, who preached the gospel of peace and whose sound went out into all the earth, preached the God whose scriptures they were fulfilling.

Finally, Tertullian speaks with precision of the millennium promised to Christians in the new Jerusalem.[63] 'For it is both just and worthy of God that his servants should exult in the place where they were afflicted for his name' (*Marc.* 3.24.5). Tertullian does this because Marcion's Christ promises a heavenly kingdom when he has no heaven, just as he appeared as a man without human flesh. The kingdom of heaven must have physical reality, because that is the only kind of reality. There is less in Marcion's Christ and kingdom than meets the eye. 'What a mirage it all is! What a hollow pretence of so great a promise!' (*Marc.* 3.24.13)

D. THE CHRIST OF THE CREATOR

In Book 4 Tertullian moves beyond the arguments from prophecy which Justin had handed on. This is necessary because Justin was arguing with a Jew, while Tertullian is arguing with a Christian, indeed a 'super-Christian'. The ground of debate must now be Marcion's only Gospel which is an edited form of Luke, to which is added the *Antitheses* which function as a hermeneutical key and divide God into two gods and scripture into two instruments or testaments.

(i) On recognizing the true antitheses

Tertullian offers, in response to Marcion, his own antitheses. There was a dispensation of the creator and there is now a dispensation of

---

[63] Recently observed, he says, in the sky over Judaea.

Christ. The two orders differ in language, moral precepts and law. But these differences are part of the plan of one God who planned and predicted a radical change: the law would go out of Zion to judge all nations. Swords would become ploughshares, cruelty would be replaced by goodness, darkness by light, imperfect by perfect, tedious complexity by decisive simplicity, old by new, thorns by pastures, temporary by eternal, temple sacrifices by simple prayer. All change produces something different and contradicts what was before. Tertullian's Heraclitean God produces change. He wounds and heals, kills and brings to life (Deut. 32.39), creates evil and good (Isa. 45.7). His world, even in one place like Pontus, is full of opposites (*Marc.* 4.1.10).[64] In creation it is plain that God's works and ways are persistently contradictory; his revelation follows the same pattern. The evidence is overwhelming that 'he whose works and ways are consistently antithetical, preserves the same pattern in his mysteries of revelation' (*Marc.* 4.1.11). These inseparable opposites provide Tertullian's philosophical response to Marcion's antitheses.

(ii) On identifying the gospel

He moves on to Marcion's Gospel which avoids opposites and aims at an inaccessible principle of uniformity. What matters for a Gospel is its apostolic origin and its agreement with an apostolic rule. Conflict over narrative sequences is of no consequence; what matters is agreement on the essence[65] of the apostolic faith (*Marc.* 4.2.2). Marcion's Gospel might be rejected out of hand because it lacks an author and a title. However, Tertullian would never stop at such a simple solution; he must seek out and destroy his enemy at every point: 'but I prefer to take issue on every point' (*Marc.* 4.2.4).

Luke lies behind Marcion's Gospel and Tertullian's attack is directed, first against this exclusive choice for an elusive uncontaminated Gospel,[66] second against its lack of antiquity and third against the implausibility of its long-postponed heretical emenda-

---

[64] 'Nec mundum saltim recogitare potuisti, nisi fallor, etiam apud Ponticos ex diversitatibus structum aemularum invicem substantiarum.'

[65] *caput*. Cf. Cicero, *Phil.* 2, 31, 77; *Ac.* 2, 32, 101; *Brut.* 44, 164.

[66] Marcion based his argument on Paul's accusations in Gal. 2.13f.

tion. 'Heresy, which is always in this way emending and thereby corrupting the Gospels, is the result of human temerity not of divine authority' (*Marc.* 4.4.5). Apostolic Gospels are linked to the four apostles – John, Matthew, Peter and Paul – and to the apostolic churches which sprang from them (*Marc.* 4.5).

(iii) Against separation: division and detail

Marcion's alterations are many, but they flow from the one principle of division – the separation of Christ from the creator, the total opposition ('magnam et omnem differentiam' (*Marc.* 4.6.3)) between justice and goodness, law and gospel, Judaism and Christianity. Against this Tertullian claims that Christ belongs to the creator because he has 'administered the creator's commands, fulfilled his prophecies, supported his laws, given reality to his promises, revived his miracles, given new expression to his judgements, and reproduced the lineaments of his character and attributes' (*Marc.* 4.6.4).

Tertullian's detail moves from the demons of Capernaum and Nazareth, to fishing for men,[67] to the conclusive title of Son of Man, to fulfilment of prophecies and to the Sermon on the Mount.[68] Principles emerge from time to time. Separation always implies continuity; no one puts new wine into old bottles unless the old bottles are his own, nor does anyone sew patches on a garment which he does not own (*Marc.* 4.11.10).

Love of strangers simply extends the older commandment to love neighbours and offers a summary which is distinctive, decisive, compendious and congenial to human freedom (*Marc.* 4.16). All Christ's acts and commands point to the creator. Who could have told his disciples to go unburdened by food or extra clothes except the one who feeds the ravens and clothes the flowers of the field (*Marc.* 4.21.1)? Even his miracles reflect the wonder of the Old Testament and his novelties are old (*Marc.* 4.21.5).

When Peter saw the miracles and confessed the creator's Christ, he drew the wrong conclusion and rejected a suffering messiah. For this error he was told to be silent. Tertullian has always a passion

---

[67] Which Jeremiah foretold.
[68] Which agrees with the creator's law (*Marc.* 4.6.4).

for paradox. Saving life and losing it is foretold by Daniel and Isaiah: 'Surely it is in no simple death or one that follows the law of common nature, but in that noble death which fights for the faith, that he who loses his life for God, saves it?' (*Marc.* 4.21.8).

(iv) On not being ashamed of the world

Christ will be ashamed of everyone who is now ashamed of him. This could never apply to Marcion's discarnate, instant Christ who never did anything which might bring a blush to the cheeks of his followers – he was never contracted into a woman's womb, never made a mess on his mother's lap or nibbled at her nipples, never wasted time on infancy, boyhood or adolescence. He was suddenly brought from heaven, all at once full grown, complete, and instant Christ, spirit and God. Lacking physical reality, he avoided the curse of the cross. Tertullian plainly loves the divine humiliation because it was done out of solidarity with mankind ('suus homo, sua imago, sua similitudo'). 'Rightly did he bring himself low for the humanity, image and likeness which belonged to him and not to another' (*Marc.* 4.21.12).

Antithesis is everywhere within the good and just God, and only careful analysis will bring understanding. Christ loves infants and declares their greatness, says Marcion, while the creator sends bears to destroy insulting children; this is a rather reckless antithesis which lumps together innocent infants and blasphemous boys who have passed the age of discretion (*Marc.* 4.23.5). Marcion's lack of subtlety is evident in his use of the lawyer's question concerning eternal life. Marcion omits 'eternal' so that the commandment, which Jesus quotes, points to an extension of earthly life. Now the lawyer knew perfectly well that such an extension was tied to the law which he was already teaching; but Christ had started raising the dead and this inspired him with hope of life eternal. Because Christ was not alien he gave no strange, new commandment for the salvation which includes present and future, but simply put forward the sum (*caput*) of the existing law, namely the entire love of God (*Marc.* 4.25.15).

Yet again Marcion misses the point when he deals with the institution of the Eucharist. 'This is my body' speaks figuratively of

Christ's body and there could be no image of a body which did not truly exist (*Marc.* 4.40.3).[69] Marcion might have it that he made a (ginger) bread body for himself to compensate for his lack of a real body; but why a body and not a simple pumpkin like that which Marcion has in place of a heart? Because Christ had already (Jer. 11.19) linked bread, body and cross just as he linked blood and wine with the winepress of Edom (Isa. 63.1). Blood can only come from a real body. 'So the proof of the body is established by the evidence of the flesh, and the proof of the flesh by the evidence of the blood' (*Marc.* 4.40.5).

Tertullian's treatment of the gospel is never tedious, despite the mass of detail. The vigour of argument carries him through to the conclusion: 'I have demonstrated Jesus as the Christ of the prophets in his doctrine, judgements, affections, feelings, miracles, sufferings as well as resurrection to be none other than the Christ of the Creator' (*Marc.* 4.43.9), because he does not lose contact with his subject: 'I pity you, Marcion. Your labour has been in vain. For the Christ Jesus in your Gospel belongs to me' (*Marc.* 4.43.9).

E. PAULINE PARADOX

When Tertullian moves to Marcion's account of Paul, it is evident that he avoids the strength of Marcion's case. A good example is his initial objection against Paul's beginning.[70] Paul is said, by Marcion, to be chosen by Christ after Christ's ascent to heaven; this is precarious, says Tertullian, because Christ might have known that he would need Paul. Tertullian finds authority for Paul in the blessing of Jacob, where Benjamin to whose tribe Paul belonged changes from a ravenous wolf in the morning to a giver of nourishment in the evening. Paul's claim to Christ has no other validation. Here Tertullian ignores the superior claim of Paul to direct appointment by God's will: Clement of Alexandria had spoken of Paul as 'God's apostle' (θεῖος ἀπόστολος) and once as 'the apostle appointed by God' (ἀπόστολος θεσπεσίος). Marcion

---

[69] 'Figura autem non fuisset nisi veritatis esset corpus: ceterum vacua res, quod est phantasma, figuram capere non posset.'
[70] Everyone but God must have a beginning.

found similar superiority in Paul's lack of earthly appointment (*Marc.* 5.1).

The argument over Galatians is intricate but more successful. The ancient law is abolished in accordance with the creator's plan and prophecies (*Marc.* 5.2.1). The faith of Abraham makes him the father of all who believe and the plain meaning of the text points away from two gods (*Marc.* 5.3.12).

In the central account of the folly of the cross, Tertullian argues intricately and inevitably on his theme of divine paradox. Paul's opening greeting to Corinthians shows us that God is not the destroyer of Judaism since he uses the Jewish greeting 'peace' and offers grace. Now grace implies an offence which is forgiven and no offence had been committed against Marcion's god. Against the creator, however, the Jews had transgressed his law and the whole race had denied natural virtue (*per naturae dissimulationem*) (*Marc.* 5.5.4); therefore grace is an appropriate greeting.

The folly of the cross must be the creator's work (Isa. 29.14 and 1 Cor. 1.19), bringing salvation to some, and perdition to others. Marcion implicitly argues that the hostile creator destroyed the wisdom of men so that they would share his hostility to the cross, yet nevertheless predicted the cross of which he was ignorant. Tertullian sees both Jews and Greeks justly punished by the jealous God who made them foolish. The cross and death of Christ are God's folly. The birth and flesh of Christ are his weakness. What is mean and ignoble on the human scale gains nobility and grandeur in the divine order. One might, as Marcion does, ridicule the creator's old testament with its sacrifices and cleansings. This distortion of Paul is turned by Tertullian against Marcion. If it is foolish then it is God's way of confounding worldly wisdom, of confusing things with their opposites[71] so that flesh should glory only in the lord. The lord here (Jer. 9.23f.; 1 Cor. 1.29–31) has to be the creator, unless the creator with his passion for paradox commanded us to honour Marcion's god (*Marc.* 5.5.5–10)!

Tertullian works through all ten letters of Paul, showing how Marcion has misused them. For example, 'the likeness' of sinful flesh (Rom. 8.3) refers to the likeness of sin not to the flesh which

---

[71] 'contraria contrariis redarguere' (*Marc.* 5.5.10).

was real (*Marc.* 5.14.1). He ends with the claim that he has produced proofs from the apostle, which concern earlier issues, that there has been no unnecessary repetition, and that whoever examines the whole work *Against Marcion* will find neither superfluity nor lack of conviction. However, the modern reader needs patience and intellectual stamina. If he should persist, he will find a consistent claim that antithesis is essential to the ways of God and to the world which he has made. As we noted at the beginning of this chapter, Marcion's antitheses would have been acceptable to Tertullian, if only they had been kept within one God and one world.

The second half (Books 3–5) of the work *Against Marcion* is the first example of sustained critical, exegetical argument in Christian theology. It is noteworthy (Books 1 and 2) that Tertullian does his theology first and then undertakes the exegetical argument which can be such a headache (*praescr.* 16.2). Why should it be a pain when he generally does it well? One problem is that the rule of faith and scripture determine one another. The rule derives from scripture and the rule determines that nothing contrary to the rule be recognized as scripture. The reciprocal validation of rule and scripture argues in a circle. Tertullian tries to break the circle by arguing from the scriptures which Marcion acknowledges. He does this well; but he knows that, with these scriptures, Marcion could also argue convincingly.

In the end he was no closer to solving the problem of evil than others had been. His exposition of the need for fear of God is rescued by the death of God (*Marc.* 2.16.3). His work against Marcion remains a remarkable achievement in early Christian literature, matched only by Origen's attack on Celsus. Those who trace its arguments will understand it better than those who list its conclusions.

CHAPTER 6

Trinity and christology

The influence of Tertullian's account of the trinity has been variously assessed. It has been claimed that through Novatian, whose work (according to Jerome) was an epitome of Tertullian, and through Hosius, Tertullian triumphed at Nicaea and the *homoousion* went on. Indeed, in Tertullian 'we first find the accurate definition and technical terms that passed over into Catholic theology, winning prompt acceptance in the West and securing – when the time came – the grudging but certain approval of the East'.[1] This is an impressive claim; but ideas rarely enjoy such unambiguous triumph.[2]

Tertullian's achievement may even be embarrassing in a climate of anti-trinitarian debate. Through him and other theologians, it is wrongly claimed that Christians lost their belief in God as 'one without further qualification', for the understanding of trinity requires such 'well informed and highly sophisticated powers of thought' that many Christians are effectively tritheist rather than monotheist. Today, 'the contrast between the apparent simple clarity of Jewish and Muslim monotheism and the apparent complexity of Christian monotheism remains a stumbling-block to Christianity's detriment'.[3] Tertullian was aware of the difficulty here raised (*Prax.* 3.1); but he insisted that trinity was the way to one God.

---

[1] J. Bethune-Baker, *An introduction to the early history of Christian doctrine*, 9th edn (London, 1951), 138.

[2] As William Telfer, who made the final revision of Bethune-Baker's work, once said, 'History is not 1066 and all that. Rather it is all that and 1066.'

[3] J. D. G. Dunn, What did Christianity lose when it parted from Judaism?, *Explorations*, 8.2 (1994), 2.

A. TRINITY A NEW FAITH IN ONE GOD

Trinity is never a mere multiplication of heavenly beings; there must be one God. Trinity is the faith of the gospel.

God so willed to renew his covenant with humanity, in order that he might be believed as one in a new way, through the son and spirit ('ut nove unus crederetur per filium et spiritum'), so that now God might be known directly, in his proper names and persons, who in times past was not plainly understood, although declared through the son and the spirit. (*Prax.* 31)[4]

Father, son and spirit, one unique deity, are the object of the same faith and adoration. This Godhead is that of the father, revealed in and by the others, as they are united with their first-principle (*Prax.* 18.5, 19.5, 22.11).[5]

Like all early Christian theology, Tertullian's first question sprang from theodicy: Is there one God, good and true, who is creator and ruler of this world of evil and chaos? The constant answer was that such a God was credible, if he had, in Jesus Christ, redeemed the world which he had made. To this answer there were two main objectors, the Jews and Marcion. Tertullian's trinitarian ideas may best be understood as third in a logic of apologetic, where his answer to the Jews made it necessary to argue with Marcion, while the answer to Marcion made it necessary to argue with Praxeas,[6] who had identified father and son.[7] It is difficult to win one argument without starting another.

(i) Jewish controversy

Tertullian claims that Jewish monotheism is spurious and that Jews are and have been idolaters (*Jud.* 1). The law, later disclosed to

---

[4] 'sic deus voluit novare sacramentum ut nove unus crederetur per filium et spiritum, ut coram iam deus in suis propriis nominibus et personis cognosceretur qui et retro per filium et spiritum praedicatus non intellegebatur'.

[5] J. Moingt, Le problème du dieu unique chez Tertullien, *RevSR*, 44 (1970), 337–62 (361).

[6] Praxeas' monarchianism was not merely a reaction to Marcion. Against all alternatives, he and others rightly wished to hold on to monotheism.

[7] As did those whom Justin attacks (*1 apol.* 63.15). Justin is the first witness to an 'identification theology'. For him the logos is ἀριθμῷ ἕτερόν τι. See L. Abramowski, Der Logos in der altchristlichen Theologie, in C. Colpe *et al.* (eds.), *Spätantike und Christentum* (Berlin, 1992), 189–202 (198).

Moses, was first given in its principles to Adam (*Jud.* 2), who did not love God or neighbour and disobeyed what he knew to be God's command. As an unwritten, natural law, it was habitually kept by patriarchs like Noah and Abraham who was the friend of God. This, not the temporary law of Moses, was the law which passed to the Gentiles. For God has always the power to reform his laws, at different times, for the one end of universal salvation. Before Moses, Adam, Cain, Noah, Enoch, Melchizedek and Lot all scored favourably.

Abraham (*Jud.* 3) had already pleased God before he was circumcised and the circumcision of his son was quite irregular. It was not done on the third day, but was an emergency operation, which gave advance notice that the Jews were going to be excluded from the holy city as a just punishment for their sins (Isa. 1.7f.) and that a spiritual circumcision (Jer. 4.3f.) would inaugurate a new covenant (Jer. 31.31f.) and new law (Isa. 2.2f.). Christians now constitute the people of God with a new law and a new circumcision. The temporal sabbath (*Jud.* 4) points to the eternal sabbath and the visible sacrifices point to the spiritual and universal worship now offered to God.

So much for the deficiency of the Jewish claim. The one question is whether Christ has come and the new covenant and law have been inaugurated. This Tertullian proves from the universal spread of Christian faith and worship. The words of Christ have gone out to the ends of the earth (Ps. 19.4), prophecies have been fulfilled (*Jud.* 7–13) and the first of his two advents has been observed. All the nations are now moving from the darkness of error, as God promised to his son (Ps. 2.7f.). Only he, the son of God, has reached the limits of the earth, given the light of his gospel through the whole world, and thus inaugurated his enduring kingdom. The economy of salvation proves the true God and his son. Jews must deny either the ancient prophecies or the evidence of their fulfilment.

Tertullian shows a remarkable change in Christian attitude to Jews. The New Testament fights against fear of Jews. 'They will expel you from synagogues. He who kills you will think that he does God a service' (John 16.2). 'Fear not those who kill the body and are not able to hurt the soul. Fear him who is able to cast soul and body into hell' (Matt. 10.28). In Justin there is still timidity, when he pleads with Jews not to ridicule the crucified Christ because by his wounds and stripes many have been healed. Tertullian is not afraid of Jews. The triumphant spread of Christian faith proves that a new covenant and a new law have been given and that in Christ and his people all promises have been fulfilled.

(ii) Marcion

The strength of the argument against the Jews made it necessary to answer Marcion who drove the dichotomy between Jew and Christian to extremes. Marcion could not affirm one God as both the father of Jesus Christ and the creator of this world; his dualism declared two Gods, one of law and another of gospel, one of Jewish scripture and the other of Jesus and Paul. At the deepest level, Marcion's denial opposed the central affirmation of Christian faith, which was that one God was only credible if he had, in Christ, redeemed the world which he had made. Marcion rejected that economy of salvation which was the theme of early Christian theology. For Tertullian and Irenaeus, God's total disgrace was the pledge of man's salvation, for it joined the end to the beginning, man to God.

To understand Tertullian's detailed argument,[8] we went to the conclusion of Book 2 where Tertullian claims that he has shown that the creator is both good and just in a way which is worthy of God. Goodness and justice (*bonitas, justitia*) must be united in God.

Marcion's move had been one of division. He had separated the divine goodness and justice, and had distinguished Christ from the creator. For Tertullian, these opposites are necessary in one God. If you remove Marcion's title (*Antitheses*) you are left with a proof of the one God who is supremely good *and* a judge (*Marc.* 2.29).

In Marcion's *Antitheses*, Tertullian recognizes his own God. These antitheses are reflected in God's world which consists of opposite elements which (as in Heraclitus and the Stoics) the highest reason regulates ('summa tamen ratione modulatus'); but the antithesis belongs in God and not just in his world ('ceterum

---

[8] See above, ch. 5.

eius erit antithesis cuius est et in mundo' (*Marc.* 2.29.4)).⁹ 'God is not, if he be not one' (*Marc.* 1.3).

(iii) Praxeas¹⁰

Just as the refutation of the Jewish argument led on to the Marcionite dichotomy, so the unity of God made it necessary to answer Praxeas. If God ceases to be God when he loses his unity, then the nature of that unity will dominate Christian theology. Behind the monarchian teaching of Praxeas, Tertullian sees the devil, who is clever enough to attack truth by pretending to defend it and who delivers an 'overkill' on dualism,¹¹ so defending the 'one lord, the almighty, the creator of the world', that he makes a heresy of the unity ('ut et de unico haeresim faciat' (*Marc.* 2.29.4)). The father became incarnate and was crucified. Further, if there is no distinction between father and son, then the spirit cannot constitute a third person in the godhead.

Tertullian is incensed¹² by the practical outcome of this teaching. When the pope of Rome had offered peace to the followers of Montanus, who gave due place to the spirit within the economy of salvation, Praxeas so maligned the followers of the New Prophecy that the offer was withdrawn. Praxeas achieved two things for the devil at Rome: he expelled the paraclete and he crucified the father (*Prax.* 1). When he had sown the seeds of his heresy, he renounced it, but the seeds are still there and need to be removed. Yet Tertullian's opposition is more deeply motivated than this. All recapitulation in Christ seems monarchian in tendency – the necessary dishonour of God is man's unique hope. He sees Praxeas' strength as he saw that of Marcion.

---

⁹ It should be noted that antithesis in God is inherent in a single subject, while in the world it may be inherent in one subject or successive within a single process. See above, ch. 4, on the strife of opposites in Presocratic philosophy.

¹⁰ The name 'Praxeas' or 'busy-body' could be a nickname for some notable person. See *Treatise against Praxeas*, tr. E. Evans (London, 1948), 184f., Bethune-Baker, *Christian doctrine*, 431f. A satisfying solution in favour of identification has been given by Allen Brent, *Hippolytus and the Roman church in the third century* (Leiden, 1995), 525–9. See also a fine discussion of the complex issue of the relation of Tertullian to the *Elenchus* and *Contra Noetum* of Hippolytus, *ibid.*, 529–35.

¹¹ Cf. Tertullian's aggression on behalf of *monarchia*: *Marc.* 3.1.2.

¹² Tertullian's anger does not affect the cogency of his argument, as we might expect. His literary output is never without emotional stimulus.

Yet the alleged crucifixion of the father points to Praxeas' fatal fault and heresy. For it is the cross which declares the divine economy and makes the doctrines of trinity and incarnation essential. All things are summed up in Christ only through the divine economy. God reconciles mankind because on the cross father and son are distinct and the forsaken son is within God.[13] This was for Tertullian and remains for all believers their *unica spes*. 'The economic trinity is the immanent trinity and *vice versa*'.[14]

B. TRINITY: THE MYSTERY OF THE ECONOMY[15]

(i) The necessity of the economy

Monarchy and economy must go together. There is indeed only one God, but the rule of faith declares the economy of salvation through father, son and spirit. Praxeas argues that monarchy requires the identity of father, son and spirit. Tertullian claims that the economy distributes unity into trinity so that the three are one in quality, substance and power (*status, substantia, potestas*), but distinct in sequence, aspect and manifestation (*gradus, forma, species*) (*Prax.* 2.4). This Tertullian calls the mystery of the economy. Trinity has to do with the internal disposition of the Godhead. Economy in Paul, Irenaeus and Tertullian has to do with the plan of salvation; a consideration of this plan causes Irenaeus[16] and Tertullian to see economy in God.

The trinitarian problem is clarified[17] by Tertullian through a

---

[13] 'Indem Gott von sich selber unterscheidet und so in Einheit mit dem gekreuzigten Jesus, als Gott der Sohn die Verlassenheit von Gott dem Vater erleidet, ist Gott der Versöhner ... Das vinculum caritatis bringt im Jesu Tod Gottes ewiges Sein als Liebe zur Geltung.' Jüngel, *Geheimnis*, 504.

[14] This claim of K. Rahner (Der dreifaltige Gott als transzendenter Urgrund der Heilsgeschichte, in J. Feiner and M. Löhrer (eds.), *Mysterium Salutis, Grundriss heilsgeschichtlicher Dogmatik*, vol. II (Einsiedeln, 1967), 328. Cited by Jüngel, *Geheimnis*, 507) opens up a new understanding of the trinity which is based on the cross.

[15] 'oikonomiae sacramentum'.

[16] *dem.* 47. There is only one God, although according to the economy of our redemption there is a son and a father.

[17] Tertullian quite properly does not so much solve the problem as elucidate it. What was lost in later discussion was Tertullian's sense of opposition between the one and the three. For one substance does not explain trinity without remainder. The three are neither attributes nor substantives, neither adjectives nor nouns.

comparison of the relation between father and son, which is similar
to that between thought and speech. Tertullian uses different terms
to describe the relation. The father utters (*edere*) the son who derives
(*decurrere, derivatio*) from the father.[18]

To understand the necessity of the economy, we may turn back
to the argument of the *apologeticum* 21.10–13. Here Tertullian
compares his claims with those of the Stoics. Zeno speaks of the
logos as 'word', 'reason', 'oracle', 'god', 'mind of Jove', 'universal
destiny' (*sermo, ratio, fatum, deus, animus Iovis, necessitas omnium*).
Cleanthes brings all these together in the *spiritus* which permeates
the universe. Christians make a similar claim that God made all
things by his word, reason, power (*sermo, ratio, virtus*),[19] to whom is
ascribed the substance of spirit. To this very substance of God
belong the word which proclaims, the reason which disposes and
the power which perfects God's work.[20] Christians say that the
word is extended from God, born by projection, so that 'God's son
is also called "God" from unity of substance'.

Visual metaphors are now added to the intellectual account.
When a ray is directed from the sun, 'it is a part from the whole, but
the sun will be in the ray', because the ray belongs to the sun. There
is an extension rather than a separation of substance, as light is
kindled from light, while the material source remains whole and
undiminished. In the same way, what comes from God is perfect: 'at
once God and son of God, and the two are one'.[21] So spirit comes
from spirit and God from God, in a sequence without change of
being, never receding but rather proceeding from the source.

Continuing the metaphor, Tertullian says that this ray of God,
as foretold of old, descended on a certain virgin 'and, made flesh in

[18] When he uses the unfortunate word 'portio' he corrects it, using the equally dangerous
word 'alius'; 'non tamen diversitate alium Filium a Patre, sed distributione, nec divisione
alium, sed distinctione' (*Prax.* 9).
[19] See Abramowski, Der Logos. The prologue of John identifies *logos* of creation with *sophia*
of Prov. 8. 'Es ist wieder Tertullian (*Prax.* 7.3) der ausdrücklich entwickelt, dass die *vis*
(Kraft), das heisst der Gehalt an Bedeutung, von sermo und sapientia derselbe sei' (192).
Tertullian rejects a possible argument of monarchian opponents from the grammarian's
definition of sermo: 'vox et sonus oris aer offensus intelligibilis auditu'. But from God
there could never come anything (*vacuum, inane, incorporeale*), but only something which
possessed *substantia* (199).
[20] 'cui et sermo insit pronuntianti, ratio adsit disponenti, virtus praesit perficienti'.
[21] 'Deus est, et Dei filius et unus ambo.' Cf. Clem. Alex., *paid.* 3.12.101.1.

her womb is born man mixed with God. The flesh formed by the spirit, is nourished, grows to maturity, speaks, teaches, works and is the Christ'.[22]

Many interpreters have gone wrong because they have forgotten that the intellectual metaphors come first and are not supplanted by the visual metaphors. Spirit is material but it is a very intellectual sort of matter. Visual metaphors are useful for those who think in pictures, but they must never hold first place.[23]

This is evident when we turn to christology in *adversus Praxean* 8. The word is an emanation (προβολή), but not like Valentinian emanations,[24] which are separate from and ignorant of the father. The word emanates from the father but, like a tree from its root, a stream from its source, is never separate. The proofs here are intellectual or epistemological. Only the son knows the father (Matt. 11.27), reveals the father's inner nature (John 1.18), hears and sees everything *apud Patrem* (John 8.38). He speaks what the father commands (John 14.31), does not his own will but that of the father (John 6.38), for who knows what is in God except the spirit in him (1 Cor. 2.11).[25] The word (sermo) is always in the father and with the father (John 14.11 and John 1.1). 'I and the father are one' (John 10.30).

So the son is (*Prax.* 8.5) a projection of reality,[26] who preserves and guards the unity of the divine reality. The son is put forth from the father and never separated from him. The trinity (*Prax.* 8.7) derives from the father 'by intermingled and connected degrees in no way threatening the monarchy but protecting the quality of the economy'. The trinity is a dispensation and internal disposition of the divine substance. It does not destroy unity but administers it (*Prax.* 3). In this way the mystery of the economy (*oikonomiae sacramentum*) is to be understood, bringing together the unity of *status*, *substantia* and *potestas* with the threefold *gradus*, *forma* and *species* (*Prax.* 2).

---

[22] 'et in utero eius caro figuratus, nascitur homo Deo mixtus. Caro spiritu structa, nutritur, adolescit, affatur, docet, operatur et Christus est'.

[23] As I think they do in Cyprian's ecclesiology, to the confusion of church order. See my, *Cyprian's Imagery*, *Antichthon*, 7 (1973), 65–79.

[24] The Gnostic view that the logos is simply God's spoken word, uttered speech, is rejected.

[25] 'Sermo autem spiritu structus est et, ut ita dixerim, sermonis corpus est Spiritus.'

[26] 'προβολή veritatis'.

For some, says Tertullian, monarchy excludes trinity, yet a moment's thought will show that, at a human level, sole rule is often exercised through agents. The solid meaning of the word must be preferred to its sound,[27] and the pluralism of Valentinus as well as the dualism of Marcion are to be rejected. There is no monarchy without trinity and no trinity without monarchy; they are mutually dependent.[28] There exists no way to one God except through trinity and no way to trinity except through one God. Those who deny the son, deny the monarchy to the father, for it is the son who restores the monarchy to the father, when he delivers up the kingdom to him (1 Cor. 15.24–8). God cannot be God without the son and the spirit. The son is even now putting the enemies under the father's feet, making them his footstool and subduing all things so that God may be all in all. The son is the source rather than a hindrance to the monarchy, which is in his hands,[29] who will restore it to the father.

Who then is the son and was he always part of the divine economy? Here we have the 'intelligent exploitation'[30] of the Stoic distinction between inner and uttered logos, applying the first to the father and the second to the son. God always had logos as reason but did not always speak ('Quia non sermonalis a principio sit rationalis etiam ante principium' *(Prax.* 5)). However as in man, who is the image and word of God, reason and discourse always go together, so in God inner and uttered speech are essential to one another. This is the crux of the argument. Only in the creative act is the word perfectly manifest as uttered, and not merely inner, thought. Divine speech was born, when God said: 'Let there be light!' The best word for this (προβολή) has been used by heretics *(Prax.* 8.1); but that is no argument against using it in another sense. Here again the visual metaphors are added. God emitted the word, as a root emits a tree, a fountain a river and the sun a ray. When the spirit is added to the series, we have root-tree-fruit, fountain-river-

---

[27] L. Abramowski, Der Logos, 199.
[28] We may recall the links which Waszink claimed between the threefold theology and the testimony of the soul which is naturally Christian. See A. Cortesi, Varrone e Tertulliano. Punti di continuità, *Augustinianum*, 24 (1984), 349–66. Cf. *REA*, Chronica Tertullianea (1979), 8.
[29] apud filium.
[30] Spanneut, *Stoïcisme des pères*, 316. The Stoics made no theological use of this distinction.

stream, sun-ray-point. The trinity flows down through intertwined and connected steps, preserving both monarchy and economy. The sequence is clear in scripture when Jesus says, 'I will pray the father and he shall send you another comforter, the spirit of truth' (*Prax.* 9.3).

(ii) Relative disposition and substantial relation

The necessity of the economy is reinforced by the genre of relative disposition. This is Tertullian's chief argument, which was taken up and developed by Augustine,[31] but has been overshadowed by the formulae which passed into fourth-century debate. Trinity is a matter of substantial relations, which require distinctness and mutual necessity between the three members of the divine economy.

Stoics listed four categories or genres: substance, quality, disposition and relative disposition.[32] They are tools for handling the diversity and unity of things.[33] Substance is applied to everything which exists as a material object. It is 'the prime matter of all existing things'.[34] As matter it cannot change. Every existing

[31] The tradition goes on, with further deviation from Tertullian, in Boethius and Thomas Aquinas.

[32] ὑποκείμενον, ποιόν, πῶς ἔχον, πρός τί πως ἔχον. Simplicius, *On Aristotle's categories* 66. 32–67.2 (*SVF*, 2.369. LongSedley, 27F). The first genre was sometimes described as 'being' or οὐσία.

[33] See J. J. Duhot, Y-at-il des catégories stoïciennes? *RIPh*, 8 (1991), 220–44. Tertullian's account is unaffected by the continuing controversy about the status of these genres. They are better not called 'categories', says Duhot, since this suggests a false relation with Aristotle and a mythical history of categories which is a doxographical illusion (221). The four genres attributed to the Stoa by Simplicius are discussed by Plotinus (*Enn.* 6.1.25ff.). The fourth genre is 'étant en quelque manière relatif' (237), but there is residual complexity. In the end

> Ces quatres concepts n'indiquent pas des états ou des niveaux de l'être, ils permettent d'articuler, à des niveaux différents l'unité et la multiplicité, l'identité et la différence, le corps et l'incorporel, à l'intérieur ou à propos de chaque être ... ce sont des concepts opératoires grâce auxquelles se resolvent les problèmes de l'un et du multiple. Ils sont au service d'une ontologie qui relie chaque être à l'essence unique que constitue la matière première. (243f.)

> The genres do not provide an ontological system and for this reason Tertullian is able to use one of them to solve a crucial problem. Eclecticism is essential for the freedom of an apologist. Philosophy is 'whatever has been well said ... an eclectic whole' (Clem. Alex., *strom.* 1.7.37).

[34] Stob., *ecl.* 1, 132, 27; *SVF*, 1.87; LongSedley, 28Q.

thing is made up of substance and quality, two material components which cannot exist alone. This means, says Plutarch, that we are all double with two substrates, substance and quality. Stoic metaphysics deals thus with particulars, individually qualified entities.

The categories of disposition and relative disposition may seem elusive[35] because of the paucity of evidence concerning them. The former 'was used to describe conditions of the qualitative substrate, not of the existential (category one) substrate of the particular'.[36] At any time, everything is in some kind of disposition and, if we wish to go beyond generalization to the particular, we need the genre of disposition.

The final category 'relative disposition' arises out of the distinction between 'sweet and bitter' on the one hand and 'father and son' on the other. The former is *relative* and consists of 'all things, which are conditioned according to an intrinsic character, but are directed towards something else'. 'Sweet and bitter' point to intrinsic qualities which are also in a certain disposition to one another. 'Father and son' do not point to intrinsic qualities but only to a disposition. This final category is *relatively disposed* and comprises 'all those whose nature it is to become and cease to be a property of something *without internal change* or qualitative alteration, as well as to look towards what lies outside'. Sense perception is relative because it is directed towards something else and has a differentiated condition. Our concern here is with things which are not subject to inherent differentiation, but are simply disposed in relation to something else. 'For son, and the man on the right, in order to be there, need certain external things.' When a son dies, the father may cease, *without any internal change*, to be a father. Similarly, when one's neighbour moves, one may cease to be the man on his right. Sweetness and bitterness present a different case. They cannot change unless their internal power (ἡ περὶ αὐτὰ δύναμις) also changes. The conclusion has striking relevance for

---

[35] That they are not elusive was proved in 1981, when, in celebration of the Council of Constantinople, a philosopher bishop, Eric D'Arcy commended substantial relations on the front two pages of *L'Osservatore Romano*.

[36] J. M. Rist, *Stoic philosophy* (Cambridge, 1969), 167f. This section is indebted to the lucid treatment in ch. 9 (152–72) of this book.

Tertullian: 'If, then, despite being unaffected in themselves they change because of something else's disposition relative to them, it is clear that relatively disposed things have their existence in their disposition alone and not through any differentiation.'[37]

Tertullian takes over this category and uses it in his own way (*Prax.* 10). Father and son have their existence in their disposition alone; therefore, when that disposition is denied, they cease to be. Father and son are no more identical than day and night. Neither can be both. A father makes a son and a son makes a father. Their relative disposition means that the father cannot relate to the father as he does to the son, nor can the son relate to the son as he does to the father. God establishes and guards relations. These relations make me what I am when I come to possess them. When they are reflexive (father-father, son-son), the members cease to exist. Since, for Praxeas, monarchy makes father identical with son, and son identical with father, both father and son are no more.

Could God not overcome this disaster, since he is able to do anything? What God is able to do and what he does are two different things. He can give wings to humans but he does not. Father and son then are distinct, but not separate (*Prax.* 11). When God says, 'my heart has emitted my most excellent word' (Ps. 45.1), this must stand unless someone can find a text where he says, 'my heart has emitted myself as my most excellent word'. Equally conclusive and impossible would be 'The lord said to himself, I am my own son, today I have begotten myself' (cf. Ps. 2.7) or, 'Before the morning star did I beget myself' (cf. Ps. 110.3 LXX) or, 'I the lord possessed myself the beginning of my ways for my own work; before all the hills too did I beget myself' (Prov. 8.22).

(iii) Redaction into one, from plurality to unity

The truth of God implies that he declares nothing to exist outside his disposition or arrangement, and that he has arranged nothing contrary to his declaration. For all his monarchy, there must be a

---

[37] εἰ τοίνυν καὶ μηδὲν αὐτὰ παθόντα μεταβάλλει κατὰ τὴν ἄλλου πρός αὐτὰ σχέσιν, δῆλον ὅτι ἐν τῇ σχέσει μόνῃ τὸ εἶναι ἔχει καὶ οὐ κατά τινὰ διαφορὰν τὰ πρός τί πως ἔχοντα. Simplicius, *On Aristotle's categories* 165.32–166.29 (15–29). *SVF*, 2.403; LongSedley, 29C.

plurality in God, else there could be no relative disposition and it is relative disposition which defines the being of God. Tertullian (*Prax.* 12) turns to the plurality which Justin had noted, the plurality of the creator.[38] Can a being who is merely and absolutely one, speak in the plural 'Let us make man after our image and likeness' (Gen. 1.26), without deceit or joking or (as the Jews claim) an angelic audience? Was he himself father-son-spirit and did he speak to himself in the plural? Rather, he used the plural 'because there was already attached to him the son, a second person, his word, and also a third person, the spirit in the word' (*Prax.* 12.3). He was making man with and like the son who was to put on human nature, and he was speaking to the spirit who would sanctify man. They were 'ministers and mediators in consequence of the unity of the trinity'. Further, God could only make man in the image of God because that image already existed in the son 'who because he was to be the surer and truer man caused that man to be called his image who at that time had to be formed of clay, as the image and likeness of the true'. The son, who is the true light of the world, came on the scene when God said, 'Let there be light.'

Now we no longer speak in the plural, because Christ has come and is known as he who once caused plurality, but who now reveals the fullness of unity. Through the divine economy, the father is more fully manifest and 'the name of God and of lord is reduced to one (*redactum . . . in unionem*)'. Through Christ, God is one.[39] This makes the issue plain for the nations who now convert from many idols to one God and for us when we face martyrdom because we refuse to swear by many gods and lords.

The son is visible and the father is invisible.[40] Yet the son is 'also on his own account, as word and spirit, invisible even now by the quality of his substance' even if before the incarnation he was visible to Moses (*Prax.* 14). Then he was visible in the incarnation and is thereby distinct from the father. The changing economy of salvation cannot be reduced to uniformity. In the Old Testament,

---

[38] Andresen showed the decisive influence of prosopographical exegesis for the understanding of the term 'persona'. Zur Entstehung und Geschichte des trinitarischen Personbegriffes, *ZNW*, 52 (1961), 1–39.

[39] Paul found faith in one God, possible, and only possible, through Christ.

[40] Note Irenaeus on this point: J. Ochagavía, *Visibile patris filius. A study of Irenaeus' teaching on revelation and tradition* (Rome, 1964).

the son was active not only in creation, but also judged, destroyed a tower, confused languages, sent the flood and rained down fire and brimstone. All the time he was learning, as God, to talk with men on earth. He knew the wide range of human affections, as he intended to take on human substance, body and soul. His mixed behaviour in those times prepared him for the human experiences which the heretics, like Praxeas, deny him and attribute to the father, because they do not know that 'from the beginning the entire order of the divine economy has come down through the son' (*Prax.* 16).[41] When the prophet (Isa. 45.5, 18) declares, 'I am God and beside me there is no other', he denies that the son is other than God. If it was said, 'There is no one else, except my son', then he would have made the son other than himself; this would be as foolish as for the sun to say, 'I am the sun, and there is none other besides me except my ray' (*Prax.* 18). While Praxeas finds a few passages of scripture to support his case, Tertullian gives an extended analysis of the Fourth Gospel (*Prax.* 21–5) and a brief reference to Matthew and Luke (*Prax.* 26) to show that father and son are distinct persons.

Later, Augustine was confronted by the Arian claim that distinctions within the Godhead must be either substance or accidents, and that since there were no accidents in God, there must be three substances. He turned to Tertullian and the Stoics for the notion of unchangeable relations or relative disposition. The three eternal and unchangeable relations within the Godhead are as real as the begetting, being begotten and proceeding, which define them. 'Therefore, although to be the father and to be the son are different, yet their substance is not different; for they are so called, not according to substance, but according to relation, which relation, however, is not an accident, because it is unchangeable' (*trin.* 5.5.6).[42]

In answer to the objection that father and son are said to be unbegotten in relation to themselves, not in relation to one

---

[41] 'a primordio omnem ordinem divinae dispositionis per filium decucurrisse'.

[42] 'Quamobrem quamvis diversum sit patrem esse et filium esse, non est tamen diversa substantia: quia hoc non secundum substantiam dicuntur, sed secundum relativum; quod tamen relativum non est accidens, quia non est mutabile.' This appears more Stoic than Tertullian's account.

another, Augustine replies that 'father' and 'unbegotten' do not mean the same thing. The father would have been unbegotten, even if he had not begotten the son. Begetting a son does not make one unbegotten. 'Begotten' and 'unbegotten' do not point to a difference in substance. Only a remarkable blindness can prevent one from seeing that no one can be said to be begotten except in relation to something (*trin.* 5.6.7).[43] A son is a son because he is begotten and begotten because he is a son.[44]

Objection can be made that the father is said to be unbegotten in respect to himself and the son is begotten in respect of himself and, since what is in respect of oneself is substance, therefore father and son are not the same in substance. But it must be replied that the son is equal to the father, not in respect of his relation to the father, but in respect of what is said with relation to himself, that is, according to substance (*trin.* 5.6.7).

Augustine draws together talk of relations[45] with unity of essence and trinity of persons. 'For as the father is God, and the son is God, and the holy spirit is God, which no one doubts to be said in respect to substance, yet we do not say that the very supreme trinity (*ipsam praestantissimam trinitatem*) is three Gods but one God' (*trin.* 5.8.9). Whatever we say of God in respect to himself, we say of each person and of the trinity itself, speaking always in the singular.

(iv) Substance and persons

For Tertullian, God is unique and of three divine persons.[46] Since the three are of one quality, substance and power, God is unique although three in sequence, aspect and manifestation. The *monarchia*, or the claim that one God creates and rules the world as its only lord, is the one issue for Praxeas (3.2) and his followers. Perhaps Tertullian's reply would only satisfy someone who could handle paradox and puzzle. The one lord is he who rules all, God the father, *and* his son who has received from his father the rule

---

[43] 'genitum vero mira caecitate non advertunt dici non posse, nisi ad aliquid'.
[44] 'Ideo quippe filius qui genitus, et quia filius utique genitus.'
[45] Augustine has developed Tertullian's account of relative disposition which he may also have learnt from Plotinus, *Enn.* 6, 1, 6–8.
[46] Moingt, Le problème, 337–62.

over all creation. Within the trinity, the father, as the origin and proprietor of power, is the greatest (*Prax.* 9.2, 14.10); *yet* the three possess in different ways the same greatness. God delegates authority to the angels; but each member of the trinity possesses *without limit* the family property.[47] The father communicates all that he has to son and spirit, so that they too are omnipotent (*Prax.* 7.3).[48]

Tertullian supplies the enduring terminology of trinitarian theology. What did he mean by one substance and three persons? Fragments of recent discussion may help. If Tertullian provided the terms for later debate, he did not supply definitions to resolve that debate, partly because that debate cannot be resolved.[49] The key concept *substantia* is elusive. According to a juridical interpretation, which has been widely rejected, the members of the trinity were 'persons of substance' (i.e. persons who possessed wealth) and the wealth which they possessed was the same.[50] There has been a general acceptance of Tertullian's appropriation of the Stoic view of substance as 'stuff'. While Tertullian may use the term for a particular thing, his more exact use points to the constitutive material of a thing. This Stoic definition is always behind the concept of God's substance and is not purely material in the commonly accepted sense of today.[51]

Unity was a matter of substance. God's substance might mean God himself, his mode of existence, his rank or character, his divinity or eternity. Another meaning suggests 'the unique stuff which is, or composes, the divine *corpus*, and which Tertullian denotes *spiritus*'.[52] Spirit may describe the whole trinity (*pud.* 21.16) or what issues from God the father (*Prax.* 26.3–4). In the metaphors of sun or spring, *spiritus* can be used either of the whole trinity or of each person. Tertullian's account displays 'a certain tension between the simple monarchian teaching traditional at Rome and

---

[47] *Ibid.*, 356.

[48] It was a principle of monotheist apologetic that there could only be one omnipotent being, since there could be no territory left for the others to rule.

[49] F. R. Tennant pointed out that what trinitarian theologians were looking for was something between a noun and an adjective, between a substantive and an attribute.

[50] This view of Harnack was rejected by Stier, Schlossmann, Tixeront and Prestige and, more recently, by Braun, Stead and Moingt.

[51] Braun, *Deus Christianorum*, 182, 194.

[52] Stead, Divine substance in Tertullian, 62.

the pluralistic theology which he adopted from the earlier Apologists and developed for the purposes of controversy'.[53] Maintaining tension is exactly what Tertullian wanted to do; but his reasons were logical rather than historical. He could speak of the gospel as 'the substance of the New Testament' (*Prax.* 31.1).

While for Tertullian 'substance' means 'stuff' or 'material', 'one physical thing',[54] it was non-material matter '*stoffloses Stoff*' and his main arguments had to do with mind and speech or with logical relations. We cannot apply a later mind–body dichotomy to Stoic matter. When it is claimed that the only sure guides to his meaning are the metaphors which he uses 'of *substantiae*, which admit of a kind of distribution, and plurality, which does not constitute a division',[55] it must be remembered that these metaphors are secondary to the arguments which they illustrate. That argument was psychological rather than visible. The *tota trinitas* of reason, passion and desire was found in the unity of the soul and the unity of God (*an.* 14).

Body was also necessary to persons. Tertullian makes the divine spirit corporeal enough to render the divine persons distinct from one another. While there is a difference between a human and a divine body,[56] he insists that God be a reality which can be displayed. The body of spirit is the thing itself, a unity of being and action. Yet Tertullian, like many others, never succeeds in defining his concept of being.[57] A first reading of *Against Praxeas* suggests that Tertullian has not avoided a division of the divine substance, and more exact scrutiny indicates that he may not have given the son and the spirit a totality of divine substance.[58]

Particularity is affirmed by certain words: *species, gradus, forma, proprietas* and, especially, by *persona*.[59] Unfortunately, *persona*, the key-word, could function *either* as part of an economy *or* as a metaphysical term in its own right. This ambiguity persists within Tertullian; but there is development in the concept of *persona*

---

[53] *Ibid.*, 65.
[54] S. Schlossmann, Tertullian im Lichte der Jurisprudenz, *ZKG*, 27 (1906), 251–75 and 407–30.
[55] Stead, Divine substance in Tertullian, 66.
[56] J. Moingt, *Théologie trinitaire de Tertullien*, 4 vols. (Paris, 1966–9), vol. II, *Substantialité et individualité*, 333.
[57] *Ibid.*, 337.   [58] *Ibid.*, 338.   [59] *Ibid.*, 431.

between the work against Marcion and that against Praxeas. *Persona* moves from the concept of 'representative person' to 'distinct individual existence (or existing individual)'.[60]

'Substance' refers to the unitive element, while 'person' designates the distinctive elements in the inner life of God.[61] It would be a mistake to think that, in the eyes of Tertullian, the two terms completely dissolve the tension between the three and the one; that tension points to the relative disposition which requires both father and son for either of them to be.

(v) Criticisms of Tertullian

Criticism of Tertullian's doctrine of the trinity has measured him against later formulations and either applauded or bewailed his achievement.[62] To many he seems to have anticipated Nicaea and later developments, to others he has succumbed to extreme subordinationism.[63] We must take some samples of this criticism, to show that it falls short of finality as much as does Tertullian.

Is he subordinationist? The equality of the three persons and the unity of *substantia*, *status* and *potestas* is his central theme (*Prax.* 2; *Marc.* 4.25; *res.* 6). The distinction in *gradus, forma* and *species* (*Prax.* 2) points to nothing more than distinction of persons and order of procession. While there is modern nervousness about the terms 'derivation' and 'portion' (*Prax.* 9,14), these words are meant to join rather than to divide. The similes of sun and ray, spring and stream point to continuity. It is as foolish to depart from the point of the simile by dividing what is continuous as it would be to link the first with Heraclitus and the second with Thales, giving Tertullian a divine substance of fire or water. Further, the contrast between visible son and invisible father makes the same point of continuity; now the son is no more visible than the father (*Prax.* 14.6). Certainly, Tertullian goes on to link the theophanies of the Old Testament with the son rather than with the father; but this is an apologetic device from Justin and most early writers. It points to

---

[60] *Ibid.*, 615.   [61] *Ibid.*, 669, citing Braun, *Deus Christianorum*, 237f.
[62] D'Alès, *La théologie de Tertullien*, 99.
[63] A. von Harnack, *Dogmengeschichte*, 3rd edn, (Berlin, 1893), vol. 1, 532, 'den ausgeprägsten Subordinationismus'.

plurality in the Godhead and was later discarded when Arians found it advantageous. As with the similes, many arguments, when placed in a different controversy, can have their meaning inverted.

Tertullian, others claim, lives within the world of second-century apologetic and meets the monarchian challenge with an account of the generation of the *logos* which republished an anachronism.[64] Perhaps we have here another example of the logic of apologetic which answers diverse objections from a store of arguments which may not be coherent with one another. The Stoic distinction between inner and uttered logos had already served Christian apologetic in the different interpretation of Theophilus of Antioch.

Any sound appreciation of Tertullian must place him in his historical context where he had to respond to monarchianism and other challenges. His trinitarian response was of value to subsequent theologians, but it could not anticipate the problems which the Greek fathers had thrust upon them. When we claim the lasting value of a contingent response, we need not forget its contingency.

Tertullian's achievement was twofold. First, he realized the strength of the monarchian position, with its insistence on the unity of the divine being; for the centre of his own faith was the necessary dishonour of God in Christ. Second, he stated more clearly than any other early Christian writer the central significance of relative disposition. God was one God; but father and son were mutually necessary to each other and never identical. Identity would destroy them; their difference was the ground of their unity. As in other debates, Tertullian grasped the main logical issue.

Among recent discussion, different ways ahead have been suggested. We may concentrate on individual, stuff or spirit. An attempt at greater precision was made by one scholar who established that divine substance was necessarily one, indivisible and incommensurable.[65] He concluded, '*Substantia*, it appears, though it might have meant "existence" comes in practice to mean an existent thing: and since God is not a species or genus, it must mean a πρώτη οὐσία, a single individual Being'.[66] All of which

---

[64] J. Stier, *Die Gottes- und Logoslehre Tertullians* (Göttingen, 1899), 79. D'Alès, *Théologie*, 103.
[65] Evans in *Treatise against Praxeas*, 38–58.
[66] *Ibid.*, 41.

establishes the 'mystery of the economy' (*Prax.* 2) as a mystery which joins the three persons of different sequence, aspect and manifestation. The precision of this suggestion must, I think, be rejected in favour of Stoic substance, the stuff or spirit which is unique to God, understood only through metaphors.

This more useful approach pays due respect to the concept of substance and its dominant place in Christian theology.[67] It begins from the two notions of absolute being and unique stuff, then moves to the basic question of the existence of God. God has been held to be either pure being or beyond being. Substance may be a category, or may apply to all categories. God may be substance and yet be held to be unique in the same way as Christian theology begins from one God. Substance without accidents is unthinkable, but a substance can remain what it is through different determinations. God as substance can make sense if the notion of a Platonic ideal or a Stoic simple source of different energies be admitted.

A third possibility takes 'spirit' not 'substance' as the dominant notion. Tertullian, with his enthusiasm for prophecy, might approve. Through the concept of indwelling spirit, sense can be made of 'God's continuing creative relationship towards human persons and of his active presence in Jesus as the central and focal point within this relationship.'[68] Christ as indwelling divine presence is not distinguishable from spirit. Fellowship in the holy spirit is no more separable from the grace of Christ than it is from the love of God. Spirit is not a second divine being who coexists with Christ nor a second divine mediator between the father and his creatures.[69] God as spirit, it is claimed, provides a better answer to fourth-century problems than do the classical accounts of trinity, with their tendency to tritheism and hierarchy. Spirit makes children of God through resurrection power which liberates the cosmos. God is for us as one God who comes to each in χάρισμα. In the articulation of Christian experience the concept of God as spirit is again more useful than the doctrine of the trinity. The divinity of Jesus Christ is affirmed 'in the sense that one God, the Creator and Saviour Spirit, revealed himself and acted decisively for us in

[67] G. C. Stead, *Divine substance* (Oxford, 1977), especially 267–80.
[68] G. W. H. Lampe, *God as spirit* (Oxford, 1979), 34.
[69] *Ibid.*, 118.

Jesus'.[70] This recent account has value for contemporary apologetic.

Tertullian's achievement is his use of the category of relative disposition, in his persistent concern with economy or dispensation[71] which springs from the need for some way of relating unity and plurality in trinity. The relation of one to three can be expressed without qualifying nouns and should not be seen as a later imposition on the simple Christian faith . The early credal formula, ἰχθύς, requires plurality in God. Son needs father as father needs son. The centrality of Christus Victor points to an economy of saving history which is mirrored in the relative disposition of father, son and spirit.

This is evident from the prologue of the Fourth Gospel through Clement of Alexandria to Athanasius. The word was with God and was God. When he became flesh, he revealed the glory of the only-begotten of the father. Whoever saw him, saw the father and no one comes to the father except through him. For Clement, neither is faith without knowledge, nor the father without the son. The great God is the perfect child for the son is in the father and the father in the son. For Athanasius, the incarnation of the word is necessary because, as word of the father, he alone was able to recreate all, suffer for and act as ambassador for all to the father (*de inc.* 7). None but the only-begotten of the father could teach humankind of the father and destroy idols (*de inc.* 20). The word of God became man that men might become divine. The triumph of Christus Victor is proof that Christ is God, word and power of God (*de inc.* 54).[72]

(vi) Persona

The most extensive treatment of Tertullian's use of *persona* and *substantia* struggles with the difficulty of assessment. On the one hand Tertullian has done more than simply introduce new terms; on the other hand he has not given philosophical definitions to these terms. He has given contours for the use of the new terms.

---

[70] *Ibid.*, 228.
[71] Cf. J. Tixeront, *Histoire des dogmes*, vol. 1 (Paris, 1915), 401.
[72] See above, p. 18.

Both refer to the inner life of God. *Persona* points to what characterizes and distinguishes that inner life. *Substantia* refers to what joins and unifies it. That is as far as his speculation goes and leaves us with his account of relative disposition. *Persona* is not a substantive thing but 'the effective manifestation of a distinct being'.[73]

The elasticity of *persona* is the second point of interest. It stretches from a transitory appearance to a substantive thing. From three substantive things (*res substantivae*), one scholar, looking to the plural *res*, concluded that Tertullian is tritheist[74] and another looked to the adjective *substantivae* and claimed that he is close to *homoousion*.[75] The contradictory assessments show that person and substantive thing cannot be the same. *Persona* is the effective manifestation of a distinct being, which puts the problem at one remove and illuminates the puzzle. Tertullian opposes *substantia* and *persona* in order to find a way between real division and purely modal distinction. When he wants to prove the reality of word (*sermo*) he thinks of the rational substance which is divine spirit.

Persona is not a metaphysical word; but it is joined in contrast to *substantia* which is metaphysical. The two words do not have a common scale. The reality of *sermo* is proved from its rational substance, while its distinctive being is indicated as the son who is related to father and spirit. When he talks philosophically, he uses ontological categories like *res*, *species*, *forma* and *gradus*.[76] Whenever he wants to indicate this entity in the biblical revelation, which is where he finds the distinction, he uses *persona*.[77]

Most recently the prosopographical interpretation of *persona* has proved helpful;[78] this has been modified by the claim that the term comes from grammarians and indicates role, communication and openness to others. Importantly it is insisted that *persona*, for

---

[73] J. Moingt, *Substantialité*, 669.
[74] Harnack, *Dogmengeschichte*, vol. I, 577; vol. II, 298.
[75] Tixeront, *Histoire des dogmes*, vol. I, 401f.
[76] Much later, scholastic theologians will place *persona* among these.
[77] 'Ce mot désigne bien ce qui est conçu dans les autres, il ne signifie pas par lui-même ce qui est formellement exprimé par d'autres.' Moingt, *Substantialité*, 670.
[78] C. Andresen, Zur Entstehung und Geschichte des trinitarischen Personbegriffes, *ZNW*, 52 (1961), 1–39.

Tertullian, involves a combination of individuality and relationality.[79] Like most controversies the discussion has gone wrong through asking wrong questions. Is *persona* a legal or a philosophical concept (as if it must be one of the two)? Tertullian never defines it in either way but he does use it in both ways.

After Tertullian, *persona* has a ragged history. Marius Victorinus does not use it in his account of the trinity. Hilary and Ambrose tell us little. Even Augustine is less than lucid on trinitarian usage. The chief problem is christological not trinitarian: how can Jesus, God and man, be one person? Leo, in dependence on Tertullian, writes of 'true man united to true God ... playing the same part in the deity of the word'.[80] It is claimed that only in Boethius, who imports the meaning of *hypostasis* does something like a philosophical definition appear. It is therefore quite wrong to see Tertullian's *persona* as providing a definition for the Greeks, who turned to *hypostasis* instead.[81]

What then did Tertullian achieve? He handed on a form of discourse, which opened the way to further development, and above all a formula, 'one substance in three persons'.[82] We return to our starting point. Trinity is less the existence of three heavenly beings, than a new way of believing in one God. 'God is believed as one in a new way – by the son and the spirit.' This is the gospel, 'the substance of the new covenant' which Praxeas had lost (*Prax.* 31.1). The three are the object of the same faith and adoration which is directed to one, unique divinity. This Godhead is that of the father, revealed in and by the others, in so far as they are united with their first-principle (*Prax.* 18.5, 19.5, 22.11).[83] At creation, God

---

[79] See B. J. Hilberath, *Der Personbegriff der Trinitätstheologie in Ruckfrage von Karl Rahner zu Tertullians Adversus Praxean* (Innsbruck, 1986), 149–254. See also A. Milano, *Persona in teologia. Alle origini del significato di persona nel cristianesimo antico* (Napoli, 1984), 65–97. While Tertullian did not follow a philosophical definition (90), he introduced speculative content (88–95) and effectively determined later usage (95).

[80] 'verus homo vero unitus est deo ... eamdem gerens in verbi deitate personam'. *Ep.* 25, cited in Moingt, *Substantialité*, 672.

[81] The later Cappadocian fathers made use of Stoic logic in replacing *persona* with *hypostasis*. The formula 'three hypostases and one ousia' emerges in the Meletian explanation at the Synod of Alexandria in 362. It enriched the homoousian position and provided a flexibility which the Old Nicene party lacked. L. Abramowski, Trinitarische und christologische Hypostasenformel, *ThPh*, 54 (1979), 38–49.

[82] Moingt, *Substantialité*, 673.

[83] Moingt, *Le problème*, 361.

could speak of plurality. Now that we have found his fullness in Christ, the name of God and lord is reduced into one (*redactum in unionem*).

C. CHRISTOLOGY

(i) *Two natures*

Besides the distinction between father and son there is the distinction between spirit and flesh, God and man in Christ. Monarchians confuse the distinctions in quite different ways. For them the word becomes flesh by transfiguration, not by putting on the clothing of the flesh. This means that a third substance is produced which is neither word nor flesh but an amalgam. As the work of Christ is understood through opposites, so is his person (*Prax.* 27). In him spirit and flesh retain their opposition. Christ puts on flesh. Here Heraclitus will give way to the later Stoic concept of 'total blending'.[84]

Stoics distinguished three different sorts of mixtures. In the first, things were simply juxtaposed with one another. In the second kind, they were so joined as to disappear into a third substance. The third kind of mixture was a total blending,

> when certain substances and their qualities are mutually coextended through and through, with the original substances and their qualities being preserved in such a mixture; this kind of mixture he (Chrysippus) specifically calls 'blending'; . . . for the capacity to be separated again from one another is a peculiarity of blended substances, and this only occurs if they preserve their own natures in the mixture.

The different mixtures are common conceptions which provide different expressions for juxtaposition, fusion which destroys and blending which preserves the natures which unite.[85] The persistence of the blended constituents was proved from the fact that they could be separated artificially. An oiled sponge, when placed in a blend of water and wine, will absorb water and leave the wine.[86] Splendid debate followed from Arcesilaus who described a severed

---

[84] κρᾶσις δι' ὅλων.
[85] Alexander of Aphrodias, *On mixture* 216.14–218.6 (*SVF*, 2.473; LongSedley, 48C).
[86] Stob., *ecl.* 1.155, 5–11 (*SVF*, 2.471; LongSedley, 48D).

leg, thrown into the sea and dissolved, so that the Persian and Greek fleets could fight a battle within it.[87]

The integrity of this concept was removed by Posidonius who misunderstood so much and who thought that the substance of a particular thing could undergo change. It is important to remember that 'Two particulars can be compounded into a new unit by total mixture, but their οὐσία does not change its quality as such'.[88]

In the debate with Praxeas the question of the trinity runs into christology. 'For, convicted on all sides by the distinctness of the Father and the Son, which we say is ordained without disturbing the permanence of the union as of the sun and the beam and of the spring and the river, they attempt to interpret this distinctness in another way, not less in accordance with their opinion, so as no less than before to distinguish Father and Son in one person, while they say that the Son is the flesh, that is the Man, Jesus, while the Father is the Spirit, that is, God, Christ' (*Prax.* 27; E. Evans, translation). Here the move is to divide flesh and spirit rather than to confuse father and son. This different kind of *monarchia* may have come from Valentinus and makes two of Jesus and Christ. Yet what is born of the Virgin is divine, for it is the son of God and was conceived by the Holy Spirit. Emmanuel is God with us, the word is in the flesh. But was the word made flesh by transformation or by putting on the flesh? Here Tertullian cannot accept a simple interchange. Spirit is not transfigured into flesh for the eternal God cannot change. The logos never ceased to be God. If he had been transformed by a change of substance then he would have been neither flesh nor spirit but a third, new substance. Tertullian uses as an illustration the mixing of gold and silver to form an amalgam (*electrum*); this is exactly what did *not* happen. Spirit remains spirit and flesh remains flesh. God remains God and man remains man: 'We see a twofold state, not confused but joined in one person, God and man, Jesus' (*Prax.* 27).[89] There is an identity of essence between

---

[87] Plutarch, *On common conceptions* 1078B–D (LongSedley, 48E).

[88] Rist, *Stoic philosophy*, 159.

[89] 'videmus duplicem statum, non confusum, sed coniunctum in una persona, Deum et hominem Jesum'. This formula was regarded as a theological miracle by R. Cantalamessa, *La cristologia di Tertulliano* (Freiburg, 1961), 168, who quotes Harnack, Tixeront, Altaner, Bardy, Grillmeier and Quasten in support of his claim. However, if the later discussion is seen in relation to Tertullian, it is simply a matter of continuity.

father and son. The word of the Gospel, 'I and the father are one', is absolute.[90] The two-nature formulae are equally striking: flesh-spirit, word-flesh, son of God-son of man, God-man, human standing-divine standing, inner substance-outer substance, substance of flesh-substance of spirit, human substance-divine substance, as each substance. There are two substances, twofold quality, two natures.[91]

The insistence on unity ('twofold quality ... conjoined in one person ... flesh and spirit can be in one')[92] is sustained through a Stoic concept of interpenetration of physical bodies, by which each retains its specific qualities and is not replaced by a third thing. For Tertullian, as for all Stoics, the phrase 'two in one' means the interpenetration of two bodies, their physical union in 'total blending'.[93] He takes his version of two natures from scripture (in particular Rom. 1.3f. and John. 1.14) and rejects both Gnostic dualism and Marcion's docetism.[94]

(ii) A modern postscript

Tertullian's account is necessary to clarify later christological controversy. Platonism, after absorbing Stoicism, was to play a role in trinity and christology. The terms 'combination' and 'unconfused union'[95] were appropriate to the two natures as they were to the trinity.[96] However it is not Porphyry's 'unconfused union' of body and soul but Proclus' account of the unity of the ideas in Nous which is influential.[97] The concept may be found in Philo, Plutarch

[90] *Ibid.*, 26f.

[91] *Ibid.*, 94f. 'caro-spiritus, sermo-caro, filius Dei-filius hominis, Deus-homo, condicio humana-condicio divina, substantia interior-substantia exterior, substantia carnis-substantia spiritus, substantia humana-substantia divina, utraque substantia. There are duae substantiae, duplex status, duae naturae'.

[92] 'duplex status ... coniunctus in una persona ... caro et spiritus in uno esse possunt'.

[93] 'Ma per Tertulliano, come del resto per gli stoici in genere, "duo in uno esse" è espressione tecnica per designare la compenetrazione dei corpi, cioé l'unione fisica secondo la κρᾶσις δι' ὅλων.' *Ibid.*, 148.

[94] His minimal achievement was to fortify the West against any monophysite tendency. *Ibid.*, 196.

[95] συνάφεια and ἀσύγχυτος ἕνωσις.

[96] See the useful discussion in L. Abramowski, *Drei christologische Untersuchungen* (Berlin, 1981), 63–109, where the author takes issue with E. L. Fortin, H. Dörrie and J. Pépin.

[97] Proclus expounds the central thesis of Platonism that the forms are distinct from one another yet one.

and above all in Plotinus.[98] Plotinus anticipates both the 'unconfused union' of the 'intelligible' and the decisive phrase of the Tome of Leo 'for each form does what is proper to it'. This Stoic idea is taken over by Porphyry. Syrian, the teacher of Proclus, unites the divine forms in 'unconfused union' and 'unbroken partnership'.[99] The clearest statement is in Proclus,[100] however, where the forms are both separate from and inherent in each other, and the intelligibles are one in the appropriate manner which is through 'unconfused interpenetration'.

Despite its condemnation by Cyril of Alexandria (*anath.* 3 and 11), the term 'combination' (συνάφεια) was widely used both in trinitarian and christological discussion. Tertullian uses, we have seen, *coniungere, cohaerere* (συνάπτω or ἐνόω) and he certainly does not depend on Neoplatonism. So he writes (*Prax.* 8.6) *coniunctae* (of root and fruit), *indivisae* (of spring and river) and *cohaerentes* (of sun and ray). The persons of the trinity are distinct yet not divided, but cohering together (*Prax.* 12.6). So father and son are one (*unum*) (*Prax.* 22.11), not in singularity but in unity, likeness and conjunction. Father, son and spirit cohere (*Prax.* 25.1). The most striking christological statement (*Prax.* 27.11) denies confusion and speaks of 'duplicem statum, non confusum sed coniunctum'.

Tertullian is the first to use technical terms for the trinity and also the first to use a similar vocabulary in christology.[101] The usage is not identical for in the trinity the three persons have one substance, whereas in christology the one person has two substances. However, the terminology suggests that Tertullian saw a formal similarity between the two problems. It is also important that for Tertullian 'combination' (συνάφεια) is understood as equivalent to 'unconfused union', for this becomes the usage of Nestorius.[102] Basil uses the same equivalence when defending the status of the holy spirit as does Gregory Nazianzus in his fifth theological oration (*orat.* 31.9).

---

[98] 'Plotin benutzt also das "Nichtzusammengeschüttet-Sein" des Wahrgenommenen beziehungsweise der Fähigkeiten auf dem Niveau der menschlichen Seele als Ausgangspunkt eines Komparativs um Verhältnisse im Bereich des Göttlichen einsichtig zu wachen.' Abramowski, *Untersuchungen*, 67.

[99] Abramowski, *Untersuchungen*, 70.

[100] Proclus, *in Parm.*, see *Opera inedita*, ed. V. Cousin (Paris, 1964), 754.

[101] Abramowski, *Untersuchungen*, 83.   [102] *Ibid.*, 86.

Now we come to a recent problem. Concern has been expressed that Augustine and Chalcedon depend on the Neoplatonic view of the hypostatic unity of soul and body[103] and that they are therefore vulnerable when Neoplatonism is rejected. However, there is no basis for this uncertainty.[104] First, while Augustine's use of 'unconfused union' goes back to Porphyry's union of body and soul, it is not an argument which Augustine uses frequently. Secondly, Augustine uses 'unconfused union' for the trinity where the unity of the νοητά in νοῦς is the relevant point. Above all, Chalcedon (Leo) is dependent on Tertullian as well as on Augustine. There is no ground for taking Augustine's commendation of the Neoplatonists as a cryptic reference to the christological use of 'unconfused union'. There remains an important difference between Porphyry and Leo. For Porphyry, the soul can leave the body; for Leo, the two natures cannot be separated. It is the unconfused unity of intellectual objects in the Nous which is important for trinity and christology.

All of which adds to the interest of Tertullian.[105] The 'twofold quality' does not allow for the subordination of one member to the other. Rather the unity of God and man in Christ establishes that all that can be said of Christ is said of one who lived and suffered as we do.[106] Despite the universal Greek insistence on an unchangeable God, this extreme claim persists. And this claim is identical with the paradox for which Tertullian is chiefly known and which proves, not the eccentricity, but the catholicity of his thought. It is the cross which declares the divine economy and which makes the doctrines of trinity and incarnation essential. What God did on the cross is the most concise account of the trinity.[107]

---

[103] E. L. Fortin, The *definitio fidei* of Chalcedon and its philosophical sources, Studia Patristica 5, *TU*, 80 (Berlin, 1962), 496f.

[104] Abramowski, *Untersuchungen*, 107.

[105] *Ibid.*, 108: 'noch interessanter und eigenartiger'.

[106] *Ibid.*

[107] Jüngel, *Geheimnis*, 498, 'Gottes Identifizierung mit dem toten Jesus impliziert in diesem Sinne eine Selbstunterscheidung Gottes.' See also 481, cited above, ch. 3, p. 303, and 504, 'So ist Gott gerade in seiner Einheit dreifach unterschieden: im Gegenüber von Vater und Sohn aufeinander bezogen als Geist. Gott bleibt im tödlichen Gegenüber *ein* Gott.'

CHAPTER 7

Prayer and the bible

A. PRAYER AS COMBAT

Trinity points to prayer, as the cross points to trinity. Jesus was the will and power of the father and yet, to demonstrate patience, he submitted to the father's will: 'Not my will, but thine be done' (*or.* 4.5). Conflict lies at the heart of prayer which is, for Tertullian, the Christian soldier's sword and shield. His short work on prayer concludes with the strife of opposites. Christian prayer is a defensive armour and an offensive weapon against the oppressive, encircling hostility of the devil. In prayer, Christians stand to arms under the standard of Christ, their General, waiting for the trumpet to sound for resurrection. Angels also pray, because they are caught up in the battle.

Prayer is natural. It belongs to this world, where nature adds her testimony to the truth and neither God nor nature lies. Cattle and wild animals bend their knees and, when they first rise from their rest, they look to heaven with a bellow or roar. Birds too, when they leave their nest, move towards heaven with wings in the form of a cross and make a sound that seems like prayer. Our lord, who is the peak of all creation, prayed (*or.* 29.4).

Yet prayer outstrips this world. The power of prayer is a spiritual power and a spiritual sacrifice. God rejected the multitude of sacrifices – the fat of rams and the blood of bulls and goats (Isa. 1.11; *or.* 28.1). The gospel teaches the true demands of a God who is spirit and must be worshipped in spirit and truth. Christian believers are true worshippers and true priests, because they pray in the spirit and offer the spiritual sacrifice which is acceptable to God. Such prayer comes from a whole heart which is marked by faith, truth, purity and love; it is brought to the altar with a procession of good works and the singing of psalms and hymns. Such a sacrifice prevails on God for all things (*or.* 28.4).

What can prayer do? It can even conquer God. The different dispensations display the superiority of spiritual prayer. While ancient prayer saved men from fire, wild animals and famine, the power of Christian prayer does not provide present immunity from suffering; but it grants patience, endurance, virtue and faith, with an understanding that such suffering is for the sake of God. As in days of old, spectacular achievements continue, when righteous prayer now holds back the anger of God and prays for persecutors. In times of drought, it brings down rain from heaven, when the gods of the heathen have failed. Prayer is the only means which can overcome God; it works only for good, recalling souls from the way of death, setting prisoners free and contending on all sides against evil in the strife of opposites. It washes away the stain of sin, resists temptations, puts out the fire of persecution, comforts the poor in spirit and gives cheer to those whose spirits are high. It guides the traveller on his way, stills the stormy waves, stops robbers in their tracks, feeds the poor, rules over the rich and lifts up the fallen. In the strife of opposites it destroys what is evil and establishes what is good, holding up those who would fall and strengthening those who stand (*or.* 29).

(i) The New Prayer

Tertullian begins (*or.* 1) from the grace of God which has made all things new. The perfection of all things in Christ means that we need to pray in a new way. Trinity, we have seen, means believing in one God in a new way. Tertullian examines the Lord's Prayer clause by clause because it is a summary of the whole gospel. It comes from the word, spirit and reason of God, Jesus Christ, who has given a new form of prayer for the disciples of the New Covenant. In summing up all things, he has both corrected what was wrong in the law (e.g. circumcision), supplemented prophecy and perfected faith. The new grace of God has made all things new. John the Baptist had taught his disciples to pray but the words of his prayer are not known for he was but an earthly forerunner of the lord from heaven. The lord taught the way of heavenly prayer, which was made in secret to God who saw and heard all things. In the simplicity of faith, Jesus gave the prayer which is an epitome of his gospel (*or.* 1.6).

The prayer begins as we call God 'father', acknowledging that faith is rewarded by the right to be called sons of God. In this prayer we recognize the father, and in calling on the father, we call on the son who is one with the father and acknowledge our mother the church (*or.* 2).

The hallowing of God's name does more good to us than it does to God. It does not mean that we wish God well in face of possible suffering and evil which may oppress him. What happens is our holiness. We are sanctified as we glorify God and prepare to take our place among the angels who cry, 'Holy, holy, holy'. We ask that God's grace may be hallowed in us who dwell in him and may spread beyond us to all men (*or.* 3).

When we ask that God's will be done on earth as in heaven, we do not suggest that God's will might possibly fail; rather we pray that his discipline may be followed everywhere. We ask that God may show us the substance of his will and grant the ability to do that will which is our salvation. We also pray for patience as our lord prayed, 'Not my will, but thine be done!' (*or.* 4.4). As we do his will, his kingdom comes in us and we look forward to the revelation of his rule at the consummation of the age. Some fear the last days and the coming of the kingdom and pray that the end might be delayed;[1] but the delay of the kingdom means the protraction of our slavery. We pray in hope for the speedy coming of the kingdom which will confound all nations and bring joy to the angels (*or.* 5.4).

After our prayer concerning heavenly things – the name, will and kingdom of God – we pray for earthly things and our daily bread. Yet even our bread is spiritual, for Christ is the bread of life, who gives us his body in the Eucharist. When we pray for our daily bread, we ask that we may continue for ever in Christ and never be removed from his body (*or.* 6.2).

After the God who gives, we come to the God who forgives. There is no point in being fed each day if we are on our way to

---

[1] The *mora finis* was a subject of controversy; some Christians wanted it, others did not.

destruction.[2] When we ask for forgiveness, we confess our guilt and show penitence before God. Since debt and guilt go together, we cancel debts and remit what others owe to us. We forgive seventy times seven (*or.* 7.3). We ask that God will not let us be led into temptation, but rather that he will keep us from the evil one who is always trying to tempt us (*or.* 8.1).

So the Lord's Prayer, in a few words, brings together many sayings of the prophets, gospels and epistles and it discharges, simultaneously, many obligations of our faith and obedience. The completeness and perfection of the prayer are no surprise because it came from God who alone could tell us the way in which we should pray to him (*or.* 9.3). After this prayer we may add other requests since our lord knows that our needs are many and told us to ask that we might receive (*or.* 10). Prayer anticipates the final union with God. The many teachings of Christ point our pathway to heaven. We cannot come before the altar of God unless we are at peace with our brethren. We cannot approach our father if we are angry with our brother. The way of prayer is not the way of anger and the law was enlarged to prohibit anger and not merely to condemn the murder which might follow from it (*or.* 11.3). Prayer must be offered from a mind which is free from all anxiety and must emerge from a spirit which is like the spirit to whom it ascends. Sinful spirit cannot be welcomed by a holy spirit. A captive spirit cannot be received by the God who is wholly free. Like is admitted to like (*or.* 12). In prayer we are not merely on the way, we are already with God and are already like him. For all the combat, perfection is near.

(ii) Practice of prayer

After explaining the essence of prayer, Tertullian gives equal space to the practice of prayer. Christians may agree on one common prayer; but they characteristically disagree on all related practices: washing, wearing coats, sitting, standing, shouting, kissing, fasting, veiling, clothing and the time and place of prayer. Many practical problems of prayer find a solution through evangelical thinking.

[2] Countless little arguments like this reveal the argumentative, sophistic flavour of Tertullian.

The washing of hands before prayer was a well-known practice, yet, says Tertullian, God requires inner spiritual cleanliness, not mere outward physical cleanliness. True cleanliness is purity from things like falsehood, murder and idolatry. There are those who make a fuss of washing their hands before prayer, as some do, even if they have just had a bath. Tertullian investigated this practice and found that it was a memorial of the surrender of our lord by Pilate. We do not want to identify ourselves with Pilate and therefore we should avoid this practice. We have been washed once for all in Christ, and there is no need for repetition after such perfect cleansing (*or.* 13.2).

The Jews washed themselves all over every day but they are never clean of the blood of the prophets or of our lord. They inherit the sins of their fathers and do not dare raise their hands to God lest the prophet Isaiah should denounce them, and Christ, whom they killed, should shudder. We hold out our hands before God as Christ held out his arms on the cross (*or.* 14).

Other practices, which our lord did not command, may also be rejected as superstitions. There is no need to take off our coats as pagans do when they come before their idols. Paul does tell us (cf. 1 Cor. 11.3f.) how we should be dressed for prayer, but there is no mention of removing coats, unless, of course, we think that Paul left his coat behind with Carpus because he had been praying (2 Tim. 4.13). God had no trouble in hearing the saints in the fiery furnace although they were wearing their trousers and their turbans (Dan. 3.21; *or.* 15).

Similarly there is no reason for sitting down when prayer is finished (*or.* 16), nor do we need to lift our hands too high but rather to raise them with modesty and restraint. The publican who prayed in humility was more justified than the Pharisee who prayed with pride. Nor should we raise our voices since we could never make enough noise to reach God. God looks on the heart and listens to the heart. He does not depend on physical sound or else Jonah's prayer could never have reached him from the belly of a whale in the depths of the sea. Noisy prayer is nothing more than noise pollution, a nuisance to our neighbour (*or.* 17.5).

Another strange custom has spread widely. Those who are fasting do not offer the kiss of peace after they have prayed together with their brethren. Yet there is no more appropriate occasion for peace, and prayer is incomplete without it. We have been taught to fast secretly, but the secret is disclosed if we do not share the kiss. However, it is perfectly proper to abstain from the kiss when *everyone* is observing a fast (*or.* 18.6).

There are problems over 'standing to arms' (*stationes*)[3] or half-fasts which end at 3.0 p.m. Some claim that the sacrificial prayers and reception of the Eucharist[4] will interrupt their guard-duty. On the contrary, such duty will be all the more solemn for those who have stood at the altar of God. Any soldier knows that he must stand to arms, whether he feels cheerful or miserable, and we are God's soldiers ('nam et militia dei sumus') (*or.* 19.3). The dress of women, as the apostles taught, should always be modest (*or.* 20.1). There is extensive (*or.* 21f.) discussion of the veiling of virgins and the precise teaching of scripture on this point. There is confusion of practice; but Tertullian insists that the veil must be worn by those who are betrothed.

Kneeling is also a matter of Christian controversy, since there are some who refuse to kneel on the Christian Sabbath. This disagreement should be sorted out and those who will not give way should avoid offending others. For Tertullian, not only kneeling, but also every 'position of solicitude' is to be avoided on the day of our lord's resurrection; similarly at Pentecost we should stand in exultation. Yet every day we should kneel before God, especially at our first prayer and at fasts. The one thing that has not been regulated is the time of prayer, since we have been told to pray at every time and place (Eph. 6.18; 1 Thess. 5.17; 1 Tim. 2.8). Can we pray in every place when we are not to pray in public? Here we may follow the example of the apostles who prayed in gaol (Acts 16.25) and Paul who gave thanks to God on a ship (Acts 27.35; *or.* 24).

Times of prayer may also be considered. The third, sixth and ninth hours were clearly important times of prayer for the apostles and we should pray not less than three times a day, because we pray

---

[3] Tertullian uses this word here and at *cor.* 3 and *praescr.* 36.
[4] He speaks of the Eucharist as 'sacrificium' (*or.* 19; *cult.* 2.2), 'panis et calix' (*Marc.* 5.8), 'convivium dominicum' (*ux.* 2.4), 'convivium dei' (*ux.* 2.9), 'coena dei' (*spect.* 13) and 'sollemnia' (*fug.* 14; *an.* 9).

to the trinity of father, son and spirit. We should pray when day dawns and when night falls. We should pray before we eat and before we have a bath, since spiritual refreshment takes priority over the flesh (*or.* 25). We should welcome and farewell a brother who visits our home with prayer (*or.* 26). Those who add to their prayers the 'Hallelujah' and responsive Psalms are to be commended. For every practice is good which brings to God greater honour and richer prayer (*or.* 27).

Tertullian's theology of prayer is built from every part of the bible and reflects his understanding of an economy of salvation which finds its consummation in Christ. The Lord's Prayer sums up prayer as Christ sums up the course of salvation. The Christian who prays is still a pilgrim, and prayer reflects his conflicts and anticipates his end in final peace with God. So there is combat and completion everywhere. The new prayer both sums up and corrects the Law and the Prophets. In calling God 'father' we recognize the son who has made us sons of God. When we hallow the name of God, it is our holiness which is at stake. When we pray for the coming of the kingdom, we are concerned with our obedience, with his kingdom in us, and we already anticipate the kingdom which is to come. When we pray for bread to eat from day to day, we are chiefly concerned with Christ our heavenly bread. As we beg forgiveness, we ourselves forgive others. We both ask not to be tempted, yet expect temptation and ask for deliverance from evil.

Therefore Tertullian's treatise on prayer reflects the central themes of his theology (strife of opposites and perfection in Christ) and offers the clearest window on his world. While he does not apply these two principles mechanically to each subject on which he writes, his Christian soldier finds thought-provoking paradox and perfection at every point.

Since we are able to dig so deep into Tertullian's mind in his short work on the prayer which sums up the gospel, it is useful to compare his ideas with contemplative Christian spirituality. In the tradition of Alexandria, prayer is concerned not with conflict, but with knowledge and mystical entry into God. Despite similar ideas, all drawn from a common biblical source, Clement's account of prayer is philosophical, while that of Tertullian is practical. Prayer is the intimate relation of the believer who prays with the first principle of the universe, the form of the Good, who is the son of God and the father who is beyond. Clement's stated intention in *Stromateis* 7 is to prove to philosophers the superior piety of the 'atheist' Christians whom they persecute (*strom.* 7.1.1), not by piling up texts but by thinking through the ideas of scripture (*strom.* 7.1.1).

Clement stresses two things: prayer as the growing knowledge of God and prayer as entry into a divine, spiritual world. Clement's account of prayer as entering into God[5] is less restrained than Origen's, partly because it is a defence against philosophers and a competitive alternative to Gnosticism. However, the tradition is the same and the contrast with Tertullian is clear. Tertullian looks to future fulfilment in the coming of God's reign on earth. Clement and Origen look to present enjoyment of the vision of God, to life as continual conversation with God who, for all his unspeakable transcendence, is known directly.

Yet the contrast is not final. Tertullian's first petition is that God's will be done in us who are both heaven and earth (*or.* 40) and his final reflection is that we must be like the God to whom we pray (*or.* 12), free from mental confusion as God is free. For God, who is a holy, joyful and free spirit cannot receive a spirit which is polluted, sad and captive. As Clement insisted, like welcomes like. 'No one receives his opposite; no one grants an audience to anyone who is unlike him (nemo adversarium recipit, nemo nisi comparem suum admittit)' (*or.* 12).[6]

B. READING THE BIBLE

Tertullian's use of the bible is evident in every part of his work and would require many books for adequate treatment. It is astounding that he and Clement had such a wide grasp of such a new bible. His general principles are governed by the summing-up of all things in Christ and are clear from his short work against the Jews (*Jud*).

---

[5] Cf. Quis Dives Salvetur 27.
[6] The two traditions will intersect at later points, for example in Augustine. Nothing could be closer to Alexandrine Platonism than the Vision of Ostia; but Monica acknowledges Tertullian's one fear that Christ might not recognize her at the end of the age and raise her up (*conf.* 9.11.28), and the story closes, as in Tertullian, with apocalyptic hope for the eternal Jerusalem (*conf.* 9.13.37).

Fulfilment of prophecy distinguishes between references to the first and second coming of Christ. Typology studies the hidden meaning of the Old Testament in *figurae* and *sacramenta*, whose secrets are revealed to those baptized into the death of Christ. Allegory is needed to transform the military messiah of the Jews into the reality of Jesus Christ. Tertullian gives a Christian version of the allegorical method employed by interpreters of Homer. Christ is present in the Old Testament where he reveals reality through the events of history, institutions of the Law and the word of the prophets; everything points to him and only through him can it be understood.[7]

Tertullian presents, extensively in his work against Marcion, his further development of Christian exegesis in which four moves are evident: concentration, elaboration, uncertain victory and an alien text. The wealth of scripture is concentrated in the rule of faith which is reciprocally dependent on scripture. It is elaborated in all the detail of prophetic prediction and fulfilment. It is exaggerated in a literalism which claims that nothing can be discarded and insecurely reconciles every part of scripture with the rule. Finally there is an irreducible strangeness in scripture.

(i) Concentration in antithesis

The unity of the biblical message must be concentrated by joining antitheses and grasping the substance of the faith. Exegesis must be critical and evangelical. Proof-texts are not to be provided for all the details of daily life (*spect.* 3.1) nor for fundamental questions like Athens and Jerusalem.[8] Marcion added, to his one Gospel, his *Antitheses* which provided a rule for interpretation and which determined the content of his Gospel, which Tertullian calls 'The Gospel according to the Antitheses' (*Marc.* 4.1.1). Marcion is as critical and evangelical as Tertullian, but uses a different evangelical criterion; that is what the debate is about. Tertullian answers with his own antitheses which distinguish but do not divide the

---

[7] A. Viciano, Principios de hermeneutica biblica en el tratado 'Adversus Judaeos' de Tertulliano, *Biblia y Hermeneutica* (Pamplona, 1986), 637–44.

[8] See above, ch. 3, p. 47, for the remarkable omission of Col. 2.9–10 which Tertullian does not cite but presents in extended argument.

dispensation of the creator from that of Christ. Between dispensations, there is a difference in language, ethical precepts and law; but all the diversity is ordered and arranged by one God who foretold what changes would come.

His law would go out of Zion and his word from Jerusalem. This new law of the gospel and new word of the apostles would bring peace on earth and light to the nations. It would perfect and abbreviate the old law into a new and spiritual covenant. This antithesis is not accidental but essential to the creator who is 'always at variance with himself'. The inhabitants of Pontus[9] have not been able to realize that the world is made of different and conflicting substances. 'But judgement is already given and that by manifest proofs, that he whose works and ways are consistently antithetical, has also his mysteries of revelation consistently of that same pattern' (*Marc.* 4.1.11). This is the concise answer to Marcion's *Antitheses*.

In short, from among the apostles the faith is introduced to us by John and by Matthew, while from among apostolic men Luke and Mark give it renewal (all of them) beginning with the same rule of faith, which relates to the one only God, the creator and to his Christ, born of a virgin, the fulfilment of the law and the prophets.

Next comes the splendid critical claim: 'It does not matter that the arrangement of their narrative varies, provided it agrees with the substance of the faith' ('dummodo de capite fidei conveniat') (*Marc.* 4.2.2). This is sufficient to discredit Marcion's alternative Gospel and Tertullian could have stopped here; but he prefers to seek out and destroy Marcion on all fronts and to state his own case as strongly as possible. All of which is no surprise to his readers.

The consistent mysteries of the creator coincide with the essence of the New Testament faith. Tertullian argues from the essence of the New Testament which ignores differences of narrative detail. As an apologist he needs clear answers. The New Testament teaches creation by a good creator whose goodness is never unjust. There is continuity between Old and New Testaments which tell of the same God's action at different times. His central claim that there is antithesis in God needs more elaboration to exclude all that

---

[9] Despite their violent differences. Tertullian is here sarcastic. Cf. *Marc.* 1.1.

he does not mean and to show that the secure answers are still available.

(ii) Elaboration

God's primitive universal law pours out endless contents which are continuous with the creator. It covers all space and time, never discarding old bottles and old clothes. The old is reformed, enlarged and improved, but not rejected. Tertullian's argument against the Jews is similar to that which he has directed against Marcion concerning the Old Testament, with a further claim that God's universal law precedes as well as consummates the Law of Moses. Because God is the creator and ruler of the universe and all mankind, he gave a primitive, universal law. This law contained all the later precepts, was unwritten and was habitually understood and kept by mankind until the disobedience of Adam and Eve (*Jud.* 2.7).

The Mosaic law which followed was in no sense final but pointed further into the future (*Jud.* 3.3). Circumcision was a sign to a stubborn people that a future obedient people would find spiritual salvation (*Jud.* 3.7). The sabbath command was temporary and like all law and ceremony predicted a spiritual fulfilment (*Jud.* 6.1).

In contrast, the finality of Christ's universal kingdom is evident to all. 'But Christ's name is being extended everywhere, believed everywhere, worshipped by all the nations whom we have listed above,[10] ruling as sovereign everywhere, everywhere adored, ... You will not hesitate to believe what we declare, since you see it happening' (*Jud.* 7.5).

The date of Christ's coming was foretold by Daniel (Dan. 9.24–7; *Jud.* 8.1). The sign of his birth and acts of power were prophesied by Isaiah (Isa. 7.13–15). Those who deny the virgin birth are proved wrong by its designation as a startling sign. The birth of a child to a young woman would not in itself be a strange portent since young women are producing children all the time (*Jud.* 9.8). There were many prophecies of the cross and of the calling of the Gentiles (*Jud.* 10–13). Why did the Jews miss all of this? They did not see the twofold characters (*habitus*) of Christ, nor his two

---

[10] Those listed in Acts 2.9f., plus Jews, Gaetulians, Moors, Spaniards, Gauls, Britons, Sarmatians, Dacians, Germans and Scythians.

advents (*Jud.* 14). All may be understood from the harmony of the scriptures and all is fulfilled by divine arrangement (*Jud.* 14.11; cf. *Jud.* 11.12f. and *Marc.* 3.20.1f.)[11]

For the longer elaboration within the Gospel we return to the treatise against Marcion who had chosen Luke's Gospel for mutilation; Luke was not an apostle but a disciple of Paul the apostle. His Gospel must come up to the requirements of the master who denounced false apostles because they perverted the truth of the gospel (*Marc.* 4.3.4). Paul knew the difference between the true and false. How can one choose between the pure and corrupted Gospels? The test is one of time. The earlier has to be true, the later has to be false. Similarly the earlier churches are true, and the later churches of Marcion are false (*Marc.* 4.5.1).

The test of time is confirmed by content. Luke's Gospel, as others have it, coheres with the other Gospels. Marcion has so violently perverted it that it stands in opposition to the apostolic Gospels. The followers of Marcion must either change the other Gospels to agree with their version of Luke or else they must acknowledge with shame that their Gospel is corrupt. These arguments of time, source and content are, says Tertullian, 'the sort of summary arguments I use, when skirmishing light-armed against heretics for the integrity of the gospel' (*Marc.* 4.5.7).

The next point is to show how Marcion's alterations are distinguished by a common aim, already defined in his *Antitheses*, of dividing Old and New Testaments. He erased everything which plainly disagreed with this opinion and left the rest. Here Tertullian defines his case. He will show that, even in Marcion's truncated Luke, Christ must belong to the creator if 'he is found to have administered the creator's ordinances, fulfilled his prophecies, supported his laws, given reality to his promises, revived his miracles, remoulded his judgements, expressed his character and his properties' (*Marc.* 4.6.4). This is the agreed presupposition[12] which the reader must keep in mind as he follows the rest of the argument of the book. Marcion can be shown to be logically incompetent because he left behind, in the one Gospel he uses, many things which destroy his case.

---

[11] 'ex consonantia scripturarum, ex dispositione divina'.
[12] *pactum, praescriptio.*

In the synagogue of Capernaum, Christ declares his fulfilment of the ancient prophets, offers his bread to the children before he passes it to the dogs and expels a demon who acknowledges him as the Christ of the creator (*Marc.* 4.7). Other demons confirm this judgement and Christ is manhandled by the crowd in a way which could not have happened if he lacked a real body (*Marc.* 4.8.3f.). The calling of fishers of men points back to Jeremiah. The cleansing of the leper points back to Elisha and to Christ's cleansing the nations of seven deadly sins: idolatry, blasphemy, murder, adultery, fornication, false-witness and fraud (*Marc.* 4.9). The healing of the paralytic points back to Isaiah 35.3 and the forgiveness of sins to Isaiah 1.18. The self-chosen title 'son of man' implies the humanity of Jesus (*Marc.* 4.10.6).

But how should we understand new wine and old wineskins, new patches on old clothes? Surely, here Marcion is right. No, says Tertullian and offers an intriguing argument. No one can put new wine into old skins if he does not possess the old skins nor a new patch on an old garment if he does not own an old garment. In separating new gospel from old law, Christ made it clear that both belonged to him.

Separation is possible because things are joined together: indeed their conjunction is its source. So he made it plain that the things he was separating had once been in unity, as they would have continued to be if he were not separating them. In that sense we admit this separation, by way of reformation, enlargement, progress, as fruit is separated from seed, since fruit comes out of seed. So also the gospel is separated from the law, because it is an advance from out of the law, another thing than the law although not something foreign, different but not opposite ('diversum sed non contrarium'). (*Marc.* 4.11.11)

All of which depends on how much you can take from a parable, and what you can infer from Christ's use of parables. Just as you can prove a speaker's nationality from his use of foreign idioms so you can prove that Christ's native speech of parable links him with the Psalmist (Ps. 78.2).

All the Old Testament allusions which remain in Marcion's Gospel as well as Beatitudes and Sermon point the same way: to the Old Testament connection (*Marc.* 4.13–17). The *lex talionis* is handled carefully. Originally it acted as a deterrent for those who did not fear the retaliation of God. The intention of the law was revealed and made intelligible when Christ commanded the turning of the other cheek. This command extinguishes more effectively all reprisals of an injury by forgetting wrong and leaving vengeance to God. It responds with an opposite, which is Tertullian's way (*Marc.* 4.16.4–7). When you turn the other cheek, you are acting out a paradigm of Christ's recapitulation which both obeys and corrects the old covenant. In all cases Tertullian argues that the law is extended and developed, yet at the same time expressed more concisely by Christ (*Marc.* 4.16.17). The centurion's faith which is greater than that of Israel points to the existence rather than absence of Israel's faith (*Marc.* 4.18.1).

The question of Christ, 'Who is my mother and who are my brothers?' shows that there were persons who had been identified in this way and that Christ was indignant that they had been kept outside while others had been admitted. When he enlarged his family to include all who believed, he simply translated the blood-relationship to those who were more nearly related to him by faith; and indeed there was no doubt as to the priority of God's word over family. Yet all this argument is lost if Marcion's denial of Christ's earthly birth is derived from the initial question (*Marc.* 4.19.12f.). The complexity displays Tertullian's general principle: that Marcion lifts words out of context, denying the coherent context which defines their sense and the dispensation[13] which is abbreviated in them.

The recurring theme of divine disgrace is another example of the same move. There is nothing in Marcion's Christ of which one might be ashamed since he shows none of the indignities of incarnation. Nor would any but the jealous God of the Old Testament deny those who had been ashamed of him (*Marc.* 4.21.10).

The parables of lost sheep and lost coin show that divine love which was of first importance to Marcion. However, they only make sense if lost humanity belonged to the seeking God. You cannot lose what has never belonged to you and you cannot rejoice in finding what you never lost (*Marc.* 4.32.2).

[13] *consonantia, dispositio.*

In this second aspect of Tertullian's exegesis, the remarkable thing is the logical directness of his argument. He does not merely quote texts and precedents; he tries to show how isolation of a text from its context is as fatal to understanding as is the neglect of its own logic.

(iii) Uncertain victory

Together with all his argument, Tertullian indulges in rampant literalism and exuberant polemic. His exegesis fails to convince when he defends the letter of the Old Testament against Marcion. This is as much a matter of his bondage to the sacred letter[14] as of his exuberant polemic. For his polemic required that he denounce heretics when they enlarge or diminish the text of scripture (*praescr.* 17.1). He denies heretics the use of scripture which does not belong to them (*praescr.* 15.4); argument with them about scripture upsets the stomach or the brain (*praescr.* 16.2) and is a waste of speech (*praescr.* 17.3). Argument must not be based on scripture, where victory will either be impossible or uncertain ('aut nulla aut incerta') (*praescr.* 19.1). Yet he could not be content with a critical interpretation of scripture according to the rule of faith; for he had to show that scripture did not contain anything which contradicted the rule and that scripture should not contradict itself. For this reason he engaged in the kind of argument which he knew he could not win.

If anything could prove Marcion right it would be the incident of Elisha and the bears (2 Kings 2.24), where two she-bears demonstrated affirmative action and devoured forty-two boys because they commented derisively on the prophet's bald head. Marcion sets in antithesis the love of Christ for little children, whom he chose as a paradigm for entry to his kingdom, and this spectacular animal orgy – the bears must have been very hungry! Tertullian (*Marc.* 4.23.5) claims the antithesis to be invalid, even shameless, since it fails to distinguish between little children (*parvuli*) and boys (*pueri*). The former belong to the age of innocence, while the latter were capable of judgement and mockery, even blasphemy. A just

---

[14] Braun, *Deus Christianorum*, 554.

God could not spare disrespectful boys, but demanded honour for their elder. Yet in his kindness to children God had spared the midwives in Egypt, as he later showed the kindness of Christ to little ones.

Jewish legend[15] claims that Elisha's healing of the waters of Jericho caused anger among those who made their living by selling good water. Elisha cursed them, a forest sprang up and bears devoured the murmuring traders. Elisha was punished for his passion by a sickness. According to the Haggadah, Elisha's mockers were not boys but adults who 'behaved like silly boys'. The leaders of Jericho were also to blame, because if they had accompanied Elisha, no one would have dared to insult him. There is little to choose between the two accounts; both sacrifice divine morality to secure the sacred text.

The spoiling of the Egyptians by the Hebrews provoked another objection of Marcion against their God. Tertullian claims that it binds the Hebrews to the Christ who taught that the labourer was worthy of his hire (*Marc.* 4.24.5). Tertullian's extended explanation (*Marc.* 2.20), like that of Philo,[16] is initially reasonable. When we judge between the two nations, we see that God was entirely fair. The Hebrews were owed enormous arrears of pay because of their slavery, the bricks they had made and the houses and palaces they had built. Tertullian acknowledges his Jewish source. 'Today, in spite of the Marcionites, the Hebrews put forward a further claim. They say that however large the amount of that gold and silver, it is not adequate for compensation, if the labour of six hundred thousand men through all those years is priced at a penny a day each' (*Marc.* 2.20.3).

Exuberant polemic takes over. There were more Egyptians living in houses built by Israelites than there were Egyptians who had lost their silver. Which is greater, the loss of the Egyptians or the gain of the Israelites? What would happen if the Hebrews brought a legal action against the Egyptians for injury in slavery? If the scarred shoulders of the Israelites were displayed in court, they would be granted the whole of the rich men's property, augmented

[15] *Sotah* 46b–47a. See L. Ginzberg, *The legends of the Jews*, 7 vols. (Philadelphia, 1909–38), vol. IV, 240.

[16] *Mos.* 1.25.141f.

by the contributions of the rest of the population. If the Hebrews had such a strong case, then the creator had an equally strong case.[17] He told his people to take less than was their due; their male children should also have been returned.

So we may see in Tertullian both critical and biblicist strains. Critically he identifies the central meaning and argues for continuity at every point. Yet reverence for the whole text drives him to biblicist hyperbole, in polemical exuberance.

(iv) Alien text

Tertullian's sensitive use of the bible, determined by his different adversaries and areas of conflict, has attracted a careful study,[18] which notes the strangeness of scripture. Marcion found an alien god in the gospel, while Tertullian finds an alien text in the bible. Biblical language is different: Tertullian explains the special meaning of such words as *sophia, sermo, moechia, fornicatio, caro, sanguis, cor, adpretiatus* and *problemata* and shows that certain words have special meanings. Biblical imagery is also different: Tertullian is sensitive to the biblical imagery of water, clothing, weaponry and athletics. Finally, biblical exegesis is different: for example, Tertullian explains the prophetic present tense which points to future events as already realized.

Of course there is some continuity between biblical and classical ways of interpretation, otherwise each would have remained unintelligible to the other. Tertullian echoes the classical theme of 'progress' in language, song, medicine, sea voyaging and clothing, as found in Lucretius and Virgil, and finds parallels for classical presentations such as Mercury, Asclepius and Minerva (*cor.* 8.2–5).[19] He uses almost every rhetorical skill and persistently practises literary analysis, especially in the New Testament where Jewish exegesis is of no help.

Tertullian sees the need for explanation of two strange sets of

---

[17] Again, it is this kind of argument, rather than any legal terminology, which suggests Tertullian's legal affinity.
[18] T. P. O'Malley, *Tertullian and the bible* (Nijmegen and Utrecht, 1967), where it is rightly insisted that many volumes would be needed to cover Tertullian's use of the bible, 173.
[19] *Ibid.,* 174f.

terms.[20] First, there are the orthodox theological terms, biblical words and proof-texts which link the Old and New Testaments (e.g. *portare, parabola, problemata, adpretiati, filius hominum,* and *ascendit in sublimitatem*). Secondly, there are Marcion's antitheses which do not, Tertullian claims, point to two gods.

Two of Tertullian's literary terms may be noted – allegory and figure. Tertullian knows that allegory is used by pagans to interpret myths (*nat.* 2.12.17) and by Gnostic Christians to rewrite the Gospels (*Val.* 1.3; *res.* passim); but he takes the term from Paul to prove, against Marcion and others, the unity of the two testaments. The principle which he follows is that if the literal sense is nonsense, then allegory must be applied, whereas if the historical sense is true, then allegory is out of place.[21]

Figura is the concept which Tertullian has defined and used as his central hermeneutical term.[22] For Cicero a figure may be *gravis, mediocris* or *attenuata* (*de orat.* 3.199). Quintilian's use (*figura* as 'figure' or 'shape') is reflected in Tertullian's 'in the shape of a man' (*in hominis figura*) (*pat.* 3.10; Phil. 2.7). He criticizes Marcion's docetic Christ (*Marc.* 5.20.3): 'not in reality and the likeness of man, not in a man and found in human shape, not in substance, that is not in flesh'.[23] Prophecy must be real and the vision of Ezekiel (37.1–14) must declare a physical resurrection, in order to foretell Christ's resurrection or the return of Israel. What is not real cannot reveal. A figure must have a basis in history in order to prefigure something. Here again the term is chiefly used to declare the continuity of the Old Testament with the Christ of Marcion's Luke and Marcion's Paul; but there is also a new use where Tertullian uses it to express the shape of Christian living as prefigured in Old and New Testaments.[24]

How does Tertullian's lust for simplicity[25] affect his use of the bible? First, he has a preference for simple, over against laboured,

---

[20] *Ibid.*, 176. [21] *Ibid.*, 157f.

[22] *Ibid.*, 158–64. O'Malley draws on E. Auerbach, Figura, *Archivum Romanicum*, 22 (1938), 436–89.

[23] 'non veritate, et in similitudine hominis, non in homine et figura inventus homo, non substantia, id est non carne'.

[24] O'Malley, *ibid.*, 164. 'Here the great axis is the relation of the two testaments; but it is accompanied also by a line which interprets Old and New Testaments for Christian life. In so doing, he appears as witness of linguistic innovation.'

[25] See above, ch. 1.

exegesis (*or.* 16.2 and 25.5; *carn.* 18.1). The text of scripture should be taken in its obvious sense (*bapt.* 11.2). He criticizes Marcion's extension of the imagery of the good and bad trees producing good and bad fruits to include not merely good and bad men but also good and bad gods producing good and evil (*Marc.* 1.2.1).

Secondly, Tertullian rejects simplicity when he considers it to be superficial. God's walk in the garden of Eden should not be taken in a literal sense (*Marc.* 2.25.2). The apostolic number twelve (*Marc.* 4.13.3) and the apostolic fishing boat (*Marc.* 4.9.1) have a deeper meaning which is not obvious and literal.[26]

In general, he claims that Marcion is too simple in his interpretation of the Old Testament and too tortuous in handling the New Testament (*Marc.* 4.19.6). The simplicity of scripture lies in the agreement of prophecy with its historical realization and in the limit placed on the meaning of parables (*pud.* 9.3). Scripture is plain, because it is direct, clear and open. It is elegant in a way later to be denied by Augustine, but retains the simplicity of truth.

Conflict remains. Tertullian can see problems in the exegesis of scripture which is not as plain as he suggests. His philosophical and rhetorical skills were needed to unravel obscurities and ambiguities. Did Montanism provide the refuge of simplicity which he could not find in the biblical text?[27] I do not think so. The whole of this investigation has pointed to Tertullian's need for both simplicity and conflict. Like Heraclitus, he found both simplicity and conflict in his world and felt remote from reality when both were not present. This saved him from the hermeneutical error, on the brink of which interpreters from Origen to Bultmann hover: that there could be one method to guide all exegesis of scripture.

---

[26] See also *ux.* 2.2; *Prax.* 5.3; *mon.* 11.11; *res.* 20.7.

[27] O'Malley, *Tertullian and the bible*, 178, ends with the claim 'Incapable himself of *simplicitas*, Tertullian nonetheless insisted on the *simplicitas* of Scripture; and he finally takes his refuge in a non-scriptural, simple solution to the problem of interpretation'.

CHAPTER 8

Mankind's two natures and a sordid church

A. SIN AS CONTRADICTION

If Tertullian finds antithesis in the world and God, he will have no trouble finding it in human beings. Everyone had found contradictions in the human person, which was racked by every kind of tension – soul/body, reason/passion, saint/sinner and free/enslaved. A part of European culture, east and west, is the history of Paul's struggle ('the good that I would, I do not: but the evil which I would not, that I do'),[1] narrowly anticipated in Ovid ('I see and approve better things, but follow worse')[2] and repeated in Augustine ('What shall wretched man do?').[3]

Always Tertullian's antitheses come, not from perversity, but from a sense of reality. His own reality was dominated by his consciousness of slavery to sin and the deliverance of baptism. At the last judgement, he would remember the adulteries with which he had once stained his flesh, and be confident that God would raise that flesh which Christ had long since cleansed in baptism (*res.* 59.3). Sin[4] was the supreme contradiction, for it denied God and destroyed humanity. Platonists like Clement could doubt the ultimate reality of evil. Heraclitean Stoics like Tertullian could only face reality when evil and sin were taken seriously. Tertullian, like Paul, thought and wrote a lot about sin. He made the first moves toward a doctrine of original sin and his views on the forgiveness of

---

[1] Rom. 7.19. See also verses 15–25.
[2] 'video meliora, proboque; deteriora sequor'. *Metamorph.* 7.20.
[3] *Conf.* 7.21.27.
[4] For an extended and excellent account of Tertullian's doctrine of sin, with attention to the difficult problem of development, see E. Polto, *Evoluzione del pensiero di Tertulliano sulla dottrina del peccato* (Biella, 1971).

sins caused conflict with the hierarchy of the church. Dissenting on behalf of the New Prophecy, he continued to affirm the church as one, holy, catholic and apostolic,[5] so that sin played a role in his ecclesiology. As well as affirming a concept of original sin, he vigorously defended freedom of will and thereby claimed a twofold origin for sin. Sin comes from a soul which is corrupt but responsible.

Mankind's likeness to God, which dominates Tertullian's ethics, was lost by Adam's sin and is restored by grace (*bapt.* 5.7). A mere ethic is inadequate, for all mankind, sprung from the seed of Adam, is infected by his sin, 'totum genus de semine infectum' (*test.* 3.2). Stoicism reinforces the physical nature of the corruption, which is passed on from every parent to every child, to produce a distortion of human nature.[6]

(i) One soul, two natures

How are we to understand the human soul? It is created and not, as Plato claimed, unmade and eternal (*an.* 4.1). The Stoics help us to understand it as corporeal, spiritual and the source of life (*an.* 5.3). Plato's arguments for an incorporeal soul are criticized and rejected (*an.* 6 and 8); but his arguments for a simple non-composite soul are accepted (*an.* 10.1). When philosophers divide the soul they are merely distinguishing its different faculties (*an.* 14.3). Rationality is the natural condition of the soul, impressed by its rational divine author. It must be rational because it is the breath (*afflatus*) of an essentially rational creator. Irrationality came later and was caused by the serpent. While it intruded at the beginning of nature, became inherent in the soul and grew along with the soul (*an.* 16.1), it is still not strictly natural because God is the author of nature (*auctor naturae*) and irrationality remains external and foreign (*extraneum, alienum*) to God (*an.* 16.2). It is the devil's work and the two elements in the soul point to two authors.

Tertullian will not diversify the soul (as Plato did) into two[7] irrational parts and one rational part; anger and desire are found in God and in Jesus so the *tota trinitas* of faculties can be rational (*an.*

---

[5] Rankin, *Tertullian and the church*, 91–110.   [6] See Spanneut, *Stoïcisme des pères*, 188.
[7] θυμικόν shared with lions and ἐπιθυμητικόν shared with flies.

16.4).[8] He distinguishes instead between a first and second human nature. Corruption from the sin of Adam is transmitted by original fault (*vitium originis*), to become a second nature, less powerful than the soul's original, rational and good nature. The devil rules over the second, later and tainted nature.

The faculties[9] of the soul are never spontaneous in their choices and acts because the devil, driven by jealousy, has darkened and deprived them. He is quite open in the way he does this; he accepts the invitation offered by superstitious birth rites. Idolatry is midwife at every pagan birth, binding wombs with demonic wreaths and consecrating the newborn child to demons. Christian parents can avoid this corruption for their child; but the need for baptism and for a second birth remains (*an.* 39.4).

As Paul taught, one Christian parent could sanctify the birth, by Christian seed as much as by Christian discipline. The children of believers are not, says Paul, unclean, but destined for holiness and salvation. 'For the unbelieving husband is sanctified through his wife and the unbelieving wife is sanctified through her husband. If it were not so, your children would be unclean, but as it is they are are holy' (1 Cor. 7.14). This hope enabled Paul to defend the integrity of marriage, to which he was entirely committed. At the same time, he could never forget the need for a second birth through water and the spirit, a new beginning of which his lord had unambiguously spoken (John 3.5).

Since every soul possesses the nature of Adam until it is born again in Christ, it is unclean and spreads, to the flesh, contamination by association. However, although the flesh is exuberantly sinful, 'nevertheless it is not shameful on its own account. For it is not of itself that it thinks or feels anything which serves to advocate or command sin'.[10] It exercises a *ministerium*, but not an active ministry like that of a servant or friend but an inert (inanimate and

---

[8] The two concepts of importance for Tertullian here are 'the corruption of the soul by sin, and the reality of the affections of God and Christ'. *de anima*, ed. Waszink, 230. Even more important is the exposition of a human trinity which is supremely one.

[9] The distinctive position of Tertullian is seen in three chapters of *de anima* (39–41). Tertullian's account makes sense when his opponents are remembered; he is moved by what he does not want as much as by what he wants to say.

[10] 'non tamen suo nomine infamis. Neque enim de proprio sapit quid aut sentit ad suadendam vel imperandam peccatelam'.

unhuman) ministry. It is but the cup from which we drink if we choose. Flesh is earthly and neither distinctively human nor a faculty of the soul nor a person. Made over like a slave for the soul to use,[11] it serves as the soul's instrument in life's duties (*an.* 40.2f.).

Soul and flesh are of different substance. Flesh cannot be virtuous or vicious without the soul, in whose crimes it serves as an accessory. All the more shame falls on the instigator when his accomplices are condemned and punished. More stripes are inflicted on the initiator of a crime, although his accessories are condemned for obeying his orders (*an.* 40.4).

Above all, there is one genus of human souls. Every soul is counted with Adam until its rebirth in Christ. Without this second birth, it is unclean, actively sinful, and spreads its corruption into the flesh which serves it. Flesh remains a cup or vessel which may be put to good or sinful use. It makes no decisions and is of a different substance from the soul, which is its ruler (*praeses*), whom it serves. It is not the distinctive property of man, and it should not be blamed for the 'works of the flesh' which come from the soul. Indeed the emotions of sin, the lusts which anticipate adultery, belong to the soul. It is plainly absurd to attribute sins and crimes but no good works to the flesh, which is always an accessory and never the instigator in each case (*an.* 40).

As well as the evil which the devil brings at birth there is an antecedent evil from his ancient corruption of our original nature, which has given mankind a second nature. Sin changes the creation which came from God. It destroys reason as it destroys nature (*Marc.* 5.5.4–6). It invades nature (*cult.* 1.8.2) to form a different, secondary and adulterous nature (*an.* 16.7).[12] The corruption of nature is a different nature (*alia natura*) (*an.* 41.1). Nevertheless there remains in the soul a higher ruling element which is good and a sibling natural to herself.[13] This shines as a light, rarely visible, from behind the thick barrier of obscuring sin. For while humans may be very bad or very good, there is always some good

---

[11] 'Addicta tamen animae ut suppellex.'

[12] Cf. *an.* 16.7: 'ne timeas et illi proprietatem naturae adscribere posterioris et adulterae'. Note that *an.* 16.7 and 41.1 are more extreme statements than that of *an.* 16.1. On the contrast see, *de anima*, ed. Waszink, 454.

[13] bonum, principale, divinum, germanum, proprie naturale.

in the worst and some bad in the best. 'Only God is without sin and the only sinless man is Christ, since Christ is also God' (*an.* 41.3). The primitive goodness of the soul breaks out in common exclamations: 'Good God! God knows! Go with God!'[14]

The sin of Adam and Eve is the source of all sin (*an.* 39–41; *test.* 3.2; *Marc.* 1.22.8, 2.2.7). A cascade of souls flows physically from one man (*an.* 27.9). Differences remain. Some seed may bestow a sanctity on a soul (*an.* 39.4), while other seed is so corrupt that no good is brought to birth. The soul is physically transmitted by sperm, so that, as Cleanthes the Stoic pointed out, we resemble our parents in mental as well as physical endowments (*an.* 25.9). Eve received both soul and flesh through Adam, else God would have breathed on her to give her soul (*an.* 36.4).[15]

While Tertullian displays the origins of the idea, one cannot attribute the later doctrine of original sin to him. He does not cite the key texts (Gen. 5.3; Ps. 51.5; Rom. 5.12ff.) nor does he see guilt and death as physically transmitted. He does not regard original sin as relevant to the question of infant baptism, speaking rather of the aweful responsibility which baptism brings (*bapt.* 18.5). It has been claimed that he gives the theory only a passing mention (*an.* 40f.).[16] However, he links original sin with physical continuity and with the soul. He does this through his materialism, which could not make a clear distinction between spirit and matter. Later writers did not share this materialism; but they accepted the consequences which Tertullian had drawn from it as the elements of a doctrine of original sin.[17]

(ii) Free will and God's indulgence

Free choice remains. What we cannot do is what we do not wish to do (*mon.* 14.7). Sin is what God forbids (*paen.* 3.2), the love of what

---

[14] Cf. *test.* 2.

[15] Spanneut, *Stoïcisme des pères*, 187f., notes other texts where soul as *tradux* is given a more passive meaning. He cites H. Karpp, *Probleme altchristlicher Anthropologie* (Gütersloh, 1950), 59–67, who following these texts hesitates to describe Tertullian as a traducianist.

[16] Karpp, *ibid.*, 62. Karpp goes on to see a modified Gnostic influence on Tertullian at this point, 65.

[17] Karpp, *ibid.*, 66. 'Tertullian hat seinen Nachfolger lediglich eine Möglichkeit gegeben, die ausgebildete Lehre von der Erbsünde auf die von der Seele anzuwenden.'

God does not love (*paen.* 4.4). Tertullian, in defence of the creator against Marcion, attributed evils to the free will of humans, who both committed sins (*mala culpae*) and were punished for them (*mala poenae*). The result was human misery, derived from the endowment which made man most like God – his free spontaneous power to produce good.

Our sin is our fault. 'It is our will, when we will the evil which is contrary to the will of God who wills the good. If you ask whence comes this will by which we will something contrary to the will of God, I shall say: from ourselves' (*cast.* 2.5). Tertullian develops this point along lines which are plainly Stoic, but which have been absorbed into his own thinking and are used because they are the best way of handling an intricate, yet intelligible, problem. Those who remarry claim that the God who gave and took away gives again a second marriage. However, faith which is good and solid does not so attribute everything simply to the divine will. We indulge ourselves when we overlook what is in our own power ('esse aliquid in nobis ipsis') (*cast.* 2.3), because God permits all that happens. If we argue that God wills whatever we do, there is an excuse for every sin and there is no ground for any Christian discipline. Indeed there is no rational account of God possible, for either he produces things which he does not will or else there is nothing which he does not will. God condemns and eternally punishes some actions, while he commands and eternally rewards others. When we have learnt from his commandments the distinction between what he forbids and what he wills, we retain the power to choose ('iam in nobis est voluntas et arbitrium eligendi alterum') (*cast.* 2.3). From the beginning, he sets before us good and evil. It cannot be his will that we choose what is against his declared will. Such volition as is hostile to God can only come from ourselves. Adam, the author of our race and of our sin ('ille princeps et generis et delicti Adam') committed sin because he willed it. The devil did not make him sin but acted as an accessory to Adam's will ('materiam voluntati subministravit') (*cast.* 2.5).

In this way, God's will came to be a matter of obedience, and so it remains whenever we freely choose the downhill path from God. The devil wants us to sin, but he does not diminish our volition, force us or impose ignorance of God's will on us. God's will was clear when he imposed death as the punishment consequent upon disobedience. The devil's work is equally clear: he puts our wills to the test. Only when we have willed to disobey God do we pass under the control of the devil; he has not caused our volition but simply taken advantage of it.

The only thing in our power is our will and the one test we face is whether we will what God wills. So we must scrutinize and seek the hidden will of God (*cast.* 3.1). First, God's pure and absolute will is not revealed in what he permits, since he makes allowance for lesser wills. Secondly, his pure will is found in the discipline by which he decrees those acts which he prefers. What he wills more (or prefers) wipes out what he wills less and prescribes what is our duty. If we do not follow his higher will, we tend to contradict his will. We may do what he wills, but still offend him; if we do what he prefers we earn a reward. In the former case, we both sin and do not sin; but we certainly deserve no reward. It is a sin not to want to deserve a reward.

Now we can see how second marriage should be understood. It is not the pure volition of God, but the will of God which is his indulgence (*indulgentia*). All this Tertullian finds in Paul when he speaks about marriage to the Corinthians (1 Cor. 7). It is better to marry than to burn and marriage is the lesser of two evils; an evil can seem good only when compared with something very bad ('non potest videri bonum nisi pessimo comparatum') (*cast.* 3.7). Goodness is best seen apart from comparison.

Something is good if it continue to keep that name without comparison, I say not with evil, but rather with some other good; so that, even if it be compared to some other good, and is overshadowed by that good, it nevertheless retains the name 'good'. If, however, it be only called 'good' in comparison with an evil, it is not so much 'good' as a species of lesser evil, which by being obscured by a superior evil has to be called 'good' ('quod a superiore malo obscuratum ad nomen boni impellitur'). (*cast.* 3.8)

The point may be grasped if we drop the comparison. Who would be rash enough to claim 'It is better to marry'? What is not 'better' cannot be 'good' when only the comparison with personal combustion provides a ground for its goodness. The comparison between marriage and burning is logically similar to that between losing one eye and losing two eyes. It is neither better nor good to lose one eye, unless the comparison of losing two eyes be introduced. Paul's argument in this chapter cannot be taken as a defence of the goodness of marriage, nor as more than a conditional permission for a specific group, namely the unmarried and the widows (*cast.* 3.10).

(iii) Blame

If there is subtlety in discerning the will of God, there is also marked variation in the culpability of the human will. Fornication is worse than apostasy because the former is willed (*voluntarius*) while the latter is not willed (*invitus*) and a response to coercion and torture (*pud.* 22.13). If adulterers are restored to the church, the stronger claim of the apostate must be respected. For no one is compelled to fornicate (*nemo nolens*) and no one freely chooses to deny his faith (*nemo volens*).

Knowledge and ignorance also determine blame. Adam had full knowledge of the sin which he chose to commit. Yet ignorance does not excuse; there is a wilful ignorance which Tertullian attributes to pagans who do not follow the way in which the evidence of Christian expansion drives them. He begins *ad nationes*:

The proof of your ignorance, which condemns while it defends your injustice, is evident in the fact that all who in the past joined you in ignorance and hatred (against Christian faith), immediately they come to know about it, drop their hatred along with their ignorance. Further, they themselves become what they had hated and begin to hate what they had been. (*nat.* 1.1.1)

This paradox is followed by the puzzle of the incurious pagans who complain about the overwhelming expansion of Christian numbers[18] yet never open their minds to the possibility of goodness in what is so successful. They do not allow themselves to be rightly suspicious; they do not want to examine too closely. This quiescent curiosity is unique ('hic tantum curiositas humana torpescit'). 'You love to be ignorant of what others rejoice they have found. You prefer not to know, because you hate and seem to know that

---

[18] Christus Victor is Tertullian's starting point in almost every confrontation.

knowledge would destroy your hatred' (*nat.* 1.1.4). Paradox on paradox points to wilful ignorance and chosen intellectual inertia.

Can the rich variety of sin be reduced to a fundamental fault? Impatience was man's first and fatal sin; as the sole source of every sin, it eclipses original sin in importance. 'In sum, every sin may be attributed to impatience. Evil is impatience of good' (*pat.* 5.2). Tertullian confesses that he does not possess patience (*pat.* 1), but God does (*pat.* 2.1), and the incarnate Christ did (*pat.* 3.1). Since Christians should imitate Christ as slaves and animals imitate their masters, they should strive for patience (*pat.* 4.1).

Impatience has the devil as its source. The devil envied, grieved and deceived man because he was lord of creation. Malice and impatience cause one another (*pat.* 5.7). Man's fatal impatience (*pat.* 5.11–13), led him who had been the innocent, intimate friend of God to fall from paradise. Murder, anger, hatred, plunder and adultery all spring from impatience. Immodesty is impatience of modesty, dishonesty is impatience of honesty and impiety is impatience of piety. How can such a many-headed serpent of sins not offend the lord who rejects every form of evil?

Patience precedes and follows faith (*pat.* 6.1). Love, the supreme sacrament and treasure of Christians is marked by patience (*pat.* 12.8). Heathen patience lacks an essential dimension; for Christian patience is offered to God in return for his patience and the patience of Christ (*pat.* 16.5).

(iv) Penance

The major controversy of Tertullian's later years concerned the forgiveness of sins, a question which had long concerned him. In his earlier work reason is, as ever, his starting point. Penitence must be rational because God, in all his acts and demands, is rational (*paen.* 1.1). Fear is not the motive (*paen.* 5). A decisive repentance which leads to baptism is the centre of faith for all who strive for God's favour (*paen.* 6.1).[19] We are not baptized so that we may stop sinning, but because we have stopped sinning. Yet there is a second repentance (*paen.* 7), which we should not be ashamed to use any

---

[19] 'omnes salutis in promerendo deo petitores'.

more than we abstain from medicine if an illness recurs. Post-baptismal sin offends God but he offers reconciliation (*paen.* 7.14) to those who confess. Such confession (ἐξομολόγησις) puts on sackcloth and ashes, mourns, fasts, prays, weeps loudly, rolls at the feet of presbyters, kneels and begs for the prayers of all believers. In this way, temporal mortification replaces eternal punishments, and self-condemnation leads to absolution, because we are concerned with God. The harder we treat ourselves the better God treats us (*paen.* 9.6).[20] We can be extravagantly humble before the community which is Christ's body, because Christ is at the centre of all that happens. 'Therefore when you throw yourself at the knees of your brethren, you are handling (*contrectas*) Christ and you beg (*exoras*) of Christ; equally when the brothers shed tears over you, it is Christ who is suffering, Christ who implores the father. What a son requests is always easily obtained' (*paen.* 10.6).

If it still be a miserable thing to confess in this way, remember that the means of healing can often be painful and unpleasant (*paen.* 10.9f.). For those who hesitate there is the judgement of eternal fire, proved by the activity of volcanoes. Nature shows the danger and also points to the cure. Irrational, dumb animals like stags and swallows know how to find a cure and do not hesitate to take it. No Christian has to endure the humiliation which the king of Babylon suffered (Dan. 4.25ff.). The shipwrecked sinner must cling to the two planks of salvation: baptism and confession (*paen.* 12.9).

Some sinners will sink despite this life-raft. Post-baptismal sin had been a problem for Christians from earliest times. Hermas gave all Christian sinners one second chance and for this reason he found supporters, but never made his way into the canon of scripture (*pud.* 10).[21] Tertullian's opposition to the readmission of adulterers and fornicators (he did not distinguish between these sins (*pud.* 4)) gained him notoriety and conflict with his bishop. As ever, an examination of his argument is necessary; this shows that he was in continuity with a strong New Testament tradition,[22] according to which there were three sins which were not re-

---

[20] 'in tantum non peperceris tibi, in tantum tibi deus, crede, parcet'.

[21] Every church council had judged it to be apocryphal and false (*paen.* 10).

[22] This is ignored by his conservative critics, like C. B. Daly, *Tertullian the Puritan and his influence* (Dublin, 1993).

missible: adultery, idolatry and murder. According to Acts, Paul and 1 John, Tertullian explains, penance cannot cure these sins.

Not only scripture, but much else prevented Tertullian from acquiescence on this point. His logic, ethics, materialism, doctrine of baptism and doctrine of the church left him no ground for agreement. In logic, we have already seen how important logical relations were to his triune God. At a different level, the relation between the three sins was decisive. Idolatry (which meant apostasy) was like a wedge which, on one side, caused adultery and, on the other side, murder. The three things could not be divided. Permit one and the other two must be there. The pressure to apostatize into idolatry was inescapable in Roman society, where the gods were woven into every part of daily life. Adultery meant a step back into the pagan world which the Christian had renounced. Whatever authority or argument readmits the adulterer or fornicator to the church has to grant the same help to his coordinates, the murderer and idolater (*pud.* 22).

In ethics, the will is all important. This makes adultery worse than idolatry. No one is compelled to fornicate. No Christian apostatizes into idolatry except under coercion (*pud.* 22). In metaphysics, Tertullian's Stoic materialism excludes the plea that spirit is willing and flesh weak. His concluding words are that there is nothing stronger than the flesh which crushes out the spirit (*pud.* 22). Flesh goes on into eternity. Of the three great sins, adultery is the most physical. Tertullian's own adulteries were committed in the same flesh which now strives for continence (*res.* 59.3).[23] In that same flesh he will face his lord.

His doctrine of baptism, with its fearful weight and responsibility, excluded sin from the life of the believer. The gospel began from the simplicity and finality of baptism.[24] The church, we shall see, must be the spotless bride of Christ.

It would be foolish to link Tertullian's own fornications to his intransigence on this point. The solid reasons, which he has given, render a psychological explanation superfluous. Unlike Augustine, he does not dwell on his early guilt in order to exalt the grace of

---

[23] 'Ego me scio neque alia carne adulteria commisisse neque nunc alia carne ad continentiam eniti.'

[24] See above, ch. 1.

God. An English poet, Lord Byron, and a French scholar, Louis
Bertrand, have blamed the climate. Byron wrote,

> What men call gallantry, and gods adultery,
> Is much more common where the climate's sultry.[25]

Bertrand was even more persuasive.[26] Tertullian would never have
agreed. First, fornication was a voluntary matter (*pud.* 22.13). There
could be no evasion of blame.[27] Secondly, a warmer climate was
beneficial to the soul, which became torpid and incapable of active
thought in colder climates.[28] Rejecting the link of soul (ψυχή) with
cold he notes that, in temperate zones men's minds are sharper
(*ingenia expeditiora*), while in the frozen north they are invariably dull
(*omnibus ... mente torpentibus*) (*an.* 25.7).

Tertullian's fornications were pre-baptismal or else none of his
argument on post-baptismal sin would stand; he would no longer
be within the church. They were also prior to his marriage, or else
the closing argument of *ad uxorem* would be impossible. Many of his
fellow Christians would come to baptism with a similar record. The
sins that continued to worry him were the lesser sins of the baptized
Christian. Temptation continued after baptism, for the Christian,
as it had for his lord. Indeed all must pass through temptation on
the way to heaven. It was on this account that he signed himself
'Tertullian the sinner' (*bapt.* 20.5). We must take seriously his
analysis of impatience as the archetypal sin to which he, a worthless
man (*nullius boni*) was prone (*pat.* 1.1). Through this fault, he became
omnicompetent in sin, a man born to do nothing but repent (*paen.*
12.9).

---

[25] *Don Juan*, Canto 1, 63.
[26] *Saint Augustin* (ET, London, 1914), 78.

> But the supple and treacherous city knew the secret of enchaining the will. She tempted
> him by the open display of her amusements. Under this sun which touches to beauty the
> plaster of a hut, the grossest pleasures have an attraction which men of the North cannot
> understand. The overflowing of lust surrounds you. This prolific swarming, all these
> bodies, close-pressed and soft with sweat, give forth as it were a breath of fornication
> which melts the will. Augustin breathed in with delight the heavy burning air, loaded with
> human odours, which filled the streets and squares of Carthage.

[27] He would have agreed with the late Lord Baden-Powell, who impressed upon his young
followers that, if they swam after a meal, they would not only drown but it would be their
own fault. 'Cramp doubles you up in extreme pain so that you cannot move your arms or
legs, and down you go and drown – and it will be your own fault.' R. S. S. Baden-Powell,
Scouting for boys (London, 1953), 72.
[28] Nietzsche held the contrary and false view.

We began with the contradiction of persistent sin; Tertullian's answer illuminates the predicament. Adam knew what he was doing and chose freely; since his fall, sin has acquired natural status and compulsive force (*an.* 16.1).[29] Sin is both universal and particular. Tertullian accepts totally the common duplicity of human souls. All are siblings under the skin, torn between natural goodness and original sin. Worship of fallible emperors and obedience to erring bishops are equally impossible to one of his temperament and beliefs. Everyone faces his own flawed choices with perpetual penitence.

B. A SORDID CHURCH

Every believer knows the struggle of Romans 7; but few are prepared for the disillusionment of an *ecclesia sordida*. Personal weaknesses may be depressing; blemishes on the bride of Christ are intolerable. Tertullian saw the antithesis more clearly because his was a martyr church which owned the tradition of Perpetua. At the same time it was a comfortable and prosperous church where many were ready to compromise (*mediocritas nostra*). The Christian community included members of senatorial families and the *ordo decurionum*. There were many rich widows and many cultivated speakers of Greek.[30]

Tertullian has suffered chiefly in the history of the church because of his polemic against bishops in general and the bishop of Rome in particular.[31] Most Christians have said negative things about bishops; but Tertullian said them extremely well and has

---

[29] 'Irrationale autem posterius intellegendum est, ut quod acciderit ex serpentis instinctu, ipsum illud transgressionis admissum, atque exinde inoleverit et coadoleverit in anima ad instar iam naturalitatis quia statim in naturae primordio accidit.' 'However, the irrational element must be taken as a later addition. The first momentous sin, although it was prompted by the serpent, thereafter inhered in the soul and grew along with it just like a natural faculty, because it happened at the dawn of nature's first beginning.'

[30] G. Schöllgen, Ecclesia sordida? Zur Frage der sozialen Schichtung frühchristlichen Gemeinden am Beispiel Karthagos zur Zeit Tertullians, *JAC*, Suppl. 12 (Münster, 1984), 268. While there are few traces of lower classes, the proportion of each caste is hard to determine. Indeed, apart from the strong evidence for wealthy Christians, the social composition of the church at Carthage is unclear.

[31] Many scholars see the bishop of Carthage as the object of attack and many are unsure. After great indecision, I am largely convinced by Allen Brent, *Hippolytus and the Roman church in the third century*, 509–17. Together with the arguments which Brent puts forward, I think it makes Cyprian's loyalty to Tertullian easier to understand.

paid the penalty for his verbal violence. The ground of his attack was episcopal handling of second repentance or the remission of sins, as it emerged in Rome and in Carthage about 220.[32] Callistus, bishop of Rome, was prepared to restore penitents for certain secret sins, among which fornication was specified. For Tertullian, such a sinner should be encouraged to confess, should be commended to the just mercies of God and then be expelled from the communion of Christ's body on earth.

Tertullian does not deny that bishops may pardon certain sins; but their authority is sufficiently new for him to be able to restrict this pardon to minor faults. He also recognizes that, in times of persecution, martyrs will be besieged by penitents who beg their intercessions. Perhaps, it has been suggested, a certain realism caused bishops to take upon themselves this enlarged power. Under persecution there was a persistent danger that expelled sinners might be arrested and, in despair, deny Christ and inform on other Christians. 'With such a prospect before his eyes, a bishop might well take any step that would put courage and confidence into the weaker brethren, while peace lasted, so that, when the shock of persecution came, it might find them in such solidarity with the Church that they would stand firm'.[33]

(i) Was Tertullian a schismatic?

Tertullian's doctrine of the church[34] presents a different kind of puzzle from that found in other parts of his thought. There is no need to reconcile opposing views; rather the consistency of his account is excessive. With one who gradually distanced himself from the rulers of the church, some evidence of change should be expected. The puzzle is one of fact: the common account of Tertullian's Montanist defection has an insecure basis. It is probable that he remained within the catholic church, despite (or because of) his allegiance to the New Prophecy. Further, his ideas on the church, its discipline and morals did not change with his increased opposition to the rulers of the empirical church which he

---

[32] See W. Telfer, *The forgiveness of sins* (London, 1959), 62.   [33] *Ibid.*, 64.
[34] This account is indebted at many points to the recent work of David Rankin, *Tertullian and the church*.

faced. Eschatological expectation may have grown more intense; but this simply emphasized that the bride of Christ must be fit to meet her lord. There was no substantial change in his view of the church which he derived from Paul and Matthew.

Opinion concerning Tertullian's relation to the church has been divided. Some claim that Montanism brought little change to Tertullian's theology. Others maintain that Montanism profoundly affected his understanding of spirit and church. An attempt at reconciliation claims that Tertullian's theology is a consistent whole, which finally found its home within Montanism which supported his rigorist practices and principles.[35] Indeed, Tertullian's theology of the spirit followed from his own theology and was not adopted from Montanism.[36] His tone and style became more strident in his later writings; but there was no change in his theological outlook.[37]

Montanism was already two generations old, before Tertullian embraced it. It may have been a negative response to the increased organization of the church catholic, which was partly a response to the challenge of Gnosticism. It is important that Montanus and his followers did not call themselves a 'church' and that they remained loyal to the church universal.[38] Their ministry shared with other churches a threefold structure; they had patriarchs for metropolitans and elders who supervised finance.[39]

Certainly within Tertullian's writings, the New Prophecy had no characteristics of a schism. There was no rival hierarchy as there was later with Novatianism and Donatism. While most catholics were psychics, not spiritual (*iei.* 11.1), Tertullian insisted that there were spiritual bishops (*iei.* 16.3) who shared his opposition to the readmission of serious sinners.[40] Cyprian (*Ep.* 55.21) wrote of these earlier bishops who held such views.[41] Cyprian would not have followed Tertullian so assiduously had Tertullian been schismatic.

[35] O'Malley, *Tertullian and the bible*, 120–3.
[36] G. Bray, *Holiness and the will of God* (London, 1979), 110, 131.
[37] K. Wölfl, *Das Heilswirken Gottes durch den Sohn nach Tertullian* (Rome, 1960), 269.
[38] P. de Labriolle, *La crise montaniste* (Paris, 1913), 60 and 136.
[39] Cf. F. E. Vokes, Montanism and ministry, *StPatr.*, 9 (1966), 306–15 (308).
[40] Rankin, *Tertullian and the church*, 49.
[41] *Ibid.*, 150. This 'is a clear demonstration that Tertullian's attacks were in the main directed more at particular bishops and their presumptuous claims than at episcopal office as such'.

(ii) Images of the church

Tertullian's account of the church draws on a wide range of images. The church is the ark of Noah, in which believers are saved from destruction (*bapt.* 8.4) and kept free from all impurity (*idol.* 24.4), the little ship in which the disciples are protected (*bapt.* 12.7) and kept from shipwreck (*pud.* 13.20). The church is the camp of light, at war with the army of pagan darkness (*cor.* 11.4), free from the contamination of sin (*pud.* 14.17) and subject to discipline in a way which the camp of heretics is not (*praescr.* 41.7). The church is a body in many senses: it is a society (*apol.* 39.1) and a threefold witness (*bapt.* 6.2). It is the unity of the charismata given in the Old and New Testaments (*Marc.* 5.8f.) and the means of reconciliation through the physical body of Christ (*Marc.* 5.19.6). Within the spiritual body the other members share the suffering of any member which is afflicted (*paen.* 10.5), and the congregation acts as Christ (*ecclesia vero Christus*) in receiving the penitent sinner (*paen.* 10.6). The church is closely linked with the holy spirit and the trinity (*pud.* 21.16f.). The church as mother goes beyond the source of nourishment (*mart.* 1.1) to represent a more exalted figure alongside God as father (*mon.* 7.9). Tertullian is the first to connect mother church with father God. The well-established image of the church as the bride of Christ is frequently found in Tertullian (e.g. *mon.* 5.7 and 11.2; *Marc.* 4.11.8, 5.12.6 and 5.18.9) as is also the image of the church as virgin (e.g. *mon.* 11.2; *pud.* 1.8 and 18.11). The church is also the school in which the pupils of Christ are taught the truth which was handed down to his disciples (*scorp.* 12.1), truth which surpasses all human wisdom (*an.* 1.6). As a sect, the teaching of the church places it beside the sects of philosophy and religion which were tolerated by Roman law (*ap.* 39.6); yet it remains superior to them (*pall.* 6.2).

(iii) Marks of the church

For Tertullian, these images point to the holiness (ark, ship, camp, mother, bride and virgin), apostolicity (sect and school) and unity (body) of the church.[42] The holiness of the church derives from the

---

[42] *Ibid.*, 92.

summons of the church to meet her lord. Throughout his writing, Tertullian had a perfectionist view of the church. Unworthy members must be excluded from its fellowship (*ap.* 2.18, 39.4). A Christian who is found in the gladiatorial arena on any charge other than that of his faith must be excommunicated. Those who do not stand firm under persecution must be expelled (*praescr.* 3.6). Tertullian rejects (*pud.* 13.25) the argument of those who will identify the Corinthian adulterer (1 Cor. 5.5) with the offender to be reconciled (2 Cor. 2.5–11). There can be no pardon for the sins of murder, idolatry, fraud, apostasy, blasphemy, adultery and fornication (*pud.* 19.25). Because the end is near, there is no place for sin within the church.

For Tertullian, the holiness of the church had to be an empirical holiness. It was to be perceived by all who saw it. Unworthy members were to be excluded (*ap.* 2.18), banished from prayer and fellowship (*ap.* 39.4). He who is not wholly a Christian is not a Christian (*ap.* 44.3) any more than he who is not orthodox (*ap.* 46.17) or he who is apostate (*praescr.* 3.6). The holiness of the church must not be compromised and grave sinners must be permanently excluded (*pud.* 18.11). For all who have committed murder, idolatry, fraud, apostasy, blasphemy, adultery and fornication, 'Christ will not intercede' and perpetual exclusion from the church must follow (*pud.* 19). Tertullian's demand for holiness is present throughout all his works. It is not derived from his later concern with the New Prophecy; but it will play a decisive role in the history of the African church.

The church must stand in continuity with the apostles (*praescr.* 20f.). For teaching received from the apostles comes from God through Christ (*praescr.* 21). Continuity may be verified by historical succession as well as by continuity of doctrine. Indeed physical continuity must be bound to authentic apostolic witness (*Marc.* 4.5.1–3). However, neither continuity of office nor of teaching is the final criterion. The question of power takes precedence.[43]

Tertullian, as heir of the apostles (*praescr.* 37.5), looked back to the founding of particular churches by the apostles and to lists of bishops who had succeeded them. Apostolic foundation and

---

[43] See below and also Rankin, Tertullian's use of the word *potestas*.

apostolic teaching were marks of the true church. The movement from an early concern for apostolic doctrine to a later concern for apostolic discipline points to the decisive move in early Christian ecclesiology. In the face of the problems of penitential discipline, the question of doctrine became secondary to the question of power. 'The question "To whom has Christ, through his chosen apostles, given his teaching?" receded into the background of Tertullian's thought. An alternative, "To whom did he give the power?", becomes the critical question.'[44]

The unity of the church had been a matter of concern since Christ called his second disciple. Indeed, Paul spoke firmly on the need for christian unity in his first letter to the Corinthians. Tertullian begins from Paul's condemnation of schism (*praescr.* 5). Apostolic churches, through their peace, brotherhood and hospitality, display their unity (*praescr.* 20.6–8). Their unity is a matter of tradition (*praescr.* 28.3). Heretics, with their lack of godly fear, gravity, diligent care, ordered appointment and due discipline, forfeit the unity of the church (*praescr.* 43.5). One God and one baptism belong to one heavenly church (*bapt.* 15.1). The one church as the single spouse of Christ provides the pattern for monogamy (*mon.* 5.7). It is most offensive for clergy to celebrate second marriages 'in the virgin church, sole spouse of the one Christ' (*mon.* 11.2). Even in his later writing, Tertullian never wavers in his belief that there is one church, from which only heretics, not carnal Christians (psychics) are excluded (*virg.* 2.2). Despite all the shortcomings of the bishops, there is only one catholic church.

The unity of the church was closely argued by Tertullian on the basis of 1 Corinthians (11.17f. and 12.12f.) and Ephesians (4.4–6). Never did Tertullian deny this truth. The one church (*una ecclesia sumus* (*virg.* 2.2)) included carnal or psychic catholics together with the followers of the New Prophecy. The unity of the church which is displayed in the peace between congregations is based upon common apostolic doctrine (*praescr.* 21.7). As the body of Christ, the church was not divided. Both catholic and new prophet were a part of the one church in heaven (*bapt.* 15.1). Yet, despite his reference to the church in heaven, Tertullian regards the true church as a

---

[44] Rankin, *Tertullian and the church*, 102f.

present historical reality. To sum up, it may be convincingly argued that, while he does not use the later formula, Tertullian confesses the church to be one, holy, catholic and apostolic.[45]

(iv) Ministry

Tertullian's theology of ministry affirms a threefold structure of bishops, presbyters and deacons. Here he takes a decisive step which was to be established within the western church from that time forward. For Irenaeus, churches were apostolic if, through their members and their ministry, they handed on the authentic apostolic faith.

Seen in its proper terms, the Irenaean doctrine contains little with which the historian need quarrel. But when this doctrine spread among the Latins, assumptions were made, and consequences drawn, for which Irenaeus was not strictly responsible. If any catholic congregation of the age that followed him believed itself to hold the apostolic faith, it assumed that all the actualities of its third-century life, without discrimination, were such as must always have been present in the life of the Church, since the days of the apostles. So these Latin churchmen created a historical myth, the unhistorical nature of which they were secure from discovering. This was to the effect that the apostles had provided for the future of the church by creating an order of monarchical bishops. The first of these they ordained, according to this myth, with their own hands, and set them to govern the several churches with which they were concerned.[46]

The practical value of this doctrine was obvious.

Apart from the three offices, Tertullian describes at least six other positions within the church – widow, virgin, doctor, lector, prophet and martyr.[47] The distinction between clergy and laity is clear. 'Office as a formally constituted rank or position, bearing a function or authority by virtue of such rank, is in Tertullian's thought applied almost exclusively to the clergy, and only rarely to the minor offices of lector, doctor and the two female "orders".'[48] The priestly class provides a pattern for other offices and deserves submission and respect.

[45] *Ibid.*, 111–16.
[46] W. Telfer, *The office of a bishop* (London, 1962), 119.
[47] Rankin, *Tertullian and the church*, 172–85.
[48] *Ibid.*, 142.

Just as, while criticizing philosophy, Tertullian did as much as anyone for the use of philosophy in Christian thought, so, while abusing the multitude of bishops, Tertullian indicated the most decisive step in early Christian ecclesiology. In him the church has acquired the magnitude which Cyprian was to expound in the classic catholic doctrine which has endured to the present. He accepted this, not in spite of his prophetic eschatological tendencies, but because of them. Since the end was near, the church must be ordered on lines parallel to Roman provincial government,[49] so that it could take over earthly rule when Christ had come. As the apostles were to sit on twelve thrones as judges (Matt. 19.28; Luke 22.30) so their faithful successors were to judge. 'By anticipation, and among the people of God, they were already seen to sit on thrones as judges... So in this shadow-empire, the Church, the bishops are seen to answer to the senatorial rank in the secular order.'[50] In ecclesiology as elsewhere Tertullian shaped the future of western christianity, affirming episcopal power and rebuking its misuse; as ever, he did this because he was able to handle ambiguous reality.

[49] See Eric F. Osborn, Cyprian's Imagery, *Antichthon*, 7 (1973), 65–79.
[50] Telfer, *Bishop*, 130f.

CHAPTER 9

Argument and humour: Hermogenes and the Valentinians

To argue or not to argue? The two targets of this chapter share a common dualism. Yet there is a striking difference in the way Tertullian confronts them. Hermogenes is met with exposition and argument; Valentinians are offered exposure and ridicule. The difference is of first importance. Like Marcion, Hermogenes presented argument; Valentinians offered fable and vision which was immune from argument. Tertullian's two diverse approaches respond to this difference. They are not explained by placing one work early in Tertullian's career, and claiming Montanist influence on the second.[1] The contrast is in logical method. For Tertullian, the laughing Stoic, his argument and his satire are equally philosophical.

A. AGAINST HERMOGENES

(i) Unicity of God

The chief objection to Hermogenes (as against Marcion), is Tertullian's axiom: 'God is not if he be not one'. Matter is introduced by Hermogenes as a second first-principle beside God, 'on the same level with the lord' (*Herm.* 1), in order to explain creation and its flaws. Tertullian gives a careful statement of the argument of Hermogenes (*Herm.* 1–3) and then sets about his refutation.

---

[1] There is no need to dispute a difference in date; see ch. 1 for order of composition of Tertullian's works. The point is that Tertullian's different criticism of the two views is based on their argument or lack of argument.

Hermogenes argued that:

A. 1. God created things either out of himself or out of nothing or out of something.
   2. He neither made them out of himself nor out of nothing.
   3. Therefore he made things out of something, namely matter.
B. 1. God was lord and, as unchangeable lord, must always have something to lord over.
   2. God, the only creator, lord of the universe, wholly other, was set in contrast to matter which was neither creator nor lord.

Tertullian replies to this argument that 'God' is the name of a substance while 'lord' is the name of a power. God was always God but lordship was a later addition. As soon as things began to exist, over which God could exercise power, from that moment of power, 'he became lord and received the name' (*Herm.* 3.4). He could not have been father before the son existed, nor a judge until there was sin to judge. God became lord through the service of the things which he had made.

Now, is this too subtle for Hermogenes? The bible offers simpler proof: God is called 'God' until he has completed creation. Then and only then, is he called 'lord' (Gen. 2.15). An even more obvious rebuttal is offered for the more obtuse: if, as Hermogenes claims, matter is neither born nor made, then matter must be free and God could not be its lord. In contrast, from Tertullian's position, matter experienced God as lord only from the moment of creation, when he exercised the lordly power which he had held proleptically all along.

(ii) Eternal matter

Hermogenes' transcendent matter has many inconsistencies because it denies the axiom of one God. First of all it is equally unborn, unmade, eternal, unbegun and without end; and this, says Tertullian, makes it equal to God who alone is eternal. If there is anything else beside him with the same attributes, he is not God. Hermogenes has produced two gods which means that he has no God (one plus one equals none), for unicity is part of being God. 'Whatever belongs to God, belongs to him alone' (*Herm.* 5.3). Hermogenes will deny this and claim that God is still first and incomparable; but 'how can he be first when matter is co-eternal with him?' (*Herm.* 6.1). Matter is equal to God in all respects, lacking no quality which is thought to be special to him.

Hermogenes replies that matter is inferior to and different from God, so the axiom of one God is not denied. Tertullian argues that what is eternal and ingenerate cannot be inferior to anything. Eternal God and eternal matter possess equally 'that complete and perfect felicity of which eternity is declared to consist' (*Herm.* 7.2). There can be no degrees of divinity because, by axiom, divinity is unique. Matter cannot properly be submitted to God without prompting matter's just complaint: 'Who submits me to a god, who is my equal in time and my equal in age? If this is done because he is called "God", then I also have my own name; or rather, I am God and he is matter, because we both are also that which the other is' (*Herm.* 7.4).

There is reason, claims Tertullian, for saying that Hermogenes' matter is superior to God, because it provided God with the material necessary for his work. Whatever one uses one needs, and whatever one needs is superior to one. Matter, rich, opulent and generous, lent itself to the God who needed it to make what he could not make out of nothing. Matter did God a great service by enabling him to be known as God and called 'Almighty'; yet by virtue of this service, it denied the omnipotence of God. Further, at the same time as performing this service, it performed an even greater service to itself by making itself God's equal and assistant.

Hermogenes has achieved this knowledge through the philosophers who are the patriarchs of the heretics. Certainly the prophets and apostles did not know all of this any more than did Christ. Tertullian's sarcastic aside is important because it shows the source of his ideas. It is from the prophets and apostles that Tertullian learns the account of God which he follows. There he finds an unqualified monotheism and this unqualified monotheism is the heart of his gospel. As for Paul, so for Tertullian, God is the God who justifies the ungodly, raises the dead and creates from nothing.

There is a further possibility that God used matter, which was evil, to achieve something for which he lacked the resources; but if he had been lord and a good God he would have transformed the evil matter into something good before he used it. If the good God used evil matter, which he owned, to make a universe, which thereby contained evil, he was not a free lord. If God, according to Hermogenes, drew on a foreign substance to make a world in which evil exists, then God is responsible for the evil which he has permitted. If he had no alternative way to make a world, he could have refrained from creation. It was stupid for him to make a world for his own glory, when the method of creation showed his debt to an alien and evil substance.

(iii) Eternal evil (Herm. 10–16)

Hermogenes claims that creation from nothing means that evil must be imputed to the creator (*Herm.* 10.1). God must cause evil. Tertullian's reply is that no theory of creation can avoid the permission of evil by the creator who thereby *appears* to be the cause of evil. Tertullian has given his own answer to the problem of evil elsewhere. It is clear that the account of Hermogenes will not do, for, on his proposal, God was either unable or unwilling to amend the evil which is intrinsic to matter. God must therefore be either the servant or the friend of evil, since he associated with and created the world out of matter.

Eternity and evil are incompatible, argues Tertullian (*Herm.* 11). What is eternal cannot be subject to anything, but what is evil is subject to evil, therefore what is eternal is incompatible with evil. God alone is God, because he is eternal. God is good because he is God, therefore God is the eternal, highest good. By contrast, there will be an end to evil and a restoration of creation in all innocence and purity. Evil has an end and must also have had a beginning.

If matter be evil we cannot explain the good things that have been made from it (*Herm.* 12–14). If we say that matter is evil by nature, we face further difficulties (*Herm.* 12). What is eternal is immutable, and for Hermogenes matter is eternal, so matter is immutable. Again, for Hermogenes matter is evil, but matter is immutable so matter must always be evil. Yet, for Hermogenes, if good things have been created out of matter, and matter is always evil, then matter must have suffered change, which is impossible because of its eternal immutability. If good things are made from evil matter (*Herm.* 13), without a substantial change in matter, there might be a discordant and good element in matter. Matter would then have no common nature; God would not be the sovereign creator even of good things; and God would be still more subject to matter.

We could avoid this problem, however, by allowing God as creator of good things to produce them by his own will without becoming subject to matter (*Herm.* 14). The difficulty with this defence is that God would also have to produce evil things from matter; he could not have done this by his own free will, and therefore he would still be the servant of matter. The subjection of God to anything is inadmissible: it would be better to have him create evil things out of nothing than to lose his sovereign freedom. In contrast, if matter contains nothing good and God freely created good, then God must have created good from nothing.

If good were made neither from matter nor from God, but of necessity from nothing, the sovereign God could still make all things (including evil) from matter (*Herm.* 15). But matter is superfluous, because it is at most the assistant of God in the creation of evil (*Herm.* 16) and God remains sovereign creator. Matter being redundant, God made all things from nothing. The notion that God created evil raises difficulties; but it would be preferable for God to have created evil freely than to have created evil from matter.

(iv) Exegesis of scripture (Herm. 19–32)

Creation from nothing may also be proved from the unicity of God, which is Tertullian's overriding concern. His sovereign wisdom is declared by scripture (Rom. 11.33ff.) and he needed no substance to guide him (*Herm.* 17). This wisdom may be seen as God's instrument, generated by him for the work of creation (*Herm.* 18). If even God's wisdom were born and created, there cannot be anything unborn and uncreated except God. God's wisdom and word cannot be surpassed by matter in the way Hermogenes wishes. Scripture dominates these thirteen chapters, and Hermogenes' interpretations of Gen. 1.1 (*Herm.* 19–22), Gen. 1.2a (*Herm.* 23–9) and Gen. 1.2b (*Herm.* 30–2) are all disputed.

To this scriptural detail another proof of creation out of nothing is added. The universe would derive ultimately from nothing, even if it were made from matter (*Herm.* 33). The rule of faith declares that God alone is ingenerate, and all else must be made by God from nothing. This belief is confirmed by the final reduction of all things to nothing, as scripture declares, and what has an end must have had a beginning. What is perishable cannot be the product of eternal matter; more fittingly, God works the other way and transforms our perishable flesh into eternal flesh, 'that we might believe that he alone raised up the universe from nothing into existence, when, since when it did not exist, it was, as it were, dead' (*Herm.* 34.4).

(v) Contradictory conditions of matter (Herm. 35–40)

Tertullian proceeds to show that the condition of Hermogenes' matter is full of contradictions which confirm its non-existence. It was not corporeal because it was a kind of motion, and not incorporeal because it produced bodies; yet there is no indication of a third class of things to which it might belong (*Herm.* 35). Hermogenes attempts another account (*Herm.* 36) in which matter is partly corporeal (from which bodies are made) and partly incorporeal (the irregular motion which governs matter). Motion, however, which will come up for later discussion, is an accident, an action, and never a substance.

The next contradiction from Hermogenes is that matter is not good and not evil: a singularly negative account (*Herm.* 37). If it is not good it must be evil, and if not evil it must be good. If God cannot improve good or evil matter, then he must be inferior to it. Again, when Hermogenes describes matter as having a place below God (*subjaciens deo*) (*Herm.* 38.1), he gives it a space and a shape, in spite of his claim that it is infinite because eternal. If his account has been modified, by a pupil, so that the infinity of matter be only an infinity in time, this contradicts Hermogenes who applies spatial categories to matter. God cannot shape matter as a whole, but only in parts.

Other contradictions arise from the way in which matter

changes. First (*Herm.* 39), the changes which matter undergoes are
only explicable if it is divisible, and this is incompatible with its
eternity. Hermogenes' more subtle claim that all the parts contain
the whole is equally impossible, because the presently existing
parts of matter differ drastically from its older constituents.
Finally (*Herm.* 40) change is contradictory, when Hermogenes
claims that (i) matter changed for the better and (ii) matter was a
model for the world. Nor can the world be a mirror reflection of
matter, for matter is unadorned and the world is an ordered
cosmos. Even if the world were a reflection of matter, the whole
of matter could not be known from its now visible parts. Another
inconsistency is Hermogenes' claim that the parts of matter
shaped by God may provide evidence of other matter which has
not been so changed.

(vi) Contradictory motion of matter (Herm. 41–3)

If the condition of matter be contradictory, so also is the motion
which is ascribed to it (*Herm.* 41–3). On the one hand, the motion of
matter is chaotic, like boiling water, and, on the other hand, this
motion is equable, evenly balanced between good and evil. While
matter kept its distance from good and evil it was determined by
them both. Further, if good and evil determine matter, they must
be local like matter, therefore corporeal, and therefore substances,
which is impossible.

How can the motion of matter both aim at formlessness and
desire to be ordered by God? How can it be unequal to God, yet
have something in common with him (*Herm.* 42)? How can the
motion of matter be both vehement and slow (*Herm.* 43)? With
further contradiction, Hermogenes claims that matter is not evil by
nature but capable of regulation by God; he then goes on to claim
that matter had an evil nature which it lost when God set it in
order.

How did creation happen? Hermogenes rejects the Stoic idea
that God pervades matter and he sees creation as the effect of
divine beauty, either through its appearance to matter or as the
effect of a divine magnet on scattered particles. If, as Tertullian

thinks impossible, these examples were relevant, there would be a point of time when God approached the world; but for Hermogenes matter and God are eternal and of one substance. God, indeed, is everywhere and could never have been far removed from matter (*Herm.* 44).

According to scripture, God made the world by his powers of word and wisdom. 'His glory is the greater because he laboured' in creation, preparing the world by his wisdom and stretching out the heavens by his understanding. God's incomprehensible judgements and undiscoverable ways (Rom. 11.33) point to one answer: 'What else do these words convey than: "How true! All things were made out of nothing!" For they could not be comprehended nor discovered save by God alone; otherwise, if they derive from matter, they would admit of discovery and comprehension' (*Herm.* 45.5f.).

(vii) Comment

To the modern reader, Hermogenes' account has its strength. God was always lord, which meant that God was always creator, which implied that he ordered a part of matter and produced a cosmos.[2] Matter was ordered by reflecting the God who appeared to it and whose beauty produced the cosmos. Creation, like a magnetic force, pulled particles into a pattern (*Herm.* 44.1).

God and matter both have a self-generated, eternal motion (*Herm.* 42.3). Matter is infinite and God regulates only a part of it; but the whole is known from its regulated part (*Herm.* 39.2). The world is the mirror of matter (*Herm.* 40.2). God shapes matter which is changeable and divisible. The motion of matter is both very swift and very slow, so that motion (like matter itself) is without quality.

The point of Hermogenes' position is that matter is not shaped in its entirety but only in its parts:[3] this limitation is the cause of evil (*Herm.* 38.3). God never stops shaping matter and there is always some unshaped matter left over. Consequently, in the world, there is always evidence and counter-evidence of God's

---

[2] Cf. Hippolytus, *Ref.* 8.10.
[3] 'nec tota fabricatur, sed partes eius'.

designing hand. In all the order of the cosmos, some of the original chaos remains.[4]

At first sight, Tertullian seems unreasonable, because he denies the propriety of contradiction in matter after having insisted that there is antithesis in all things.[5] However, he is arguing for the inconsistency of Hermogenes, for whom as a Platonist contradiction implies non-existence and whose matter is ideal and transcendent. As a Stoic, Tertullian could give a different account and still preserve the unicity of God and the transcendence of a creator. The immanence of divine seed in the world did not preclude the independence of the creator from his creation.

B. AGAINST THE VALENTINIANS

This short work raises problems for the modern reader who has access to many Gnostic works. The library of Nag Hammadi is more abstract than the Valentinian story which Tertullian discusses, although Nag Hammadi writings are still descriptive rather than argumentative.[6] Tertullian cannot add greatly to our knowledge of the Gnostic movement; he shows that the forms of Gnosticism which flourished in his time and place were more vivid than those which survived in later devotional reading. This is what we should expect and there is no incompatibility between the two forms. For example, the *Gospel of Truth* presents the same narrative

---

[4] Neander wrote of Hermogenes:

> Die Bildung der Materie durch Gott ist eine unendliche Aufgabe, und immer bleibt ein der Bildung widerstrebender Rest zurück. So, sagt er, lässt sich, wie das Ganze in den Theilen, die Materie als das zum Grunde liegende in der Welt erkennen, theils was sie durch die göttliche bildende Kraft werden konnte, theils was in ihr das aller Bildung Widerstrebende ist. Das alte Chaos lässt sich bei aller Schönheit und Ordnung in der Welt doch immer noch als das zum Grunde Liegende erkennen; es scheint durch mitten durch die hergestellte Ordnung. (God's shaping of matter is an unending task and there is always a residue which resists formation. So, Hermogenes says, as the whole may be known in the parts, matter may be recognized as the substructure of the world, partly as that which comes from God's ordering power and partly as that which resists every tendency to order. The ancient chaos can be recognized as fundamental in all the world's order and beauty; it appears throughout the established order.) *Antignostikus*, 347. Cited *Treatise against Hermogenes*, tr. J. H. Waszink, *ACW* (London, 1956), 94f.

[5] See above, ch. 4.

[6] The translation of *Republic* 588f. is innocent of all logical understanding, but illuminates the imagery of the *Gospel of Thomas*, 7. See, *The Nag Hammadi Library in English*, translated under the direction of James M. Robinson (Leiden, 1977), 290f.

movement as the Valentinianism of Irenaeus and Tertullian – the phase of extension is followed first by a phase of concentration and then by a phase of dispersion and return to unity through the saviour.[7] There is no ground for dissociating popular Gnosis from its great leaders.[8] In any case, it was popular Gnosticism which troubled Tertullian and Irenaeus. There is much to learn from this short work, although modern Gnostic investigators find it distressing, because it does not cover the wide scope of the Gnostic movement as it continues to emerge today.[9]

Why does Tertullian mock the Valentinians and not try to reason with them? First, Gnostics mocked ordinary Christians as naïve and stupid; Tertullian had to bounce the mockery back. From Paul onwards the folly of the cross was ridiculed by Greek and Jew. The mocking of the saviour was part of every Gospel passion narrative. Justin begs the Jews (*dial.* 147.1): 'Do not speak evil of him who was crucified and do not mock at his stripes, for by them all may be healed, as we have been healed.' Secondly, simplicity not sophistication is the way to know and declare God; by itself, wisdom does him violence and betrays him. The children did not shout 'Crucify' (*Val.* 2,3.1). Thirdly, Valentinians claimed immunity from argument which they declared was superficial. Their ideas were too profound for reason. Their professed logical immunity and their preference for aesthetic[10] rather than logical considerations made them vulnerable to humour. Fourthly, this kind of theosophy arises for those who can handle story or picture, but not logic. It offers entry into a higher world. Feigned superiority masks deficiency and should therefore not be taken seriously. Finally, incarnation was foolishness to the Gnostics because it mixed language about the pleroma with language about the world, God-talk with world-talk. Tertullian wanted to show that if you stayed in the transcendent realm, it was even easier to talk nonsense.

---

[7] Cf. F. M. Sagnard, *La gnose valentinienne et le témoignage de saint Irénée* (Paris, 1947), 144f.

[8] As Harnack sought to do and was refuted by K. Koschorke, *Die Polemik der Gnostiker gegen das kirchliche Christentum* (Leiden, 1978), 6.

[9] As, very recently, in the fine work of A. H. B. Logan, *Gnostic truth and Christian heresy* (Edinburgh, 1996).

[10] See H. U. von Balthasar, 'Der ästhetische Mythos', in *Herrlichkeit, eine theologische Ästhetik*, vol. II (Einsiedeln, 1962), 33–45. ET *The glory of the Lord* (Edinburgh, 1984), vol. II, 33–44.

At the same time, Valentinians could not be ignored, because they were partly right. They had put the divine economy into the being of God, which is exactly what Tertullian did. They did not see how far it had to be demythologized[11] into something like a theology of the trinity (with three persons and one substance). Recapitulation is explicitly transformed by Clement of Alexandria with the Middle Platonic Nous (*strom.* 4.25.155–7). Both Tertullian and Clement keep some mythology but they make many logical moves as well.

Tertullian follows Irenaeus at many points but there are differences. Irenaeus reports without satire except for the tears of Sophia (*haer.* 1.4.3f.) and specimens of Valentinian exegesis (*haer.* 1.3.6, 8.1) whereas Tertullian omits Valentinian exegesis because it is incompatible with the literary genre he has chosen. Tertullian is more concise and clear, for a *narratio* must be short, clear and have some probability.[12]

Tertullian has direct knowledge of Valentinianism. He has read the *Syllogisms* of Alexander (*carn.* 15.3 and 17.1) and at least parts of the *Psalms* of Valentinus (*carn.* 17.1 and 20.3). It is unlikely that he had read the *Gospel of Truth*: he does not cite it whereas he does cite Marcion and Alexander; he must have known of its existence from Irenaeus; but perhaps he did not want to give publicity to it, or perhaps he took the title as a reference to the abstract truth of the gospel and not to a specific writing.

What does Tertullian tell beyond that which we may learn from Irenaeus? He tells of Valentinus' ambition, disappointment and rupture from the church (cf. *carn.* 1.3). He gives us new names of members of the school: Theotimus an exegete, Axionicus who stayed faithful to Valentinus and Alexander who wrote *Syllogisms*. We also learn (*Val.* 11.2) that the division of the eastern followers (Theodotos, Bardesanes and Mark) from the western followers (Ptolemy and Heracleon) occurred because of the account given of the procession or function of Christ and the holy spirit. The former were more faithful to Valentinus than the latter. The parallel which he draws with the Eleusinian mysteries is restricted to the point of secrecy. *Scorpiace* sets out the Valentinian attitude to martyrdom.

---

[11] As J. Daniélou claims for Tertullian's eschatology, *Latin Christianity*, 394.
[12] *Rhét. Hér.* 1.14. 'brevis, dilucida, veri similis'.

What Tertullian tells of the Valentinian incarnation (*carn.*) and resurrection (*res.*), coheres with what we learn from the *Gospel of Philip* and the *Epistle to Rheginos*.

Most important of all, we may note that Tertullian is again influenced by his opponents. The terms *demiurgus*, *substantivus*, *substantivalis* and *innascibilis* show Valentinian origin, while he uses μονογενής for Valentinian teaching and *unicus* and *unigenitus* for orthodox doctrines.[13] His account of the trinity used the terminologies of forms and persons, and *prolatio* for the movement from father to son. Even *trinitas* itself probably came from the Valentinians. The relation of *persona* and *substantia* (*Val.* 4.2, 7.3, 7, 5) is not found in Irenaeus or elsewhere in these three specific contexts.[14] Of course there is no mere transposition and the final form of the idea is different. This is evident in *adversus Praxean* 8.1 where he defends his use of the borrowed term.

(i) Story and satire

Tertullian follows the form of a *narratio*, a literary genre which can be appropriate to events which invite humour. Cicero[15] handles humour with care, so as to preserve dignity and gravity. The form follows similar demands of decorum.[16] *Narratio* in Tertullian looks to the place of the story in a discourse, the form of an actual narration, and to the procedure followed in discrediting it. This threefold character of *narratio* (*historia*, *fabula* and *argumentum*)[17] sets the limits and ensures Tertullian's originality and success. He treats the myth as a 'drame bourgeois' and provides not a parody, but 'une adaptation romancée' which is convincing and not a piece of buffoonery.[18] A *narratio* should possess brevity, lucidity and verisimilitude.[19]

Tertullian is more concise and precise than Irenaeus was in his

---

[13] See Braun, *Deus Christianorum*.
[14] *Ibid.*, 152f., 223f., 295f. See also Moingt, *Théologie trinitaire de Tertullien*, vol. II, 668f.
[15] *de oratore* 2.264, cf. J.-C. Fredouille (tr.), *Contre les Valentiniens*, SC, 280 (1980), 16.
[16] 'il suffit à la "narration" littéraire de prendre le ton de la comédie ou de la satire', Fredouille, *ibid.*, 17.
[17] *Rhét. Hér.* 1.12f., cf. Cic., *de invent.*, 1.27.
[18] Like the *Apocolocyntosis*.
[19] *Rhét. Hér.* 1.14.

attack on Valentinianism. He tells a better story with a sustained
and lively rhythm.[20] There was always some danger that his
criticism would not be taken seriously. However, he had earlier
argued against specific aspects of Valentinianism. In *de carne Christi*,
he attacked a docetic christology; in *de resurrectione mortuorum*, he
defended the resurrection of the flesh; in *de anima*, he refuted the
doctrine of three natures and the dualism of spirit and soul; in
scorpiace, he attacked Gnostic objections to martyrdom; and in
adversus Praxean, he rejected Gnostic aeons.

Valentinians have abandoned truth, he says, in order to indulge
their gift for telling stories; they lack a controlling discipline which
might give order to their doctrines or practices; and their solemn
secrecy underlines the guilt which lies behind their practice.
Tertullian compares their teachings with those of the Eleusinian
mysteries where secrecy is a cover for shame, the five-years period
of initiation and the subsequent vow of silence place beliefs beyond
scrutiny, the mystery of the sealed tongue signifies virility.

Freedom from logical control has enabled Valentinians to take
the rich variety of scripture, with its names, titles and teaching, and
concoct for their own pleasure figments which are as unreal as they
are foul. When confronted by sincere investigation, they make
three different responses, all of which avoid logical disputation.
They may knit their brow and state solemnly, 'The subject is
profound' (*Val.* 1.4). They may take advantage of the ambiguities of
their terminology and claim, 'But we agree with you.' When
someone who knows their teaching questions them, they affirm
their innocence through ignorance, claiming, by self-immolation,
'We know nothing.' (Their method is to persuade first and then
teach. The disciples of truth teach first in order to persuade.)

Common Christians are simple, Valentinians claim, not wise.
But a little simple wisdom is better than bad wisdom ('minus sapere
quam peius') (*Val.* 2.2). Christians are both doves and serpents;
indeed the dove is better than the serpent because the dove loves
the simplicity of high open places, the light and the east which is the
sunrise of Christ, whereas the snake wriggles into secret holes and
labyrinthine obscurities (*Val.* 3.1).

---

[20] Fredouille, *Contre les Valentiniens*, 23.

Truth is open and unashamed as it turns from many gods to one God (*Val.* 3.2). But to turn from many gods to another crowd of gods, to turn from what is clear and open to what is hidden is an offence to faith. When the whole new story is told, recollection of child-hood fairy-tales is followed by bewilderment at the many aeons, their marriages and their offspring, 'the fables and endless genealogies' of which the apostle (1 Tim. 1.4) spoke. Their composers are not simple but 'clever' in the bad sense, as they churn out stories, without clear defence or instruction. This is their cleverness, yet the simple have but to uncover their evil system to destroy them. For the 'simple' know it all and when they display the evil secrets the whole, elaborate construction falls to the ground.

Who, he asks, are the Valentinians (*Val.* 4)? They do not like their name because they have disowned their founder, without deserting his teaching. Valentinus, when he failed to be chosen as a bishop, set about to destroy the truth.[21] He picked up a clue from an ancient source and worked on it with subtlety. He described many aeons within God whereas Ptolemaeus put these aeons outside God. Others introduced their own variety (except for Axionicus of Antioch who stuck by Valentinus). Heresy, like a prostitute, wears a different dress each day, and so the Valentinians hail each novelty as a new revelation and trace each innovation to a spiritual gift. In the resulting chaos, despite their dishonesty, they admit their evident disagreement (*Val.* 4.4).

Tertullian therefore must go back to the original statements of the first teachers and not be content with peripheral extravagances (*Val.* 5.1). There are carefully written accounts of their teaching which come from their contemporaries: from Justin, Miltiades, Irenaeus (an exact investigator) and, closer to home, Proculus who combines dignity, chastity, old age and Christian eloquence.

Tertullian's complaint against the Valentinians is that they used words without logical control. For they gave no reasons for their procession of aeons (*Val.* 6.1; cf. Irenaeus, *haer.* 1.11) and anyone could make up a list of names which had no basis in reality and was backed by no kind of argument. Furthermore, there were strong

---

[21] On Valentinus himself, see the strong case for his orthodoxy presented by C. Markschies, *Valentinus Gnosticus?* (Tübingen, 1993).

arguments against the many aeons. As Irenaeus had pointed out, they depended on the fallacy of infinite regress, since each enthusiast added a few more ultimate aeons to show his higher knowledge. They denied the logical necessity for one ἀρχή, namely, that if there are two or more beginnings, there has to be another, more ultimate, first-principle to determine the relation between them.

The multiplication of hypostases was to prove, after Iamblichus, the pattern of later Platonism. Iamblichus and Proclus provided argument for the move, insisting on the need for imparticibles (ἀμέθεκτα). Their case has been supported by one recent writer with the claim that multiplication of intermediaries makes the first-principle both more transcendent and more accessible.[22] The logic is, however, suspect since it can be twice as hard to move A-X and X-B than to move A-B. Two relations have to be proved instead of one. I have called this 'the bureaucratic fallacy' and it explains why some later Platonists lapsed into silence. Who has not, in modern times, been reduced to helpless silence by an interminable bureaucracy?

In exegesis, the place of logic had been emphasized by Irenaeus and later by Clement. The chief pursuit of exegesis was the ἀκολουθία of scripture. Irenaeus compares Gnostic exegesis with the concoction of widely separate lines of Homer (*haer.* 1.9.4). Genuine lines of Homer are used to tell a story Homer never told.[23]

The Gnostic substitution of myth for dialectic was equally abhorrent to Clement of Alexandria, for whom dialectic was the highest way to truth. In the end, logic gave way to vision and participation; but it was not permissible to opt out of the logical process at the beginning rather than the end of the quest. Clement produced a handbook of logic which has historical significance in the development of Christian theology and European thought.

---

[22] A. C. Lloyd, The Later Neoplatonists, in A. H. Armstrong (ed.), *The Cambridge History of later Greek and Early Medieval Philosophy*, (Cambridge, 1967), 272–325 (282). This claim can certainly be defended by the need for psychological acclimatization. Awareness of transcendence begins near and ends afar.

[23] A similar concoction comes from the speaking statue of Alexandria. See G. Kaibel, *Epigrammata dedicatoria* (Berlin, 1878), 1,009; J. Daniélou, *Message évangélique et culture hellénistique* (Tournai, 1961), 82–4; R. L. Wilken, The homeric canto in Irenaeus 'Against Heresies', 1.9.4, *VC*, 21 (1967), 25–39; J. Mansfeld, *Heresiography in context* (Leiden, 1992), 157ff.

The failure of Gnosticism was in irrational method more than in false conclusions.

We may note, in passing, that any modern account of Gnosticism, Christian theology and philosophy must take account of three insecure dichotomies. The first concerns the dichotomy between speculation and argument. For idealists of the early twentieth century, philosophy was a matter of system and speculation, while for the analytic philosophy which has dominated recent thought, philosophy is a matter of argument. This argument may be dug out of writings which are not normally considered philosophical;[24] but it has to be argument. For logical analysts, Gnosis is theosophy not philosophy, whereas idealists find a system of thought in Gnosticism and put it alongside philosophy.[25] While following an analytic position, it remains possible to see the point which idealists were making, partly because some argument is usually found in speculative systems and partly because there is always some continuity across the most drastic philosophical change. Gnostics mixed philosophical and biblical terms to produce a speculative system.[26]

The question of definition is reflected in the approach to Gnosis in different parts of the world. In England, there has – with notable exceptions – been less enthusiasm because of the empirical and logical concerns of philosophy. In North America, there has been real enthusiasm because of a phenomenological approach, the heritage of nature mysticism from Thoreau and Emerson,[27] and the flight from authority.[28] In Germany, because of existentialism or idealism there has been interest in Gnosis as *Religionsphilosophie,*[29]

[24] As Bernard Williams has done with Homer. See his, *Shame and Necessity* (Berkeley, 1993).
[25] As does H.-J. Krämer, *Der Ursprung der Geistmetaphysik* (Amsterdam, 1964).
[26] See C. Markschies, Die Krise einer philosophischen Bibel-Theologie in der alten Kirche, oder: Valentin und die valentinianische Gnosis zwischen philosophischer Bibelinterpretation und mythologischer Häresie, in R. Berlinger und W. Schrader (eds.), *Gnosis und Philosophie: Miscellanea, Elementa,* 59 (Amsterdam, 1994), 227–49.
[27] I owe this point to a comment of Gilles Quispel.
[28] Jeffrey Stout, *The flight from authority* (Notre Dame, 1981), 2f.
[29] See Markschies, Die Krise, 237–9, where he rejects, with good reasons, the existentialism of Hans Jonas and goes on to present a modified Hegelian idealism. Jonas also finds a close affinity between Platonism and Gnosticism (Delimitation of the Gnostic Phenomenon, in U. Bianchi (ed.), *Le Origini dello Gnosticismo* (Leiden, 1970), 90–108), also Jonas, *Gnosis und spätantiker Geist* (Göttingen, 1964, 1966). Note also H. Strutwolf, *Gnosis als System* (Göttingen, 1993).

as a speculative extension of theology, in contrast to philosophical analysis or natural theology.[30]

The second dichotomy is between picture and argument, between aesthetic and logic and between myth and reasoning. In Plato's *Republic* there is a mass of close argument which is held together by powerful imagery or myth. While there is commonly no picture without argumentation and no argumentation without picture, there is a marked difference between myth with minimal argument and argument with minimal myth. When this distinction is overridden in a theological aesthetic,[31] the relation between Gnostics and theologians is hard to elucidate. Tertullian saw the difference and that is why he treats Gnosis as inaccessible to argument and vulnerable at the point where it believed itself to be secure.

The third dichotomy is historical. Gnostic writings include little argument; but Tertullian classes them with the philosophers who discuss endlessly the problem of evil and nature of man. Basilides is explicit in his argued objection to Christian faith on the grounds of Christian suffering. It is clear from Hippolytus that there was a connection between Gnosis and philosophy. Gnostic commentaries on Presocratic philosophers were important in the decades prior to Plotinus: we may 'make a picture' of their account of the beginning of things and of the ideas. Even at this sophisticated level, there is a speculative rather than a logical approach.[32] Finally there is the downward slide of later Platonism in the theurgy of Iamblichus and others, where thought is replaced by magic as the way to the gods.[33]

---

[30] This threefold distinction is useful. '1. Religionsphilosophie als spekulative Weiterführung einer Theologie ... 11. Religionsphilosophie als philosophische Analyse ... 111. Eine rationale oder natürliche Theologie, die sich nicht damit begnügt, wie die Typen 1 und 11 die gegebenen Religionen zu hinterfragen, sondern die darüber hinaus die Grundlinien einer philosophischen Gotteslehre entwirft.' H.-J. Krämer, Überlegungen zu einer Religionsanthropologie, *PhJ*, 102, 1 (1995), 156.

[31] As in H. U. von Balthasar, *Herrlichkeit*, vol. 11, 33–45.

[32] 'Die geradezu dogmatische Betonung der Drei-Prinzipien-Lehre musste der nächsten Generation die plotinische Prinzipienlehre als geistesverwandt erscheinen lassen.' L. Abramowski, Ein gnostischer Logostheologe, Umfang u. Redaktor des gnostischen Sonderguts in Hippolyts 'Widerlegung aller Haeresien', in *Drei christologische Untersuchungen*, 56.

[33] 'With that the whole basis of the Plotinian intellectual mysticism is rejected and the door stands open to all those superstitions of the lower culture which Plotinus had condemned in that noble apology for Hellenism, the treatise *Against the Gnostics*.' E. R. Dodds (tr.) in Proclus, *The elements of theology*, 2nd edn (Oxford, 1963), xx.

(ii) The duty of derision: 'risus officium est'

For those who are new to Tertullian, the chief surprise is that his humour is based on sound philosophical reasons and not on popular effect. He wishes to explain. To avoid confusion through so many strange names, which have been invented at will, Tertullian says he will use the original Greek names. He will show weakness rather than inflict wounds. Where there is something silly it will be proper to laugh. Truth has no fear and readily ridicules that which is empty of content. Gravity is out of place and decent mirth a duty (*Val.* 6.2f.).[34]

The whole account is punctuated by humour. The Valentinian myth turns the upper echelons of the universe into 'rooms to let' (*Val.* 7). The massive multiplication of names which show the grandeur of the system is like the achievement of the rhetorician Phosphorus, a very cool fellow, who celebrated his own valour. 'I come to you, O noble citizens, fresh from battle, where I gained victory for myself and happiness for you. I come, loaded with honour, covered with glory, fortune's favourite, the greatest of men, decked out in triumph.' His pupils shouted in admiration, 'Ah!' Similarly, let the followers of Ptolemy shout in wonder for the thirty aeons, 'Ah!' (*Val.* 8.3f.). But why stop at thirty? Surely the generating power and desire of the aeons are not finished? Another hundred or fifty should not be too much to expect. Surely aeons need the consolation of friends and companions?[35] After all, it is a multiplication of names without reality and there is no controlling reference to fact.

First, we shall examine Tertullian's jokes in the light of philosophy. A useful account concludes that the universal characteristic of humour is that it points to something inappropriate.[36]

---

[34] 'Congressionis lusionem deputa, lector, ante pugnam; ostendam, sed non imprimam vulnera. Si et ridebitur alicubi, materiis ipsis satisfiet. Multa sic digna sunt revinci, ne gravitate adonerentur. Vanitati proprie festivitas cedit. Congruit et veritati ridere, quia laetans de aemulis suis ludere (quia) secura est. Curandum plane, ne risus eius rideatur, si fuerit indignus; ceterum ubicumque dignus risus, officium est.'

[35] Irenaeus makes similar suggestions that he should ornament the emanations of the pleroma with pumpkins and cucumbers, and that the tears of Sophia should produce something different from her sweat.

[36] D. H. Monro, *Argument of laughter* (Melbourne, 1951). See especially 'The Inappropriate', 235–56. Humour has aesthetic value which means that its inappropriateness is, in some way, fitting. 'There exists an element of appropriateness in the inappropriate, when it is

While much that is inappropriate is not funny, all that is funny is inappropriate. The variety of incongruity is great and there are many useful theories proposed by Hobbes, Leacock, Bergson, Kant ('frustrated expectation'), Schopenhauer, Eastman ('collapse of a pattern'), Freud and others. The inappropriate element in humour smashes stereotypes, offers relief from monotony and opens up new possibilities of thought. It also destroys by satire, offers relief from restraint, unmasks pretence in favour of humaneness and may relish the misfortune of others. Tertullian presents almost every variety of humour in his examination of Valentinian doctrine.

(1) Humour explores new possibilities. Tertullian *enjoys* the intricacies of Valentinian doctrine, developing ironically all the details of the 'fountain of ulterior fecundity' (*Val.* 7.8). The implanting of spiritual seed in man and in the Saviour are elaborated (*Val.* 25–7). The details of the way in which two kinds of matter are derived from Achamoth are not neglected (*Val.* 15).

(2) Relief from monotony. Valentinian preaching is, oddly, a form of concealment, an illumination which obscures (*Val.* 1.1). Achamoth turns up surprises when she goes on to bear fruit with still greater results, producing three different natures (*Val.* 17).

(3) The first two kinds of humour usually imply incongruity in the linking of disparate elements. *Buthos* or depth is among the highest (*Val.* 7.3). Horos stands in the way of Sophia with the cry IAO or 'Out of the way, Quirites!' (*Val.* 14.3). The demiurge is ignorant but suspects the existence of a creator (*Val.* 21.2). Sophia should be able, like a hen, to produce offspring from her own energy (*Val.* 10.1). Tertullian is worn down by the 'cramming' of the Gnostic hierarchy (*Val.* 27.2) and the ignorance of the demiurge who has to learn from the Saviour how to succeed to his mother's place (*Val.* 28.1).

(4) This incongruity or disparity has a disruptive effect, mixes attitudes and changes universes. Heretics persuade before they instruct instead of instructing in order to persuade (*Val.* 1.4). Derision becomes a duty (*Val.* 6.3). The devil emerges as an exalted

funny. It is not merely a question of something intruding where it does not belong, but of something which plainly does belong, but is not allowed for by our pre-existing attitude' (255).

person which is just what should be expected among heretics (*Val.* 22). The demiurge moves into the apartment of his mother, a mother whom he has never seen (*Val.* 31.2).

(5) Satire, which is common in Tertullian, may be of two kinds: conservative or radical. In each, A is followed by a satirical comment B, and the satire may be directed against either A or B. Conservative satire implies that B is wrong and A is sound. Fifty years ago, an American teacher of English was asked what he did for a living and was alleged to have replied, 'Look, man, my bag is, I'm into teaching English.' Here the structure and practice of teaching English is unassailed; a particular way of describing it is shown to be absurd. Radical satire implies that A is wrong and B is sound. When Winston Churchill was rebuked for finishing a sentence with a preposition, he replied: 'This is the sort of pedantry up with which I will not put.' Here the comment B revealed the inappropriateness of the stultified syntax A against which it was directed. In some cases satire can work both ways. The Englishman may ridicule the foreigner who shoots a fox for sport; the critic of blood-sport will see inappropriateness in the preference of one form of animal butchery before another. Paul uses radical satire against the legalist Galatians; if circumcision is a necessary addition, let the trouble-makers go further and practise castration (Gal. 5.12). The satire 'rises naturally and inevitably from the humour'[37] from which it can only be distinguished in theory.

Conservative satire is found in Tertullian when the formation of the pleroma is followed by applause appropriate to the end of a play (*Val.* 13.2) or when the garden of paradise is set in heaven when everyone knows that trees have to be planted in the ground (*Val.* 20.3). Radical satire is more frequent. The storeys on storeys of the Gnostic deities are an indulgence in high-rise construction (*Val.* 7.1). The rhetorical self-indulgence of an orator, Phosphorus (*frigidissimus*), like the fantastic accumulation of aeons, excites satirical wonder with the cry 'Ah!' (*Val.* 8.4). The sight of the saviour, with his retinues and fasces, is enough for Achamoth to draw a veil upon her face (*Val.* 16.2). The fire in elements and

---

[37] *Ibid.*, 244.

bodies must have come from Sophia whose vexations were such as to make her hot and feverish (*Val.* 23.3).

(6) There is release from restraint in the capricious elements of the Gnostic system: only Nous knows the Father, while all the other aeons sadly pine in ignorance. When Sophia tries to gain this knowledge she is almost destroyed by her desire (*Val.* 9.4). However, when the whole pleroma gains unity of knowledge (or ignorance) and repose, all celebrate with the father their liberation, in the way we see sailors celebrating every day (*Val.* 12.2). No painter could depict anything more extravagant than the female Achamoth who is a picture of her father, the demiurge who is ignorant of his father and his mother, the angels who are replicas of their lords (*Val.* 19.2).

(7) Unmasking, again, may be conservative when it retains respect for convention and shows up one who denies it, or it may be radical, when it destroys convention. The pretence of the Gnostic solemn claim to great profundity is uncovered (*Val.* 1.4). The whole elaborate myth is reminiscent of fairy-tales and lullabies (*Val.* 3.3). The claim to revelation is shown to be a presumption and the claim to spiritual gifts is plainly a perversity (*Val.* 4.4). Celestial marriages are but an excuse for earthly sexual indulgence (*Val.* 30.3). At the end Tertullian asks whether his daring exposure of the myth has been rash and foolish. Should he have laughed at the Valentinian mystery? Will he make Achamoth go mad, Theletus burn with rage and Fortune be angry? Let it be so, and Tertullian will stand by his Maker in whose protection he trusts (*Val.* 32.5).

(8) From all humour, a wider human view may be gained,[38] in which the interplay of human poses, emotions and aims will become clear. The solemn myth is a set of outlandish names arranged at pleasure (*Val.* 6.1). Simplicity gains new value (*Val.* 2.4). The aeons have no order and control. Why should there be thirty and not one hundred and fifty of them? How in heaven can each aeon be born in two places (*Val.* 35.2)? The system of Secundus commends itself as being more human (*Val.* 38.1).

(9) The misfortunes of the aeons play a small part in Tertullian's account. Perhaps we might mention the tears and fever of Sophia.

---

[38] What Monro calls a 'god's eye' view.

But there is little 'custard-pie' comedy in Tertullian. He lacks the crudity of Irenaeus' discussion of Sophia's watery emissions.

We may conclude that Tertullian's humour covers a wide range of this genre and is used with remarkable persistence and acumen. He enjoys burrowing into the detail of the Gnostic myth. While he disowns it as a truth possibility, he applies his mind to every twist and turn. It is fun; but it is also philosophy 'throwing on a ravaged and distorted world those saving and unsparing Socratic search-lights – a touch of humour and a turn for irony'.[39] It is entirely predictable that Tertullian's most serious philosophical comment should come in humorous form. We all need critics to jolt us out of private reveries and self-indulgent fantasy.

(iii) Logic, coherence and aesthetic

The link between humour and argument is further illuminated by a comparison with Irenaeus, whose humour was rougher and more obvious.[40] For Irenaeus, coherence is the link between logic and aesthetic. There is one truth which depends on the truth of the gospel. In response to Gnostic theory which is *incredibile, fatuum, impossibile* and *inconstans* (*haer.* 2.10.4), Irenaeus sets out what is *credibile, acceptabile* and *constans*.[41] There is nothing *incomtum* or *intempestivum* with the son and nothing *incongruens* with the father (*haer.* 3.16.6–8). The coherence of truth springs from faith in one God ('Omnia enim ei constant et in unum Deum omnipotentem fides integra') (*haer.* 4.33.7). The daily exercise of sound reason, with zeal and love of truth, leads to truth (*haer.* 2.27.1). He who receives the truth finds the connections which hold together the whole biblical revelation. 'For Irenaeus the one thing that matters is the ability to see, not the differences, but the great connections.'[42]

The relation of logic to aesthetics is complex. Plato was dedicated to following the wind of logical argument wherever it led him and to a love of truth. Yet for all his logical stringency he used

---

[39] A. Boyce Gibson, *Should philosophers be kings?* (Melbourne, 1939), 43.
[40] In the physical world, all waters, including the hot and acrid, come from different parts of Sophia's heavenly body (*haer.* 1.4.4).
[41] N. Brox, *Offenbarung, Gnosis und gnostischer Mythos bei Irenäus von Lyon* (Salzburg and München), 202.
[42] *Ibid.*, 208.

myths and imagery of great power and beauty. He banished the
poets from his city because they were a bad influence and worked
in counterfeit; yet his own account of beauty has inspired many
across the centuries since he wrote. His message was a simple one.
Logic and aesthetic must not be confused and one must not be
abandoned to leave the other alone. The whole Greek heritage tells
a similar story. Philosophers wrestle with the problems of human
destiny, freedom and evil; yet what they have to say cannot replace
the truth conveyed by the great tragedies of Sophocles. Each genre
must be allowed to do its own work; neither is adequate by itself.
Within philosophy argument is prior; but there has to be something to hold the long strings of argumentation together and to
make a philosophic life possible. Aesthetic underlines and unites
what logic has established.

Plato left this dual heritage and when later Platonists abandoned reason for the occult, they were false to their tradition. The
Platonic underworld of the second century contained the Gnostics
who were the chief target of Tertullian and Irenaeus. They
abandoned discursive reason at the beginning of their deliber-
ations, rather than, like Plato, at the summit.[43] It could well be, as
a recent critic of theism has suggested, that religious belief might
be seen as a 'subjective passion'; but this claim can best be made
after nearly four hundred pages of argument.[44] The Gnostic
alternative bypasses dialectic. The powerful attraction of theosophy has waxed and waned. Platonism continued until the fifth
century with some allegiance to logic. Then, for a time, it gave
way to magic and silence. The transcendent One was declared by
physical silence, like a student expecting a first-class honour for a
blank paper.[45] Philosophical silence is much more complex than
physical silence.

Logic had needed a negative kind of aesthetic, which would
move the intellectually inert. The point of Tertullian's and
Irenaeus' use of humour is that their opponents were not vulner-

---

[43] For the characterization of this key distinction I am indebted to Iris Murdoch. See
especially, *The fire and the sun* (Oxford, 1977), 66.

[44] Richard Gale, *On the nature and existence of God* (Cambridge, 1991), 387.

[45] See R. Mortley, *From word to silence*, vol. II (Bonn, 1986), 253. Note also Mortley, 127, where
Damascius is unwisely commended for avoiding analogies when he speaks of κενεμβατεῖν
or 'putting one's foot in it when it is not there'.

able to reason. Argument was necessary for the wavering believer but quite irrelevant to the hard-line Gnostics who claimed to be at a deeper level.[46] Therefore humour was the only way to keep others from sloppiness and sentiment. Since their orientation was aesthetic, humour could challenge their position. It became the negative aesthetic which backed a positive logic.

(iv) Recapitulation as the great inversion

In Tertullian[47] there was also a positive aesthetic which, unlike Gnosticism, was joined to endless argument. Having attacked mechanical encrustations and shattered Gnostic formulae and stereotypes, it set in its place a world accessible to reason, imagination and faith, a world where all things were made new by the inversion of what had been there before. So the move from the comic inversions of phrase[48] to the cosmic inversion of recapitulation was a small one. God becomes man that man might become God. The credible is the inept. The *ineptum* is *aptum* because only an opposite can balance the beam. The place of imagination in theology joins that of reason. The connections for which Tertullian argued were available to imagination, that faculty which is able to understand what is there in terms of what is not there. For Paul as for other Christian theologians this kind of inversion is not peripheral; he knew one thing only, Christ and him crucified. The scandal and folly of the cross were the power and wisdom of God. This begins as the word-play which is important for Bergson in removing the mechanical encrustations on living. It inverts accepted standards which stifle and it brings a 'god's-eye' view. A mere protest against rigidity is not enough because the discarded code can be quickly replaced by another. Inversion is necessary.

To achieve a 'god's-eye' view, we need to see new links, delight in what is new and discover hidden proprieties. All these are as

---

[46] Some Gnostics did argue on particular issues, despite their general rejection of reason. There are some exceptions to every rule in the history of ideas. See discussion of the three dichotomies, above p. 198.

[47] See above, ch. 3.

[48] On arrival in England during a freezing January, an Australian schoolboy pronounced, 'O to be in April, now that England's here!'

much a part of humour as they are of theology for Tertullian. We
see new links: 'Our laughter expresses, often enough, the simple joy
of exploration. It pleases us to find, or to play at finding, these
unexpected links between apparent disparates.'[49] This imaginative
exploration is central to Christian theology which is about the
death and resurrection of Christ who by dying destroyed death,
about Adam, Christ and a new creation. Belief in one God (Rom.
4) implies the justification of the ungodly, the resurrection of the
dead and creation out of nothing, for God can need no second
thing to do his work.

Recapitulation, indeed all theology, is about finding new links.
Paul defined a Christian attitude to Jewish law. Two objections are
levelled by Jews against Justin's Christians: those who do not keep
the whole law are accursed and he who dies on a cross is accursed
(*dial.* 10). The same objections are found in Paul (Gal. 3.10–14) and
were the reason why, as a Jew, he spent himself in the liquidation of
Christians. Then, on the Damascus Road, the link between these
two curses overwhelmed him; the curse of the cross had been
accepted on his behalf by Christ who died for those who had not
kept the whole law. In persecuting Christians he was attacking the
Christ who had died for him; so it became his one concern to join
Christ on the cross. The crucial link between the two ideas changed
Paul's world.

The delight in the new and the rejection of the tedious are parts
of humour and of theology; Clement of Alexandria described
Christian life as a perpetual springtime and Christ as the one who
had turned sunsets into sunrises. However, 'Humour upsets the
pattern by abruptly introducing something inappropriate. But it
must not be wholly inappropriate. There must be some hidden
propriety as well.'[50] The impropriety of Tertullian's satire points to
the propriety of rejecting Gnostic pretensions and irrationality in
favour of the folly which is, for him as for Paul and Irenaeus, the
wisdom of God.

We may conclude that the initial thrust of Tertullian's logic
against Gnostic irrationalism is supported in two ways by aesthetics, one negative and the other positive. Humour shows where the

---

[49] Monro, *Argument of laughter*, 133.   [50] *Ibid.*, 241f.

Gnostic myth is inappropriate. Recapitulation shows how the gospel has the last laugh through the divine comedy of all things in Christ. This is the alternative vision which Tertullian offers.[51]

---

[51] Tertullian does not offer a competitive gnosis like that proposed by Clement of Alexandria; he simply sees that his arguments are insufficient without a vision of the cosmic Christ.

CHAPTER 10

Promise of laughter, judgement of hell: apocalypse and system

A. MONTANISM

The New Prophecy emerged in Asia Minor in 157 or perhaps as late as 172. Our chief accounts of the movement derive from fourth-century sources (Eusebius and Epiphanius) which are marked by later orthodoxy. Earlier in the second century, Papias (130) preached a colourful chiliasm and Christian Asia Minor was strong in prophetic tradition and practice. According to Eusebius, Montanus was only a recent convert, when, in a village of Phrygian Mysia, he was seized with ecstasy and prophesied strange things which were not consistent with the tradition of the church.[1] Some rejected him as a false prophet, but others were aroused and turned from the true faith. Two prophetesses joined him in enthusiastic frenzy and their influence spread, until, says Eusebius, their sayings were examined and they were expelled from the church.[2]

According to a source in Epiphanius, the Montanists accepted what became the two testaments of the Christian bible, a trinitarian faith and the new prophecies of Montanus, Priscilla and Maximilla, with the requirement that others must exhibit the same spiritual gifts (*Pan.* 48.1.4). Yet Maximilla claimed inconsistently that after her there would be no more prophecy and that the end would come (*Pan.* 48.2.4). The oracles attributed to Montanus (*Pan.* 48.4, 10, 11) professed the passivity of a lyre under a divine plectrum, claimed to be God almighty in human form and pointed

---

[1] Eusebius, *H.E.* 5.16.7.   [2] *Ibid.*, 5.16.10.

to new heights of spiritual excellence when even the little ones would shine brighter than the moon.

Maximilla declared herself to be word, spirit, power and not a wolf who destroyed the flock.[3] To hear her was to hear Christ (*Pan.* 48.12.4). Her threefold office of partisan, revealer and interpreter is exercised over toil, covenant and promise (*Pan.* 48.13.1). She had power over others whether they willed it or not (*Pan.* 48.13.7). Priscilla stressed the need for purity and holiness which led to visions, saving oracles and open secrets (*cast.* 10.5). Either Quintilla or Priscilla claimed to have slept with Christ who told them that Pepuza was the site for the heavenly Jerusalem (*Pan.* 49.1).

In Tertullian, the influence of the New Prophecy confirmed the ascetic views which he held on martyrdom, marriage, fasting and forgiveness of sins. The highest calling is to martyrdom which, because it is a death in Christ and not in Adam, opens the gate of paradise (*an.* 55.5).[4] The paraclete calls to martyrdom (*fug.* 9.4), denounces those who flee (*fug.* 11.3). and leads along the narrow way to suffering, not to flight. It is not possible for him who fears suffering to belong to the lord who suffered; whereas he who does not fear suffering will be perfected in love, even the perfect love of God. Therefore the paraclete encourages all who endure, helping them in their suffering and speaking for them when they are interrogated (*fug.* 14.3).

The nearness of the end, Paul tells Tertullian, makes marriage inappropriate. While heretics rigidly abstain from marriage and unspiritual believers or 'psychics' marry without restraint, neither the compulsory continence of the former nor the indulgence of the latter is acceptable to God. For the spiritual believer, either continence freely chosen or single marriage is acceptable to God. One marriage is suitable to the followers of one God. Psychics do not receive the spirit or the things of the spirit, but choose the things of the flesh. There can be no compromise between flesh and spirit, for the flesh lusts against the spirit and the spirit fights against the flesh (*mon.* 1.1–6).

Psychics[5] claim that single marriage is an heretical innovation.

---

[3] *Ibid.*, 5.16.17.
[4] Perpetua saw only martyrs in paradise.
[5] 'Psychici' are mediocre Christians who are not yet spiritual.

Has not the paraclete inaugurated a new and excessively harsh discipline? These objections are answered, by Tertullian, from the lord's promise of the holy spirit who would lead into fullness of truth. When new truth is revealed, it may appear onerous and difficult; but the continuity of the paraclete with the gospel is evident because there is no change in the rule of faith. Heretics always first corrupt the rule of faith and only then pervert the practice of discipline. Since there is no such corruption of doctrine, the new discipline stands as authentic (*mon.* 2.1–3). The paraclete testifies to Christ and to God the creator in accordance with the rule of faith and then goes on to reveal the new discipline which may be onerous, but is certainly authentic (*mon.* 2.4).

Indeed, the paraclete might have now demanded virginity or complete continence, not even allowing one marriage to cool down the fire of the flesh. Such a demand need not be considered an innovation, since the lord, himself a eunuch, opened the kingdom of heaven to eunuchs (Matt. 19.12), and the apostle Paul, *ipse castratus*, preferred continence (1 Cor. 7.7); from such anticipations, the spirit leads on to the time of celibacy. He calls us away from marriage because the time has been shortened (1 Cor 7.29) and it is even shorter now, one hundred and sixty years later. The apostles had predicted this discipline and holiness. The paraclete foretold it before he defined it and held it back until the time came for it to be pronounced. The paraclete, as comforter, has moderated his demands to single marriage out of consideration for human weakness (*mon.* 3.1, 10, 11, 12).

Scripture shows that the discipline of monogamy is no strange novelty; grounded in antiquity, it is now restored as the special possession of Christians (*mon.* 4.1). As ever, the economy of salvation is central to the argument. From Moses to Christ, divorce had been permissible because of the hardness of human hearts. As the new law of Christ removed divorce, so the New Prophecy of the paraclete took away second marriage. The weakness of the flesh can now be overcome, through the presence of the paraclete (*mon.* 14.4–7). There is nothing harsh and nothing heretical in making second marriage equivalent to adultery. Those who indulge the flesh and its weakness wrongly claim that it is heretical and harsh.

Singleness of marriage is matched by frequent fasting, while both marriage and eating food are preserved. The paraclete teaches that we should fast frequently but not marry frequently. His followers extend their fast days into the evening, abstain from flesh, fruit, juice and wine, and in further concern for dryness keep away from the bath (*iei.* 1). The fasting of the New Prophecy finds a parallel in the precepts of some bishops; so there can be no objection to fasting and dry food, when practised for the paraclete (*iei.* 13). There is no common ground between heretics like Marcion and the paraclete; for Marcion teaches perpetual abstinence in hostility to the creator, while the Montanists eat dry food during only two weeks of each year and return to eating normal food when this time is over (*iei.* 15).

Further, the New Prophecy denies the forgiveness of sins to certain offenders. The church is able to forgive all sins but does not do this lest such indulgence should encourage further sin. The paraclete does not forgive fornicators because of the harm such forgiveness will bring on most believers. The right to forgive sins belongs to the church under God; 'but it is the church of the spirit, by means of a spiritual man, not the church which is a number of bishops'.[6] The decision to forgive belongs to God, not to the priest, to the master and not to the servant (*pud.* 21.17).

Tertullian's relation to New Prophecy and the catholic church raises historical questions which cannot be settled without remainder.[7] He had shown ascetic tendencies in his earliest writings but these tendencies were not strengthened by the New Prophecy before 207. Probably Tertullian had no personal contact with Montanists from Asia Minor or from Rome and when he encountered their ideas in Carthage they were already modified by their African setting.

As we have seen reason to doubt Tertullian's supposed 'schism' under the 'New Prophecy', much more should we doubt his supposed break from the Montanists to form his own sect.[8] From the beginning, he had stressed the transcendent spiritual nature of

---

[6] 'sed ecclesia spiritus per spiritalem hominem, non ecclesia numerus episcoporum'.
[7] R. Braun, Tertullien et le Montanisme: Église institutionelle et église spirituelle, *RSLR*, 21 (1985), 245–57.
[8] Augustine, *de haer.* 86. See Barnes, *Tertullian* (1971 and 1985), 258f.

the church (*bapt.* 6.2, *corpus trium*; *ap.* 39.1, *corpus sumus*; *pud.* 21.16, *ecclesia spiritus*). This conviction was strengthened rather than instigated by the New Prophecy, for the continuity and coherence of Tertullian's thought on this point are evident.[9]

New Prophecy was an extension of Tertullian's initial theme of the divine economy. Beyond the rule of faith which is perfect and complete and which declares one God and the saving work of Christ, there is scope for novelty, because the grace of God continues to advance until the very end. The devil is hard at work and the paraclete must also work. The holy spirit leads into all that truth which human mediocrity could not grasp at once (*virg.* 1.5–7). As in creation wheat and fruit grow to maturity, so the righteousness of God has passed from nature to law to prophets, to the youthful vigour of the gospel and then to the maturity of the paraclete who continues to speak what Christ commands (*virg.* 1.9–11).

The economy does not merely advance but also corrects what has gone before. The end and the beginning belong to the same God. Marriage, which was first commended (Gen. 1.28), is now forbidden (1 Cor. 7.29). This does not mean that because the tree of marriage is cut down, marriage is an evil thing (*Marc.* 1.29.5), but rather that the time has come, when, for the sake of holiness, it should be surpassed. In a similar way, the earthly Jerusalem will be replaced by Jerusalem on high, wherein the saints will live for a thousand years (*Marc.* 3.24.6).

Marriage and holiness do not go together, while sexual abstinence develops a taste for spiritual things. Among these things, prayer leads on to holiness, which is preserved by abstinence from a second marriage (*cast.* 10). The peak of holiness is found in prophetic ecstasy, which Peter, not knowing what he said, experienced on the mount of transfiguration (Luke 9.33). The New Prophecy offers the gift of ecstasy which is above reason and mind (*Marc.* 4.22.5). In such ecstasy, it is possible to talk with angels and with the lord and to see and hear secret things. For one sister, this ecstasy has occurred in the spirit in the church during the Sunday service (*an.* 9.4); it is not a schismatic phenomenon.

---

[9] On this question, see earlier discussion in ch. 8.

B. APOCALYPTIC EXUBERANCE

Tertullian was indeed a theologian of hope.[10] He was safe because he was not ashamed of the incarnate God who was the *unica spes* of every believer; his *apologeticum* culminates in the claim that, while an earthly judge condemns, at the same time a heavenly judge reverses the verdict. From these two elements – incarnation and final judgement – springs the rich, extended and severe account which he gives of the last things. It is important not to become lost in detail which derives from the denseness of the Apocalypse, Paul, Gospel sayings of Jesus and other parts of scripture, but to see the overruling optimism of one who believed in a good God who had created a good world and who was already restoring it to its first promise.

The chief objection to faith, for Tertullian as for other Christians of his time, came from the fact of martyrdom. How could a sovereign, good creator reward his faithful worshippers with a cruel death? Tertullian's rule of faith, from his early (*praescr.* 13.1–6) to his late works (*virg.* 1.3; *Prax.* 2.1), preserves a stress on God's final judgement when all would be set right.

Tertullian's anthropology for all its complexity[11] is consistently twofold: soul and body, flesh and spirit, flesh and soul, spirit and body. Patience is a matter for soul and body (*pat.* 13.1–3) and saves both flesh and spirit (*pat.* 13.6, cf. 14.3 and 16.2). For martyrs, prison means incarceration of body, but freedom of soul (*mart.* 2.6). The two substances, body and soul (*ap.* 22.5), of man must be distinguished (*res.* 35.5).[12] Yet the two substances are not separable,[13] and are generated simultaneously (*an.* 37.1). Only death breaks this unity (*Marc.* 5.9.3) and souls exist separately, waiting for incorporation in resurrected bodies. The soul of Samuel was in this intermediate state when consulted by Saul (*an.* 57).

In the *apologeticum*, Tertullian regards the soul as incorporeal and in need of a resurrection body to receive rewards or suffer

---

[10] A detailed analysis of Tertullian's eschatology is to be found in A. Fernandez, *La escatología en el siglo II* (Burgos, 1979), 307–98.

[11] 'verdaderamente sinuosa', *ibid.*, 310.

[12] 'animae corpus opponitur ... distinguitur corpus ab anima'.

[13] 'las ingeniosas oscuridades del africano!' Fernandez, *La escatología*, 316. Rather, for the Stoic Tertullian, everything had two *substrata*.

punishment (*ap.* 48.4). A similar view is found elsewhere (*test.* 4.1 and *Marc.* 4.34.12f.). However, in *de anima* (7.1–4) the need for a physical soul is argued. This change in opinion enables the soul to suffer immediately after death and not merely to suffer through the physical corruption of the body in the fires of hell; but it does confuse the position of Tertullian and indicates the lack of a clear, consistent psychology in early Christian thought.[14] There is a constant affirmation of the immortality of the soul (*res.* 34.5f., 35.2), whether it is material or not. Souls repose in the bosom of Abraham (*ap.* 47.13 et passim) and do not transmigrate as Pythagoras had claimed (*test.* 4.2). The constant theme behind multitudinous detail is that man is a unity of body and soul, which is dissolved at death and joined again in glorified flesh at the final resurrection.

The second advent of Christ is pivotal in Tertullian's eschatology, but the four main elements (return of Christ in glory, resurrection of the body, universal judgement and a renewed earth) are not discussed in every place. The second coming belongs to the rule of faith (*praescr.* 13.15) and the distinction between the two comings is clear in the prophetic writings (*Jud.* 14.1–10). No earthly spectacle can compete against the coming of the lord with his angels and the reign of the righteous (*spect.* 30.1–7). The survival of the Roman empire delays the end which will follow upon its collapse (*Scap.* 2.6; cf. Irenaeus, *haer.* 5.26). To describe the resurrection of the flesh, Tertullian has used many new terms.[15] He does not distinguish between 'resurrection of the flesh' and 'resurrection of the dead' but has a mass of brilliant images: to rebuild and reconstitute the tabernacle of the flesh ('reaedificare et restituere tabernaculum carnis') (*res.* 11.3), to summon the flesh to appear ('evocare carnem') (*res.* 11.9), to put breath in bones ('dare spiritum in ossibus') (*res.* 29.7, 15), fruit-bearing flesh ('fructificatura caro') (*res.* 52.10) and many others. For in the words of Isaiah, '"Your heart shall rejoice and your bones shall spring up like grass", because grass also is renewed by dissolution and the

---

[14] *Ibid.*, 332.
[15] *Ibid.*, 350f.: according to P. Puente Santidrián, La terminología de la resurreción en Tertuliano, dissertation (Valladolid, 1978), 88, new terms, of which the most frequent are *suscitare, resuscitare, vivificare, restituere* and *restitutio*.

corruption of its seed' (*res.* 31.4). While Tertullian acknowledges that it is easier to believe in one God than to believe in the resurrection of the flesh (*res.* 2.8), he frequently attacks the alternative account of transmigration of souls into other bodies (e.g. *nat.* 1.19.4). 'But how much more acceptable is our belief which claims that they (souls) will return into the same bodies! And how much more futile is your tradition that the human spirit will dwell in the flesh of a dog or a mule or a peacock!'

Aware of Paul's question (1 Cor. 15.35) 'How will the dead rise? With what body will they come?' (*Marc.* 5.10.2), Tertullian replies that they will blossom like the phoenix bird and conquer death and ashes (*res.* 13.3). As Ezekiel saw, the spirit will enter their bones anew (*res.* 12.10). Behind this belief lies Tertullian's persistent Heraclitean optimism that nothing perishes except in order to be saved ('nihil deperit nisi in salutem') (*res.* 12.6). Nothing is impossible with God the creator for whom it is easier to remake than it was first to make a world from nothing (*res.* 12.10).[16] There are ascetic consequences! Fasting is a good thing because a slender body will slip through the narrow gate and lighter flesh will rise more quickly (*iei.* 17.7).

There is a clear distinction between the judgement of each soul after death and the final universal judgement which will follow the resurrection of all bodies (*res.* 17.9). Judgement is the reason for resurrection (*res.* 50.2) since our present bodies cannot inherit the kingdom of heaven. The final judgement is linked to the parousia of the 'son of man coming as judge on the clouds of heaven' (*Marc.* 4.10.12f.; cf. *virg.* 1.3; *Prax.* 2.14; *praescr.* 13.5). When God judges, there can be no conflict between God's goodness and his justice (*Marc.* 2.11.3f.). God is always father and always judge (*Herm.* 3.3). Christ is 'equal to all, universal king, judge, lord and God' ('omnibus aequalis, omnibus rex, omnibus judex, omnibus dominus et deus') (*Jud.* 7.9).

The spectacular millenarianism of Irenaeus finds but one, albeit extended, reference in Tertullian's writings (*Marc.* 3.24.3–6). A kingdom is promised on earth, a city let down from heaven (Rev. 21.2–10). Such a city, foretold by Ezekiel (48.30–5) and John (Rev.

---

[16] Justin used the same kind of argument to justify belief in resurrection, comparing a drop of human seed to the fully formed human body.

21.10–26) has been announced by the New Prophecy and was observed in Judaea each morning during a period of forty days. This city has been provided by God for his risen saints in order to refresh them with all spiritual blessings and to compensate them for all that they have not enjoyed in this world, 'because it is both just and worthy of God that his servants should have their joy in the same place where they suffered affliction for his name's sake'. Within the thousand years, the saints will rise sooner or later according to their deserts (*Marc.* 3.24.6),[17] then the world will be destroyed in conflagration, all shall be changed into incorruptible, angelic substances and translated into the kingdom of heaven. The purpose of the millennium is to provide the reward of joy in the presence of God.

Eternal life in heaven means entry and participation in the kingdom of God (*res.* 32.6 et passim), winning the crown (*mart.* 3.3; *cor.* 14f.), achieving victory (*ap.* 50.2) and gaining the reward (*res.* 40.9). For the martyrs, joys far outweigh former sufferings (*Scap.* 1.1; *scorp.* 6.4f. and 13.8), consolation and laughter are promised ('risus promittitur', *pat.* 11.7) and heaven brings the vision of God who is our father (*Prax.* 23.4) and meeting with Christ, which is the unrestrained desire of all Christians. While to know Christ in the spirit is life eternal (*cast.* 10.5), Tertullian normally understands it as the final state reached after death (*paen.* 6.6). Christians die gladly in the hope of this (*ap.* 8.4) which is their final triumph, their attaining to God and their eternal reward (*ap.* 50.2 and 18.2f.). Their lord will return to receive them into life eternal (*praescr.* 13.4).

There are no degrees of fullness in this future life which is granted to all believers (*mon.* 10.6). Yet, as we have noted, there are differences in the order of resurrection, early or late, into the millennial delight of the saints (*Marc.* 3.24.6). Those who have striven harder will receive greater rewards ('sed maiora certamina maiora sequuntur praemia') (*Scap.* 4.8). There will be different levels of accommodation. The many mansions in the father's house correspond to the many degrees of merit gained in toils, suffering, tortures and death (*scorp.* 6.7f.). The wonder of an angelic crown

---

[17] This is an attractive idea. Early risers will enjoy the freshness of the first hundred years. Others will emerge about the year 200; but many should not be expected before 950.

awaits the martyrs (*mart.* 3.3). Despite all differences, heaven means the communion of saints. Those, who are united with one God, will be together, however varied their mansions and their rewards; more than one spouse will be an embarrassment for those who have remarried and for the God who has joined them together (*mon.* 10.5). Paradise is a real place (*locus*) of heavenly joys (*divinae amoenitatis*) for all the saints (*ap.* 47.12). The bosom of Abraham is also a definite place, not in heaven, but higher than hell, a place of rest for the righteous souls until the final consummation (*Marc.* 4.34.12f.).

Tertullian seems even surer of hell than he is of heaven and writes with passion of the punishment of persecutors and of those who have denied the true faith. His ground is optimism. Unless God is an avenging God who will set right and balance the evils of this present age, he cannot be truly God – omnipotent, just and good. The hardest evidence against a good God is the present persecution of his righteous people. Tertullian repeats terrifying descriptions of what he calls 'gehenna', 'eternal torture', 'endless sorrow', 'inextinguishable fire', 'punishment of eternal death', suffering 'in the house of the devil', 'death', 'bondage' and 'eternal condemnation'.[18] Here all evil is consumed. Tertullian invents nothing, but draws on the whole range of biblical imagery, because of an optimism that can only believe good of a God who, for the present, allows so much evil to prevail in his world.

In the splendour and horror of the final judgement (*spect.* 30.1–7), it is easy for his readers to miss the essence of hell, which is an absence of God and a rejection by Christ (*scorp.* 9.8–13, 10.4–6; *fug.* 7.1 et passim). This is death or 'second death'. With it there is physical pain. Christ comes 'to punish the wicked with eternal fire' (*praescr.* 13.1). To the nature and persistence of this punishment, Tertullian continually returns. Hell has no end: eternal torture (*cast.* 2.3), eternal fire (*nat.* 1.19.6) and perpetual condemnation (*paen.* 12.2f.) continue in fulfilment of the words of Jesus (*ap.* 18.3).

How does Tertullian solve the tension between the perfect saving work of Christ (*idol.* 5.2) or the ultimate divine mercy (*Marc.*

---

[18] Fernandez, *La escatología*, 382.

3.24.1) on the one hand and the judgement of God (*Marc.* 2.11.3–6) on the other? Impenitent sinners are lost eternally (*paen.* 6.5). Penitence is necessary for salvation (*pat.* 12), to escape ultimate rejection (*paen.* 5.11). Yet at the same time, God seeks the lost sheep and welcomes the lost and penitent son with a love beyond all other fathers ('tam pater nemo, tam pius nemo') (*paen.* 8.7f.). Tertullian makes, we have seen, a clear distinction between those sins which may be forgiven and those which may not: idolatry, fornication and murder. 'Sins we divide between two outcomes. Some may be remitted and others may not. Consequently it is plain to all that some deserve castigation, some condemnation. Every sin is discharged either by pardon or by punishment: by pardon as the result of castigation or by penalty as the result of condemnation' (*pud.* 2.12f.).[19]

Once again, Tertullian chooses disjunction. Salvation or damnation, heaven or hell, are final choices, final verdicts and final destinations (*ap.* 11.11, 47.12f.; *test.* 4.1). There is no third option: one confesses or denies Christ, one saves one's life or loses it for Christ (*scorp.* 11.2). The alternatives are terrible, for hell is a real place in which one suffers separation from God and physical pain, a subterranean prison of mysterious fire (*ap.* 47.12). More optimistically, Tertullian gives an extended account of purgatory, where the soul anticipates the punishment or consolation which is to come (*an.* 58). Only martyrs go direct to God. For the others, purification is possible and prayer can be effective (*or.* 29.2) and the anniversary of a death is an appropriate time for the offering of sacrifices (*mon.* 10.4; *spect.* 12.2).

It should here be evident why Tertullian has so few friends. His New Prophecy and millenarianism, like his apologetic theme of the balance of justice, all spring from a confidence in the goodness of God and commend that goodness to his readers. Yet the pain and cruelty of persecution drove him to extremes of melancholy optimism, which may be justified from scripture but not by the subsequent history of Christian thought and practice.

---

[19] 'haec dividimus in duos exitus. Alia erunt remissibilia, alia inremissibilia. Secundum quod nemini dubium est alia castigationem mereri, alia damnationem. Omne delictum aut venia dispungit aut poena, venia ex castigatione, poena ex damnatione'.

C. APOCALYPTIC SYSTEM

The exuberance of Tertullian's eschatology is a response to objections of psychics, heretics and philosophers. In rebutting the catholic objections to New Prophecy, Platonic and Marcionite objections to creation and resurrection and docetic objections to incarnation, he sets out a detailed account of soul, death and resurrection, judgement, heaven, hell and millennial bliss. Apocalyptic vision is the last place for the modern reader to expect systematic thought. Yet it is precisely in this area of Tertullian's thought that a distinguished theologian found what he calls 'Tertullian's System'.[20] Tertullian, it is claimed, 'is astonishingly original and personal' yet displays the qualities which are to mark Latin Christianity: a respect for matter, concern for the inner life of the soul and pessimism in the battle against sin. His individual genius showed less in 'its cultural or linguistic contribution than in a certain intellectual quality'.[21] These comments are important because they, in turn, came from an imaginative and penetrating mind and because they challenge the common disjunction between apocalyptic and systematic thought. Since the purpose of the study of other thinkers is the overcoming of conceptual parochialism, it is here that we are likely to learn something fresh. Tertullian's system moves through six consecutive parts: trinity, creation, soul, incarnation, intermediate state and resurrection.

His account of the trinity, as we have seen, finds plurality in the inner organization of one divine substance and also in a plurality of existents which depend upon the will of the father. The divine wisdom is found in three states: first in undifferentiated unity with God, secondly as constituted within God with a view to the work of creation, and thirdly as articulated and proceeding from God.[22]

The creation of the world is described in Tertullian's criticism of Hermogenes' uncreated matter,[23] and his literal exegesis of Gen. 1.1f., where he defines the attributes of God (*Herm.* 4.1) and the inferior status of matter (*Herm.* 7.3).

---

[20] Daniélou, *Latin Christianity*, 361–404. [21] *Ibid.*, 341.

[22] *Ibid.*, 364f. Daniélou owes this account to A. Orbe, Elementos de teología trinitaria en el Adversus Hermogenem, cc. 17–18, *Greg.*, 39 (1958), 706–47. He notes the objections of Moingt to Orbe's account.

[23] This was a distinctive element of Middle Platonism. See J. H. Waszink, Observations on Tertullian's treatise against Hermogenes, *VC*, 9 (1955), 129–41.

The soul comes from the breath (*flatus*) of God, having its own level (*gradus*), above matter but below God who is spirit (*spiritus*). It is 'immortal, corporeal, having shape, simple in substance, susceptible of its proper functions, developing in different ways, having freedom of choice, affected by external events, changeable in its faculties, rational, dominant, capable of presentiment' (*an.* 22.2). Tertullian's profoundly original account of the soul was to have great influence on subsequent Latin theology, especially that of Augustine who longed only to know God and the soul: 'Nothing more? Nothing whatever' (*sol.* 1.27). After Tertullian, the human person and its inner life will have a place in systematic theology.[24]

Against Marcionites and Valentinians, Tertullian defends the flesh of Christ. Here Alpha is joined to Omega, the beginning to the end.[25] The Virgin Birth or 'new nativity' ensures that 'the flesh born of the old seed is taken up without the old seed in order to be remade by a new, spiritual seed, free from old stains' (*carn.* 17.3).

The intermediate state between death and resurrection derives importance from the fact that perfection is reached in the renewing of the body, and not, as Gnostics thought, in escaping from it. After death, souls live in the lower regions (*inferi*) under the earth. Sinners are in prison, the righteous are in Abraham's bosom, where they find comfort (*solatium*), rest (*requies*) and refreshment (*refrigerium*), but (except for the martyrs) are not yet in heaven. Tertullian takes general ideas from apocalyptic and defines them to express his own views, in a coherent way.[26] His location of the intermediate state, beneath the earth, was not adopted by those who came after him; but his account of *requies* and *refrigerium* passed into the common thought of Christendom.

The resurrection of the dead is Tertullian's final theme. In his treatise on this subject, he uses earlier terminology with greater clarity and confidence.[27] Against Marcionites, he concentrates on Pauline theology and identifies God's goodness with his justice.

---

[24] Daniélou finds affinity at several points between Tertullian and Pascal.

[25] See above, ch. 3.

[26] 'In other words, he takes a mythical theology and changes it into a rational theology.' Daniélou, *Latin Christianity*, 394.

[27] 'It is this which gives the treatise its exceptional character, making it, in my own view, not only his masterpiece, but that of his works which has the most astonishing relevance for today.' Daniélou, *Latin Christianity*, 395. Daniélou draws heavily on P. Siniscalco, *Ricerche sul 'De resurrectione' di Tertulliano* (Rome, 1966).

Against Gnostics (as exemplified in the *Epistle to Rheginos*), he points to a future resurrection of the body rather than a present spiritual conversion. The 'flesh' in this work means 'natural physical body'. He begins from creation and the claim that God who made the body will find it easier to remake it (*res.* 11.10). Making and remaking are part of the cycle of the world which turns from day to night, light to darkness, life to death and then returns to light and life (*res.* 14.2). Creation guarantees the goodness of the flesh, which God will not reject. Rather God makes flesh the hinge on which salvation turns ('caro salutis est cardo') (*res.* 8.2).

God shaped the flesh with his own hands, in his own image, breathing life into it, making it supreme over the rest of creation and making it his own possession. He could never reject what is the sister of Christ (*res.* 9.2). Body and soul cannot be divided and 'whatever goes on in the heart is the activity of the soul in the flesh, with the flesh and through the flesh' (*res.* 15.3). Therefore both body and soul must face judgement. From these three arguments for the resurrection of the body (God's creative power, the dignity of the flesh as sister of Christ and the unity of soul and flesh), Tertullian returns to scripture. Does scripture justify this belief or should resurrection texts be given a Gnostic spiritual sense only? Against the Gnostic spiritual and the Jewish literal interpretation, Tertullian argues that some prophecies are to be taken allegorically and others are to be taken literally. His exegesis of Paul follows the same principle, which gives him a freedom which his critics would deny. The flesh and blood which cannot inherit the kingdom of God are not the physical body but man's evil works (*res.* 49.11).

Tertullian shows originality in this coherent account, following the tradition of Asia Minor rather than the Greek Apologists, drawing on scripture and philosophy, but defining everything in his own way. While his conclusions sound strange in a secular world, they indicate the working of an original mind, which met the objections of different groups with more coherence than apologetic can usually maintain.

Two problems remain to be noted: the vividness of Tertullian's imagery which is never remote from reality and the severity of a loving God toward sin. The vivid imagery can be defended, for there is no other way of describing unearthly realities;[28] however, Tertullian's language is too readily linked to earthly reality, because he cannot abandon the creator. The severity of divine judgement is intensified in Tertullian for two reasons. First, because the greatest barrier to belief in an omnipotent, good God is the suffering of innocent people, especially, for Tertullian, the horror of martyrdom. If God be God, he must reward and punish in a way that will presume to wipe out this wrong. Secondly, for Tertullian, as was seen in his argument against Marcion, it is important that the one God dispense good and evil to the just and the unjust. God is not God if he be not both good and just. God is not just if he does not punish evil. On each of these points, Tertullian is describing divine realities in terms of his rule of faith or final vocabulary. Most people would judge him to be wrong in the severity of his God. The important thing for our understanding is to see all these elements as coherent with the vocabulary which he uses.

In *de resurrectione*, the simmering controversy prepares for Tertullian's climax. The mass of detail argues the entire integrity of the human person who stands before God. How can we sing the new song (Rev. 5.9 and 14.3) if we do not know who we are who give him thanks (*res.* 56)? Here Tertullian's final vocabulary comes alive for the individual. Everything centres upon humanity, for whom God has destined fire or everlasting joy (*res.* 59). Deny the transformation of the world into a new age and you disclose a false priority, since the renewal of humanity does not have to fit into a future dispensation; but the future dispensation has to fit around humanity, for whom God makes all things new. As Paul promised, recapitulation falls upon us: the world, life, death, things present and things to come, all are ours (1 Cor. 3.22). The flesh in which we sinned, the flesh in which we struggle, that same flesh shall see God's salvation or damnation (*res.* 59.3). Do we doubt God's power to renew in order to judge? We have seen a ship whose decaying hulk had been so smashed by storms that it barely limped into port; yet once renewed, refitted and transformed, it rode the waves as

---

[28] 'The promise of God's dealing with us through grace can be set before us in nothing but images, for we have not yet experienced the reality.' A. Farrer, An English Appreciation, in H. W. Bartsch (ed.), *Kerygma and Myth* (London, 1957), 212–23 (222).

before (*res.* 6of.). That act on which our perfection depends, the joining of flesh to spirit, has already been perfected in Christ (*res.* 63.1f.). In his own self the two natures have been joined. That alone is the reason why we shall rise, our flesh entire and our identity intact. Flesh and spirit are joined as bridegroom and bride.[29] The great plan of redemption comes home to each human life. A modern Christian and Heraclitean poem celebrates the same mystery of recapitulation:

In a flash, at a trumpet crash,
I am all at once what Christ is, since he is what I am, and
This Jack, joke, poor potsherd, patch, matchwood, immortal diamond,
Is immortal diamond.[30]

[29] The use of this metaphor here would be impossible for a hater of marriage.
[30] 'That Nature is a Heraclitean Fire and of the comfort of the Resurrection', in Gerard Manley Hopkins, *A selection*, ed. W. H. Gardner (London, 1953), 66.

CHAPTER 11

Ethics of conflict

We began with Tertullian's twin claims for simplicity and perfection. Simplicity did not last long in the apologetic battle against diverse opponents. Athens turned out to have a lot to do with Jerusalem, and the Christian message of credible ineptitude made demands on understanding. Antitheses in God and a divine trinity left the 'simplices ne dixerim imprudentes et idiotae' well behind. Prayer took place in conflict and the demands of the bible could not be reduced to uniformity. The simplicity of baptism did not produce transformed lives. Not even sin was straightforward: Tertullian the sinner disagreed with bishops on the fate of exuberant sinners. Those who rose above this confused world, as Valentinians did, finished with greater confusion and muddled fantasies. Even death did not solve all puzzles, for the resurrection of the flesh was contradictory and essential.

Above all, Tertullian wanted to live and to help others to live a Christian life in a complex world. The excellence of Christian example first drew him to a church whose corporate mediocrity (*mediocritas nostra*) repelled him. Besides this conflict, there was a deeper puzzle. The recapitulation of all things in Christ meant both correction and perfection. If someone struck you, retaliation was cleverly reconstructed. In giving a cheek for a cheek, you supplied the second cheek yourself and achieved correction and perfection. Ethics lay at the heart of the Christian mystery. The love command summed up the law. Loving enemies was the way to become like God. The ultimate event of the cross, the summing-up of all things in Christ, was found, said Irenaeus (*haer.* 3.16.9 and 3.18.5), with the words, 'Father, forgive them'.

This final mystery was simple and inseparable from conflict.

Tertullian was determined to live by this simplicity in a complex and conflicting world. His ethics will be considered under three paradoxes: love and fear, denial and affirmation of the world and natural law and apocalypse.

A. LOVE AND FEAR

The early apologists found a powerful argument for Christian truth in the excellence of Christian lives. Atheism was, for ancient Romans, a moral rather than a theological failing; disbelief in the gods made people unreliable and a danger to the state. Tertullian paints a glowing picture of Christian morals and reports that he and others were first converted by observing the courage and faithfulness of Christians. If pagans encountered unimpressive Christians, the apologetic enterprise was subverted and a main apologetic argument destroyed.

(i) Love as ultimate command and Christian perfection

Tertullian, a Stoic in his commendation of reason and law, compassion, chastity and patience, found all these virtues to be present in Christians. Yet love remains the supreme sacrament, treasure and final perfection of the Christian (*pat.* 12.8; *fug.* 14.2). 'See how they love one another' is the sign of the Christian family (*ap.* 39.7). Love of God and neighbour is the ultimate command, a universal law which is not the peculiar property of Israel (*Jud.* 2.3). Given in the beginning to Adam and Eve, it needed no expansion and would have been sufficient if it had been followed. All the other commandments are generated by it. Adam and Eve would not have disobeyed God if they had loved him. They would not have inflicted death upon each other if they had loved their neighbour.

The persistent precept of love shows that the same God spoke through Moses, Christ and the apostles (*Marc.* 5.8.9). Love of enemies brings the ancient law to completeness in Christ and points to the coming end. It is distinctively Christian and derives from one God. 'For this is our perfect and proper form of goodness, not something which is shared in common with others. For all love their friends, but only Christians love their enemies. So they who know the future and see the signs of things to come must preach unwelcome truths out of love, and for the salvation of enemies' (*Scap.* 1.3).[1] When Christians pray, 'Hallowed be thy name', they pray for the hallowing of God's name both in those who are in him and in all, including their personal enemies (*or.* 3.4), for whom God's grace is waiting. Love of enemies is a divine command. There are people who give good reason why they should be hated and cursed; but God has commanded that they be loved and blessed (*spect.* 16.6).

No principle of ethics was immune, Tertullian found, from misuse. Some Christians used the love command to avoid fasting. Faith and the love of God and neighbour suffice, they claimed, for Christian obedience; an empty stomach adds nothing. Such specious reasoning protects the indulgence of psychic Christians (*iei.* 2.8). However, right use of the command has endless relevance. The flesh is the neighbour who must be loved. Resurrection is a certain hope, simply because God could never consign that flesh which bears his image, which is the work of his hands and the sister of Christ, to destruction (*res.* 9.2).

Another part of neighbourly love is modest dress. Provocative clothing incites harmful lust. 'Are we then to display ourselves so that others perish when it is said in this respect: you shall love your neighbour as yourself. It is surely wrong to give so much attention to one's own concerns and not to care for the other' (*cult.* 2.2.5). While humankind is a unity (*ap.* 37.10), 'with how much more reason are they called and considered brothers, who recognize one God as father' (*ap.* 39.9). The love command is here linked to Stoic universalism, just as it is linked elsewhere to Platonic hope.[2]

Love marches on. Perfection is not a static state but a continuous surpassing of what may be expected. Love of the enemy, who is a stranger, increases our love for our neighbour. Love which goes beyond what is due enlarges the kindness which is due (*Marc.* 1.23.5).

---

[1] Similarly Justin points to the newness of love for enemies in contrast to harlots who love and tax-collectors who give for the sake of reward (*1 apol.* 15).
[2] Clement of Alexandria, *strom.* 2.22.131–6.

(ii) Love replaced by fear and hope?

For the other side of Tertullian's paradox, we may conveniently turn to a modern critique, which attacks the negative aspects of his ethics.[3] The enormous length of the work indicates a struggle to understand the mass of detailed ethical prescription. Tertullian, we are rightly told, gave morals a central place because he thought that they were the special concern of God. Faith is revealed by manner of life, and doctrine is displayed by conduct (*praescr.* 43.2). True innocence belongs to Christians because, taught by God, they follow what was revealed by the true teacher and ordained by the judge whom none may defy (*ap.* 45.1). Apart from God all is perverse (*cult.* 2.1.3). Christians are recognized by the lonely excellence of their moral achievement which produces more disciples than do the empty words of others (*ap.* 50.14–15). They are governed by the scriptures (*praescr.* 38.4) which are *dei litterae* (*an.* 2.5).

They had their critics. Celsus had maintained that there was nothing in scripture which had not already been said by the Greeks, who had not needed the promises of a god or son of god.[4] Origen replied that Christian teaching went beyond an élite and was more effective; Christians also had the advantage of being always united to God (*Cels.* 7.51). Origen does not deny Celsus' claim for similarity of content, but simply underlines the central place of God.

The crunch of the criticism is that Tertullian speaks statistically less about love than does the New Testament. While the question is, we are rightly told, too complex to settle by counting words, there is a puzzle in Tertullian's comparative neglect of love when benevolence was highly praised in his cultural environment. Rambaux notes that the controversy with Marcion sets Tertullian in opposition to the solitary divine ideal of love; he does not see that this could be enough, given Tertullian's belligerence in debate, to explain the whole phenomenon. Such a conclusion would have been correct but might have deprived us of the remaining four

---

[3] The example taken here is that of C. Rambaux, *Tertullien face aux morales des trois premiers siècles* (Paris, 1979). This large book is not a convincing account of Tertullian's ethics; but it is stimulating and provocative and presents a vast quantity of useful material.

[4] *Cels.* 6.1. καὶ χωρὶς ἀνατάσεως καὶ ἐπαγγελίας τῆς ἀπὸ θεοῦ ἢ υἱοῦ θεοῦ.

hundred pages, and would have bypassed a problem which is essential to the understanding of Tertullian. What is clear is that Tertullian's chief concern is devotion to one God.

Love, it is claimed, has been replaced by fear and hope. He who accepts Christian beliefs is compelled to be better, through fear of eternal punishment and hope of eternal bliss (*ap.* 49.2). The two motive forces behind morality are fear and hope; of faith, Tertullian says that under persecution there is no room for anything but fear and hope (*fug.* 1.6). God must be feared beyond all others because his judgement is more rigorous and less qualified (*nat.* 17.29; *ap.* 18.3; *res.* 15.8; *an.* 33.11; *paen.* 3.9, 4.4 and 5.4; *mart.* 2.3). There is neither pardon, nor appeal nor notice of date (*pud.* 9.10; *an.* 33.11). The sentence will be more severe than in earthly courts (*paen.* 12.1) and the punishment will last forever (*nat.* 1.7.29, 1.19.6; *ap.* 18.30) because of God's anger and cruelty (*test.* 1.5; *Marc.* 2.11.1, 13.2, 27.8, 4.7.13). So Tertullian exults in the future prospect of persecutors in hell (*spect.* 30f.) and sets Christian obedience in proportion to the severity of the threat and the liberality of the promise under which it lives (*pat.* 4.1f.).

Another 'word-count'[5] shows that fear does much better in the Old Testament than in the New Testament. Yet it is claimed that Tertullian does not say anything new about God's anger; he simply omits the qualifications which his environment had introduced.[6] He is indeed consistent in his rejection of the glories of this world. His humility is offered to God alone with none of the horizontal, communal consequences which the New Testament requires.[7]

Fear destroys love. On marriage, Rambaux claims that Tertullian sets himself against scripture, Judaism, catholic Christianity and most philosophers, lining up together with Jewish sects, Christian heresies, Neoplatonists and devotees of Isis.[8] But Tertullian's position is better understood from his own arguments which derive from one God who wills our sanctification. 'For he wills that we who are his image become also his likeness, that we may be holy as he is holy'. There are different kinds of sanctification – virginity

---

[5] Rambaux, *Tertullien*, 97.
[6] *Ibid.*, 126. This account of Rambaux will hardly do; either Tertullian is more violent than his contemporaries or he is not.
[7] *Ibid.*, 168.   [8] *Ibid.*, 257.

from birth, virginity from second birth and continence within marriage (*cast.* 1.3f.). Tertullian rejects all violence, all killing even by soldiers or by courts of law, any form of abortion and even attendance at the amphitheatre. Yet this is still not, says Rambaux, the radical morality of the Sermon on the Mount which rather requires the removal of the inward disposition to kill; Tertullian retains a disposition to anger and hatred. On the contrary, Tertullian's position is clear and is simple obedience to the sixth commandment: Thou shalt not kill! His obsession with one God comes out again in his restriction on the forgiveness of sins. We may forgive sins committed against ourselves, but not sins against God (*pud.* 2.10). God pardons only under strict conditions – sins committed in ignorance (*paen.* 5.2), for which penance has been done (*paen.* 6.4) and baptism received (*paen.* 6). After baptism there can be only one further forgiveness and this must follow severe penance (*paen.* 7.2 and 10, 9.1 and 4). Tertullian never admitted the possibility that God might pardon freely.

The greatest virtue is patience (*pat.* 1.7) which safeguards all God's decrees and commands (*pat.* 15.2). For patience allows God to be God. 'Vengeance is mine and I will repay' (Deut. 32.35) means 'Patience is mine and I will reward patience' (*pat.* 10.6). The creator teaches the patience which waits on the divine patience (*Marc.* 4.16.3). The omnipresent will of God implies that persecution should not be avoided. It cannot happen without the will of God (*mart.* 3.3–4; *scorp.* 2–7; *fug.* 1–4). Martyrdom testifies to God (*mart.* 3.1), gives glory to him (*pat.* 14.4). There was a widespread desire for heroic death, supported by legend and example; but Tertullian is simply following the logic of divine omnipotence in confidence of eternal life. His loyalty to one God may be summed up in total dedication of heart, strength and mind to the God of the bible.[9]

This final verdict has, I think, returned to the centre of Tertullian's ethic. The clarity of this perception is lost in the concluding pages where it is claimed that Tertullian has introduced new elements and omitted central parts of the New Testament.[10] As a result, his conversion and that of those who followed him from

---

[9] *Ibid.,* 415. 'il n'y a pas de vie "innocente" en dehors de l'obéissance à ses commandements'.
[10] *Ibid.,* 417.

paganism was more illusion than reality. They were able to go on living as before but under a different label.[11] This has not been substantiated by the earlier evidence which indicates that Tertullian was at logger-heads with most of his contemporaries. The verdict of 'innovatory conformism' is a tribute to his achievement, his sense of paradox and the untidiness of a creative mind. While he begins as a zealous monotheist who tried to hold on to both Old and New Testaments, especially the Old which Marcion wanted to take away, his acceptance of Stoic values represents another dimension of conflict and enrichment.[12]

(iii) From fear to obedience and love

Monotheism is the key but not the whole answer. The paradox of love and fear is linked with the paradox of goodness and justice in God, which is the stuff of the argument against Marcion. It is not simply a matter of contradictory sources in Old and New Testaments. Nor is it a surrender, as has been claimed, of the New to the Old. Above all, a paradox is never simply the juxtaposition of contrary claims. If God be God, he is to be feared. If he is to be feared, he must be obeyed; but his one command is to love. Love springs from the fear which perfect love casts out.

Love and fear are linked by the concept of shame. In Tertullian's best-known paradox,[13] shame is the dominant spur to Tertullian's choice. We considered two clauses of the great paradox: epistemological ('credibile quia ineptum') and metaphysical ('certum quia impossibile'). Discussion of the ethical clause ('non pudet quia pudendum') was postponed until we came to Tertullian's ethics; but, as the first clause, it sets the tone for the earlier discussion and indicates the orientation of Tertullian's life. The necessary dishonour of faith is the hope of the world. Whatever is unworthy of God is to our benefit. We are safe if we are not confused about our lord, who said that he would be ashamed of those who had been

---

[11] 'Comme Tertullien, la société gréco-romaine a adopté une nouvelle religion plûtot que des valeurs de vie nouvelles.' *Ibid.*, 423.

[12] In the interests of proportion, the discussion of Rambaux's book has been abbreviated. An extended critique by Ch. Munier may be found in Tertullian face aux morales des trois premiers siècles, *RevSR*, 54 (1980), 173–83.

[13] See above, ch. 3.

ashamed of him. Through his lord's disgrace Tertullian is 'shameless in a good sense and felicitously foolish' ('bene impudens, feliciter stultus'). For the son of God is crucified; 'I am not ashamed because it must be a shameful thing' ('non pudet, quia pudendum est'). The intellectual subtlety, which the earlier chapter explored is not the ultimate part of Tertullian's claim. Rejection of divine shame could only end in human perdition. Behind all that Tertullian wrote lay the fear that, if he were now ashamed of Jesus, on that last day, the only day that mattered, Jesus would be ashamed of him. Here again Tertullian was as classical as he was evangelical, for

shame continues to work for us as it worked for the Greeks, in essential ways. By giving through the emotions a sense of who one is and of what one hopes to be, it mediates between act, character, and consequence, and also between ethical demands and the rest of life … This was in substance already the ethical psychology even of the ancient Greeks, and, despite the modern isolation of guilt, it forms a substantial part of our own.[14]

The achievement of Tertullian is that, when he is most biblical and evangelical, he is most classical and Stoic, and that he never leaves his sources unchanged. The shame of God inverts the classical and secular claim; the ultimate shame is failure to share that shame of God. Only a survivor within a martyr church could feel the intensity which, for Tertullian, unites love and fear. 'He who fears to suffer cannot belong to him who suffered; but he, who does not fear to suffer, will be perfected in love, that is the love of God. For perfect love casts out fear (1 John 4.18) and therefore many are called but few are chosen (Matt. 22.14)' (*fug.* 14.2).

B. DENIAL AND AFFIRMATION OF THE WORLD

(i) World-denial: martyrdom, virginity, modesty, fasting

Tertullian explains to martyrs why they are better off in a gaol which separates them from the world which is the true prison. For many reasons, the world is a darker place than gaol: it blinds human hearts not eyes; it chains souls not bodies; its air is fouler

---

[14] Bernard Williams, *Shame and necessity* (Berkeley, Los Angeles, London, 1993), 102.

with the stench of lusts; it contains more criminals (all are sinners); and its occupants are to face the highest Judge and not a mere proconsul. All this means that martyrs are at an advantage in prison, despite the darkness, chains and smells. They may have lost some pleasures; but, as in business, short-term loss is the way to greater profits. As soldiers of Christ they endure hardships, as athletes they train for a contest where the prize is life eternal (*mart.* 3).

With apocalyptic clarity, martyrdom unveils the issues which govern human life. Everyone who denies Jesus and his gospel will be denied by him (*cor.* 11.5). Each Christian lives the life of a martyr, through testimony to Jesus in every part of his life.

The coexistence of martyrdom and mediocrity brought distress to Tertullian and to many thoughtful believers. The Revelation of John celebrated martyrs and denounced Laodiceans, who were neither hot nor cold but hard to stomach (Rev. 3.15f.). If God be God, then the death of martyrs must be balanced by their eternal glory and universal veneration. The attitude of Tertullian to comfortable Christians is like the attitude of any soldier to those who keep far from battle. The tensions produced by persecution and death of comrades are reproduced in every struggle which the church has faced. While Tertullian takes an extreme view, that the sovereign God actually wills the persecution of his people, martyr-dom was only consistent with a Christian God if the end were near. It was impossible that a good God could allow such suffering without doing something about it. So great was the contradiction between a faithful, loving God and the cruelty of his demands, that nothing short of an *eschaton* could suffice. With the end would come judgement, for which all Christians needed to be prepared. The powerful presence of the spirit confirmed the nearness of the end, heightened ethical demands and gave strength to meet Christ as victor and judge.

Virginity and celibacy are of prime importance (*cast.* 1) and give grounds for Christian credibility. Sexual abstinence within mar-riage is praised (*ux.* 1.6). Widows and widowers should seize the opportunity, which bereavement has given them, to reject the flesh and gain the spirit (*cast.* 10). One God is dishonoured by successive marriages (*mon.* 1.1) and celibacy serves him best (*ux.* 1.3). Tertullian's account of spiritual marriage – *nubere deo* – points to a passionate and intense dedication to God,[15] in a contemplative life, which seeks him by intimate prayer in the company of angels. Virginity and continence are more effective than rational inquiry, for continence prepares the body to wear the garment of incorruption (*ux.* 1.7.1). Tertullian speaks of the spiritual affection of those who are married to Christ or God (*ux.* 1.4.4f.) and the attractiveness of those (*speciosae puellae*) who are his (*ux.* 1.4.4). This is all spiritual (*cast.* 10.2). In the last days, he who has a wife should be as he who has none, when God draws near in special intimacy.[16]

Such marriage is the clue to chastity and to the continence of all in the orders of the church. They have restored honour to the flesh and they are children of the age to come when, free from passion, they enter the paradise which was lost by passion (*cast.* 13.4). Nor is their chastity foreign to the higher ideals of paganism where virginity and monogamy imitate, on Satan's side, the virtues owed to God (*cast.* 13.3).

Modesty is closely linked with salvation (*cult.* 1.2.5). Fleshly lust and worldly greed deny the superiority of spirit over flesh (*ux.* 1.5.4). Continence leads to life eternal (*ux.* 1.7.1). Female finery is inappropriate and leads along the path of the fallen Eve (*cult.* 1.1.3). Cosmetic care is a form of prostitution (*cult. passim*). Women beguile through magic, gold, jewels and cosmetics (*cult.* 1.2.1). Female clothing may point in opposite directions; plain dress indicates purity, ornament indicates impurity (*cult.* 1.4.2).

Gold, silver and precious stones are useless and only valued for their rarity (*cult.* 1.7.1). God and nature deny the alteration of natural colours (*cult.* 1.8.2). Christian women will not only be modest but will appear so (*cult.* 2.1.2), not only avoid sin but shun every stimulus to sin (*cult.* 2.4.2). Beauty is not itself to be feared; however it is so inferior to holiness that it is superfluous and should be obscured (*cult.* 2.4.1). Men must, under God, equally avoid ornament. *Gravitas* governs all and is the ground of masculine

---

[15] C. Tibiletti, Vita contemplativa in Tertulliano, *Orph.*, NS 2 (1981), 320–39 (332).

[16] *Ibid.*, 339, 'La visione cristiana della vita risulta in Tertulliano unitaria, pur tra contingenti fluttuazioni. Lo anelito escatalogico, che associa celibato e vita contemplativa, pervade e anima il suo pensiero, dalla conversione alle ultime opere a noi note.'

modesty (*cult.* 2.8.1). Christian women should try to seem poor because they possess such spiritual wealth. They do not want to appear voluptuous and have renounced the wickedness of the present age (*cult.* 2.11f.). If, by following Roman and Christian manners, women remain quietly at home, clothed in uprightness, holiness and modesty, then God will be their lover (*cult.* 2.13.6).

Modesty is never a negative virtue, but outstrips even patience as 'the flower of manners, the honour of our bodies, the grace of our sexes, the integrity of the blood, the guarantee of our race, the basis of holiness, the foretaste of every good thing' (*pud.* 1.1). The recent collapse of purity through the episcopal sanction of adultery and fornication (*pud.* 1.6) is a sign that the end is near. For the custom of the church has always been on the side of modesty, and in the churches founded by apostles or apostolic men virgins have worn the veil. There is diversity in the African use of the veil; but the truth sees the unveiling of virgins as a form of rape (*virg.* 3.4). Indeed scripture, nature and discipline, which all come from God, defend the veil. The law which comes from scripture is confirmed by nature and required by discipline (*virg.* 16.1). To these authorities, Tertullian adds angelic guidance. To the followers of the New Prophecy (*nobis*), an angel has spoken through one of the sisters, telling her that the uncovering of her neck is as bad as the uncovering of the rest of her upper body.

So, rigorism rules all. Patience stands in the centre of morals, giving strength to faith, love, humility and penitence, while it restrains flesh, tongue and hands from evil (*pat.* 15).

Fasting caused controversy and here again nature, scripture and discipline are considered. Nature shows that the many marriages of the psychics are linked with gluttony because of the proximity of the relevant members of the body (*iei.* 1.1). In scripture, the first command to Adam was that he should not eat (*iei.* 3.2). In discipline, from Moses and Elijah to Paul, the examples and prescriptions of abstinence are many (*iei.* 6–8).

Discipline trains the soul for times of trial through fasting. It is ludicrous when heretics feed their martyrs so well that instead of confessing their lord, they belch and hiccup (*iei.* 12.3). Even spiritual bishops and people need to be warned against gluttony which will bring them to Hades in company with Dives rather than to paradise in company with Lazarus. Those who criticize Christian fasting as an imitation of pagan practice should recognize their inferiority to those pagans who fast before their idols, while psychic Christians refuse this service to the living God. Carnal Christians have, for a god their belly, for a temple their lungs, for an altar their paunch, for spirit the smell of their food, for spiritual gifts their seasonings and for prophecy a hearty Christian belch (*iei.* 16.8). The Christian athlete must wrestle against worldly powers. The glutton will be more attractive to bears and lions than to God; but if he is to meet them without disaster, he needs to train as an athlete of God (*iei.* 17.9).[17]

(ii) World-affirmation: loyalty to creator, marriage made in heaven, finality of the flesh

Tertullian's rigorism has attracted much attention and it is easy to miss its constant qualification through loyalty to the creator and to the flesh in which he has clothed humanity. Enjoyment of sounds and sights, in their proper pagan place and time, is an offence to true religion and the true God (*spect.* 1). However, we do not lose God simply by being in the world (*saeculum*), but only by sinking into its sin; in the temple of Serapis or the theatre we desert the God who made us and 'polluted things pollute us' (*de contaminatis, contaminamur*) (*spect.* 8.10). No one writes with more enthusiasm of the beauty of God's creation (*Marc.* 1.13.4–14.1f.).

Tertullian's denigration of marriage has drawn much attention because of the violence of his views. Yet he rightly claims to present a middle way between heretics who abolish marriages and psychics who multiply them. Those who are spiritual and continent honour the law of marriage where the one God prescribes one marriage (*mon.* 1.2). Few writings have been worse understood than Tertullian's letter to his wife where he lists the disabilities of marriage only to end with a splendid eulogy of the marriage which he and his wife have known. There are no words to tell of the happiness of the marriage which the church blesses and which angels recount in heaven. One in flesh and in spirit, two people pray and serve God

---

[17] Other ascetic teaching of Tertullian has been discussed in the previous chapter under Montanism.

together, sharing all things in the joy and peace of Christ. Paul left these things to be understood and they are not capable of repetition in a second marriage (*ux.* 2.8.6–9).

Tertullian, who is so fierce in his renunciation of the world, nevertheless defends the flesh and the goodness of the creation with stronger claims than any other early Christian writer. The flesh is the hinge on which salvation hangs, 'caro salutis est cardo' (*res.* 8.2) The heretics despise the flesh and think only of the resurrection of the soul; in this they despise the lord of the flesh (*res.* 2.12). Against these views, Tertullian speaks positively of the flesh. In the order of divine creation, the human flesh was prior to the soul (*res.* 5.8). God has mixed the breath of his own spirit with flesh and one cannot say whether flesh carries soul or soul carries flesh (*res.* 7.9). The flesh fights for the name of Christ and is exposed to human hatred. It will go to prison, suffer every privation and in the end offer itself in death for Christ. The flesh must be most blessed and glorious when it can fully repay its Master the vast debt it owes (*res.* 8.5f.).

The whole of faith is acted out by the flesh. The mouth utters holy words, the tongue refrains from blasphemy, the heart avoids irritation and the hands both give and work (*res.* 45.15). The manner of our life in the flesh must be changed to a way of holiness, righteousness and truth (*res.* 49.7). The transformation of our bodies to the likeness of Christ's body preserves the substance of the flesh, so that the same flesh which is torn by martyrdom will wear the crown (*res.* 56.1). Bodies which have been mutilated before or after death will at the resurrection recover their perfect wholeness (*res.* 57.2). At the resurrection the flesh will become capable of a new kind of life without losing its essential identity (*res.* 59.1f.). God's judgement will destroy sinful flesh and save that which is continent. Tertullian is convinced that in the same flesh as he once committed adultery he now strives for continence. It is in our power to mow down the sinful flesh which is grass and to preserve the flesh which God will save (*res.* 59.3f.). The usefulness of the resurrected flesh is not in question because in the presence of God there will be no idleness (*res.* 60.9). Both flesh and spirit are united in Christ who has joined them together as bride and bridegroom (*res.* 63.3).

Once again Tertullian's paradox says something important. The paradox of world-denial and world-affirmation reflects the divine economy which moves from creation to resurrection, for which life must be lived in freedom from sinful lusts and in the fullness of the flesh which will rise again. Body and soul exist in harmony and have a common future in the resurrection. God has arranged creation for man who is both soul and body (*res.* 5). Although man is made of both body and soul, his life is an undivided unity, the flesh of man cannot be discarded; and his final end must relate to both soul and body and not just to one part of him.

C. NATURAL LAW AND APOCALYPSE

The final paradox in Tertullian's ethics is between natural law and apocalypse, between creation and consummation, between beginning and end. 'It is a long way', writes Spanneut, 'from conscience and law to the revelations of the paraclete... However, if the truth of prophecy gains an ever larger place through Tertullian's growing adherence to Montanism, conscience and nature keep their force to the end.'[18] At first look, Tertullian unites dry moral theology with charismatic exuberance. Who would think of reading Aquinas on natural law in the middle of a charismatic celebration? The contradiction is, like everything in the theology of Tertullian, clarified by the perfection of all things in Christ, where the end becomes the beginning, and the *eschaton* is paradise (with natural law) regained.

(i) Natural law: conscience, law and nature, discipline

We have seen that Stoicism formed both Tertullian and the world which he sought to convert. He did not have to pretend to be Roman. Metaphysics of spirit and a Stoic logic of relative disposition and paradox defined his thought. Ethics were a special concern to Stoicism and we must expect to see strong influence here. Stoic ethics are ruled by the concepts of conscience, law and nature.[19]

---

[18] 'De la conscience et la loi naturelle jusq'aux révélations du Paraclet la distance est grande... Si la vérité prophétique prend de plus en plus de place avec l'adhésion progressive de Tertullien au montanisme, la conscience et la nature ont cependant gardé jusq'au bout leur valeur.' M. Spanneut, *Tertullien et les premiers moralistes africains* (Gembloux, 1969), 18.

[19] *Ibid.* These two paragraphs are indebted to the monumental works of Michel Spanneut.

Conscience for Tertullian begins as such common knowledge which may be directed to moral and ethical issues (*res.* 2.8; *cult.* 2.1.2; *Marc.* 4.17.12 and 2.25.1) and depends on natural law (*iei.* 6.1). It judges ethical matters, present and past (*paen.* 3.16), and guides concrete actions (*cult.* 2.13.3). Without conscience as a common ground, apologetic could make little progress (*ap.* 9, 10). It may be sensitive (*nat.* 2.1.5 and 7.8), secure (*cult.* 2.2.2), sound (*spect.* 29.2) and soiled (*ap.* 30.6), or even criminal (*ap.* 8.1); but it stands for what is essentially human in contrast to all that is superficial (*res.* 56.3).

Conscience learns from nature (*test.* 5) such 'common notions' (*res.* 3.1) as the existence of God, the immortality of the soul (*res.* 3.1) and the difference between good and evil (*Marc.* 4.16.15). Conscience is God's primordial gift (*Marc.* 1.10.3) and nature teaches by recalling what the soul already knows (*Marc.* 1.17.4). Soul is the pupil, nature is the teacher and God teaches the teacher (*test.* 5.1).[20] One must believe nature who is the sister of truth as one believes in God and the soul. 'Neither God nor nature lies' (*test.* 6.1).

God teaches the teacher through the text of scripture which provides a legal corpus of ultimate authority. Critical use of scripture is necessary, because in the law of Moses there are temporary and permanent provisions. While the Sabbath command has no permanent validity (*Jud.* 2.10), the command to love enemies belongs to both testaments and, contrary to Marcion, even the law of retaliation can be consistent with the kindness of Jesus (*Marc.* 4.16.5). But the ritual requirements of the ancient law were annulled by the very creator who first gave them. He who gave the law plainly preferred the circumcision of the heart to that of the flesh, for the spirit came to take precedence over the letter (*Marc.* 5.13.7). There is a difference between what God allows and what he wills. This is clear in Paul's first letter to the Corinthians, chapter 7 (*cast.* 3.2f.), where a second marriage may be lawful, but all lawful things are not expedient (*cast.* 8.1).

When the thunder of the gospel had shaken the ancient law, the apostles preserved only the prohibitions of sacrifices, fornication and blood (*pud.* 12.3f.). All sexual intercourse outside marriage is forbidden by both testaments, and adultery has always been linked

---

[20] Spanneut, *Tertullien*, 14. Soul becomes almost synonymous with nature.

with idolatry (*pud.* 4f.). Yet Christians were seen by Jews and Gentiles to be profoundly legalist. Tertullian describes a cartoon in which a Christian is depicted as a book-reading donkey dressed in a toga (*nat.* 1.1.14). Similarly a Jew like Trypho could read and admire the Gospel, yet declare to Justin that its precepts were too hard for practice (*dial.* 10).

Natural law reproduces the law of God and has its own legal status (*cor.* 6). It is the law given by God to Adam and Eve which is the matrix of all divine precepts (*Jud.* 2.4) and which patriarchs followed instinctively (*Jud.* 2.7). Only the devil defaces nature which is God's perfect work (*cult.* 1.8; *spect.* 23) and since God is nature's author, everything unnatural is monstrous and sacrilegious (*cor.* 5.4). Natural law is the source of common wisdom and discipline (*cor.* 5.1, 7.1) and it is free from the historical limitations of the law of Moses which is surpassed and completed by the New Testament, whose new law contains the integrity and fullness of all *disciplina* (*or.*1.1f.).

In Tertullian as elsewhere, the claims for natural law may strike us as sometimes sound, sometimes absurd. Unnatural sexual practices have no place in the church because they are 'monstrosities' rather than sins (*pud.* 4.4); God could produce purple and blue wool on sheep if he wished to do so; since he did not wish to do so, it is wrong for humans to produce wool of an unnatural colour (*cult.* 1.8). The sexual claim is reasonable: the guide to correct dress is not.

Mixing scripture with nature can be equally confusing. Man is the image of the creator and Christ is the head of man (*Marc.* 5.8.1f.). Consequently, differences arise between what is required of men and women. On the one hand, a man should not cover his head because he has no excess of hair and may shave or have his hair cut. His head is Christ. Women on the other hand should cover their heads because they have too much hair and Christ is not their head in the same way (*virg.* 8.1).

Tertullian is wise enough not to identify nature with Christian law. While Christian practices are supported by nature (*cor.* 5.1), the declarations of the lord are not of universal application. We are told to give to all who ask, yet our lord himself refused those who asked for a sign (*fug.* 13.2). There is a difference between what God allows and what he wills. This is clear in Paul's first letter to the

Corinthians, chapter 7 (*cast.* 3). While a second marriage may be lawful, all lawful things are not expedient (*cast.* 8.1).

Discipline

To scripture and nature is joined the discipline of the church. They are the three guides in moral matters. They all belong to God and are the ways in which he confronts humans (*virg.* 16.1). Discipline[21] embraces the practical precepts which come from scripture, nature or the life of the church. 'The majesty of the scriptures takes concrete form in practical rules: *disciplina* or *disciplinae*'.[22] It takes precedence over custom and tradition (*ux.* 2.7.3; *virg.* 16.1; *or.* 18.1; *cor.* 3f.), both of which have their place. Any good custom must be respected when it is practised within the brotherhood of the one body of the church (*virg.* 2.1). Yet custom must be validated by argument or reason (*cor.* 4.7, 10.9; *iei.* 3.1, 10.9). Reason is manifest in the revelation of the paraclete who brings wholeness of truth. Truth has ultimate authority and no time, place or person can override it. Custom may be contrary to truth; 'but Christ our lord is called "truth" not "custom". If Christ is forever and prior to all, truth is equally ancient and eternal' (*virg.* 1.1f.). Sin is irrational, diabolic and hostile to God (*an.* 16.1), and the soul does not lack intellect at any stage of its life (*an.* 19.1).

(ii) Apocalypse: renewal of lost image, last Adam, idolatry as reversal of assimilation, end and beginning

How does natural law, primitive and universal, join with the particularity and promise of the gospel? The perfection of all things in Christ, the dominant theme of early Christian theology, pointed to the one goal: that what humankind had lost in Adam might be regained in Christ. Ethical renewal meant a return to the image and likeness of God as found and then lost in Adam, and finally found again in Christ. Every ethical issue was seen in this perspective. Our maker is our remaker. All must be fulfilled in each life, where the whole economy of salvation runs its course. In the

---

[21] Tertullian uses the concept nearly 200 times.

[22] Spanneut, *Tertullien*, 16, refers to V. Morel, 'Disciplina' le mot et l'idée ... dans les oeuvres de Tertullien, *RHE*, 40 (1944–5), 5–45.

end we must find our beginning. Montanism claimed that the final stage of the divine dispensation, the outpouring of the spirit, was a present event. Through the spirit, believers could complete their journey to the end which, in Christ, was a new beginning. They could recapture the innocence of Adam, and be formed anew in the image and likeness of God.

Tertullian's optimistic account of the beginning[23] is always worth recalling. God created the world, not for himself, but for humankind (*Marc.* 1.13.2). Animals (*pat.* 4.3) and indeed all things should serve, in some way, the interest of mankind (*nat.* 2.5.18). Humanity is *dominus* of all mortal things (*ap.* 48.9), which serve and submit to him (*an.* 33.9). Human flesh, formed from the dust, was glorified by the breath of God (*res.* 7.7), and formed in love by one who knew that his son would one day dwell in it: 'Christus cogitabatur, homo futurus' (*res.* 6.3). Divine breath (not spirit) makes an image of God which is free, rational and intelligent (*Marc.* 2.9.4). Tertullian makes much of the concept of image in this way.[24]

There is a distinction, never easily maintained in any language, between image and likeness.[25] The water which once healed sick bodies, now heals spiritual sickness by baptism. The divine image, which is a matter of *form*, has survived; the likeness, which is the *eternal quality*, was lost through Adam's sin and is restored by the spirit at baptism (*bapt.* 5.7). God wills that sanctification by which, in us, his image is restored to God's likeness (*cast.* 1.3). This is possible through the great exchange when God became human that humans might become divine, when God became small that man might become great (*Marc.* 2.27.7). We put on Christ (*fug.* 10.2); we are coins struck in his likeness, bearing his name, bought with his blood (*fug.* 12.10). By following Christ we add his heavenly likeness to the earthly likeness of our common humanity, as we copy his holiness, righteousness and truth (*res.* 49.7).

Idolatry as reversal of assimilation

Such assimilation to God is driven by fear as well as by love. God commands what is good; our obedience follows not from the

---

[23] See above, ch. 5.
[24] *virg.* 8, 10; *cult.* 1.1.2; *Marc.* 2.4, 5.6.11 and 5.8.1; *cor.* 10; *spect.* 2.3, 4; *an.* 37.4; *pat.* 5.
[25] Because likeness is what enables an image to be an image.

perceived goodness of his prescription, but from submission to God's authority, majesty and power (*paen.* 4.6). Fear of judgement and hope of life eternal go together (*pud.* 1.5); sound faith follows a perfect fear (*metus integer*) (*paen.* 6.17). 'Be ye holy as I am holy!' The image of God is holiness and therefore he wills our holiness (*cast.* 1.3). Because assimilation to God is the ultimate good, idolatry is the ultimate evil (*idol.* 2.1). Idolatry reverses the moral direction by making God in the image of sinful humanity instead of restoring man again to the likeness of God. The recapitulation of all wickedness, the reversal of creation and the gospel, it can be practised without a temple or a visible idol.[26] This claim brings Tertullian close to the negative theology of Clement of Alexandria.

Both the making and the worship of idols are condemned by God (*idol.* 4.1) He who makes an idol offers up his mental ingenuity and his physical sweat to the idol; this is already an act of worship (*idol.* 6.3). The hands that have made idols cannot be brought into church and offered to God (*idol.* 7.1). Yet, in folly and ignorance, Christians compromise with idolatry, lighting lamps and placing wreaths on their doors (*idol.* 15.1).

End and beginning

To return to the chief puzzle of Tertullian's ethics: it is a long way from conscience and natural law to the revelations of the paraclete; but however strong the power of prophecy grows, conscience and natural law never lose their force.[27] The answer is clear. Natural law and apocalyptic must go together because the beginning in creation is joined to the end in the paraclete who brings no strange novelties but testifies to Christ 'with the whole order of God the creator' (*mon.* 2.4). As *restitutor* rather than *institutor*, the paraclete restores mankind to its ancient beginning (*mon.* 4.2). Monogamy is part of this beginning; for example, even the animals in the ark went in two by two (*mon.* 4.5). The end is joined to the beginning by Christ, who is both Alpha and Omega, and brings mankind back to paradise (*mon.* 5.3). If the beginning passes to the end and the end passes back to the beginning, the last Adam meets us in the same form as the first. Christians renew their origin in Christ, by

[26] See J. C. M. van Winden, Idolum and Idololatria in Tertullian, *VC*, 36 (1982), 108–14.
[27] Spanneut, *Tertullien*, 18.

assuming the monogamy of Adam and Eve, of Christ and his church (*mon.* 5.7).

What is new and true is necessarily old, since the truth, which is Christ, is eternal. The rule of faith is one and unalterable, but discipline is always renewed and revised as the grace of God leads on to the end. The paraclete makes all things new, directs discipline, illuminates scripture, reforms the mind and leads on to better things. Everything has its stages of growth: from seed to shoot to sapling to tree. Tertullian, like Irenaeus, has both a catastrophic and an evolutionary view of human history.

So also righteousness (for the God of righteousness and of creation is the same God) was first in a primitive condition, possessed of a natural fear of God, and from that stage it advanced through the law and the prophets to infancy; from that stage it passed through the gospel to the fervour of youth; now through the paraclete, it is settling into maturity. He will be, after Christ, the only one to be called and revered as master; for he speaks not from himself, but he speaks what is commanded by Christ. He is the only prelate, because he alone succeeds to Christ. They, who have received him, set truth before custom. (*virg.* 1.1)

The paraclete regains paradise by perfecting the divine dispensation.

The paradox of natural law and apocalypse restates the oldest puzzle in ethics: is there a natural law and are there natural virtues? For Plato every virtue must be connected to the Good before it can be valid. For Aristotle and for Aquinas natural virtues could be recognized as inferior to those perfect virtues which are connected to the End or God. There is no simple account of the relation between natural and perfect virtues. Continuity and disjunction are both arguable. Virtue may be evident in those who deny the Good. Yet that were

> the greatest treason:
> To do the right deed for the wrong reason.[28]

Tertullian has grasped this point and links natural law with knowledge of the End which is also the beginning, through the summing-up of all things in Christ.

On the one hand, Tertullian appeals to nature, conscience and

---

[28] Another St Thomas, in T. S. Eliot's *Murder in the cathedral* (London, 1935), 44.

the divine image in which humanity was made. On the other hand, martyrdom and the paraclete bring him to the last days. His Heraclitean solution is that in the end is our beginning. We begin from and end with God; when we see him we shall be like him.

> What we call the beginning is often the end
> And to make an end is to make a beginning...
> We shall not cease from exploration
> And the end of all our exploring
> Will be to arrive where we started
> And know the place for the first time.[29]

[29] T. S. Eliot, Little Gidding, *Four Quartets* (London, 1944), 42f.

Conclusion

Most thinkers write under the stimulus of controversy, and Tertullian was fortunate to have many opponents to make him think. He denied the existence of eirenic theology. Confrontation was a fact of life and the only way to maturity (*Marc.* 2.29.4). Life and thought for a Heraclitean (*PP* 211, 212) were adversarial (*Marc.* 1.25.6).[1] Durability in disputation clarified his opinions, for propositions are understood from the proofs which support them. Like his contemporaries in philosophy, he chose a criterion or rule of truth and used ideas which were consistent with it.

We note first the limits of his achievement. Tertullian's loyalty to his rule and to scripture,[2] together with his desire to destroy his opponents, brought mistakes. These came when he felt a need for answers which left no remainder, a need which derived from his logic of apologetic,[3] and from the pressures of controversy and persecution. His answer to Marcion, that justice and goodness were united in one God, pointed back to the antitheses of the Sermon on the Mount and is confirmed in the universal Christian plea for divine mercy. However, in loyalty to this answer, he went further and felt obliged to argue that only a God who inspired fear could keep sinners from sinning; love could not conquer all. Even the notorious case of the bald Elisha and the brutal bears came down to this. For any advocate could prove a difference between

---

[1] 'porro nihil sine aemulatione decurret quod sine adversario non erit'.

[2] He is utterly subordinate to the text of scripture and will not allow any ground for Marcion's objections. Every Old Testament barbarity has to be defended. He is no longer, as were New Testament writers and Justin, afraid of the Jews, because he cites to them the judgement of their own scriptures. This failure of Christian forgiveness, derived from the unity of scripture, was to have serious consequences.

[3] See above, ch. 1.

the badness of boys and the innocence of infants; unlike Augustine, he does not condemn the latter for original sin.

Divine retribution solved the problem of evil. Tertullian scorned philosophers and heretics who tossed this question about and never found an answer. He found his solution in the vengeful God of the Deuteronomist. There were two kinds of evil: guilt (*mala culpae*) and punishment (*mala poenae*). The first was self-inflicted and freely chosen. The second was God's unvarying response to sin. The strength of Tertullian's answer, he rightly claimed, was that God was always present, either to bless or to blame; God had become contingent.[4] The weakness of his answer was that God so frequently smote the wrong people; against this he would argue that God would have an ultimate word. His praise of the last judgement as a spectacle for wonder and even derision wins him no friends (*spect.* 30). The laughing judge belongs to the Old Testament (Ps. 2.4 and 59.8); but Psalm 2 links very closely the divine son who was central to New Testament apologetic with the derisive destruction of the nations, and Christians do not forget this.[5] Nor is there any doubt in the Apocalypse (Rev. 16.5f. and 19.1f.) about that divine retribution for the deaths of martyrs to which Tertullian looks. A modern theologian indicates a better answer. While 'It is necessary to remember the martyrs, so as not to become abstract'[6] the true God is 'not recognised by his power and glory in the world and in the history of the world, but through his helplessness and his death on the scandal of the cross of Jesus'.[7]

Were Tertullian's dubious answers the result of impatience, to which he confesses, or insensitivity to the wider implications of his words? His Stoic world made it easier for him to write austerely to his wife or martyrs. For an apologist, indeed, impatience can be a virtue. Philosophers elucidate problems; apologists have to come up with some kind of an answer. Tertullian cannot luxuriate at length in problems. In order to get on with the business of living, his people need the best answers he can find. Theology never loses this tension and contingency. Many objections to Christian belief, like

[4] 'Here it seems he remains a Christian more of the Old Testament than of the New.' H. von Campenhausen, *The fathers of the Latin church* (London, 1964), 35.
[5] Thanks to G. F. Handel's *Messiah*.
[6] J. Moltmann, *The crucified God* (London, 1974), 278.   [7] *Ibid.*, 195.

the problem of evil, point to problems which no one has solved, despite perpetual discussion (*praescr.* 7.5).[8] As an apologist, Tertullian has frequently to give answers and destroy objections, not mounting, like the Platonists, ever closer to ultimate truth. His Heraclitean task is one of horizontal strife, in the name of the logos which flows through all things.[9] However, we cannot overlook his mistakes, since they resemble the kind of short-cut which he attacks in others and they are not consistent with his dominant claim for a suffering, compassionate God.[10]

Do his errors have a common pattern? They occur when his final vocabulary or rule of faith conflicts either with the scripture he proudly claims as exclusive Christian property or with reality as he knows it. He cannot afford to renounce either scripture or his rule. He refuses to see that the jealous, vindictive God of the Deuteronomist is not the helpless, compassionate figure on the cross, and he could never disown the latter. In his loyalty to the rule, he was, strangely, too systematic for his own good. He could not say, with William Blake, 'Thinking as I do that the Creator of this world is a very cruel being, and being a worshipper of Christ, I cannot help saying "The Son, O how unlike the Father." First God almighty comes with a thump on the head. Then Jesus Christ comes with a balm to heal it.'[11]

A thinker's mistakes often indicate his central concern more clearly than do his extended arguments. Tertullian's anxiety is that either the Marcionite subdivision or the monarchian 'identification' of God will remove the divine disgrace which is mankind's salvation. He therefore goes on to clarify the rule of faith or the gospel. Christian theology is concerned with the being of God.[12]

---

[8] There can be virtue in Tertullian's straightforward answer as there is in a simple deist response. The deist can move the mysteries of providence to an impersonal, natural order and put the problem of theodicy one step further away.

[9] Not even when the long day's task is done, and he takes the philosopher's cloak, does he abandon disputation in the better philosophy. He has fought the good fight, but wears no crown, for a crown is unchristian and unnatural (*cor.* 5.1). God alone will give him his crown when the end comes (*cor.* 15.1) and not before (*ap.* 41.3).

[10] In fairness, it should be noted that Tertullian does relate the anger of God to God's own possibility and death (*Marc.* 2.16.3).

[11] A vision of the last judgement, in *The portable Blake* (New York, 1953), 670.

[12] No one in recent times has seen this central point with the same clarity as Christopher Stead. See his, *Divine substance*.

Nothing else provides a basis for faith. Tertullian, like others, came to faith through the moral excellence of Christians, the fulfilment of all things in Christ and the spread of the gospel. Each of these grounds he found to be flawed: Christians do bad things, another parousia is needed and falsehood as well as truth spreads over the face of the earth. Faith must rest on the being of God, without abandoning its three beginnings.

The first question of Christian theology is therefore about God: 'Is there one God, good and true, who is creator of this world of sin and evil?' and its answer concerns divine being: 'Only if that God acted in Jesus Christ to redeem the world which he had made.' Consequently theology faces a problem of inclusiveness or micro-engineering: how to put the gospel into the being of God. Proposed in the New Testament, tackled by Tertullian and others in the second century, it has remained central.

Most Christians followed (and still follow) Tertullian's path. They began with simplicity and perfection – with a simple faith in one saving God and the particularity and universality of Jesus Christ, son of God, saviour.[13] Their criterion of truth was God's saving work from creation to the summing-up of all things in Christ. There was no diminution in its claims as it joined the end to the beginning and united humanity with God. Recapitulation ends in the being of God. When he spoke to pagans, Tertullian began from a sense of God, which, like the Stoics, he found in all humans. When humans heard the scriptures and the gospel message, they recognized Jesus as the God they all had dimly known. What looks like paradox (a soul naturally Christian still has to become Christian) is a common path for believers. The awareness of one God found content in the story of salvation.

Tertullian owed most to his two great opponents. How, challenged Marcion, could Jewish scripture and Christian gospel be fitted into one God? Tertullian followed the lead of the antitheses of Matthew's Sermon on the Mount. There were real antitheses between the Old and the New, but they belonged within one God, just and good, creator and saviour, judge and father. The theme of

---

[13] ἰχθύς. Particularity is found in Jesus Christ, universality in the saviour who is son of God. 'And after all, it was an instinct for the truth and universality of Jesus that carried them away.' T. R. Glover, *The conflict of religions in the early Roman empire* (London, 1912), 194.

the Christian bible was the economy or history of salvation. This was the mystery (Eph. 3.9) hidden in God from all ages. Tertullian pointed out to Marcion that this mystery was hidden *in* God, and not, as Marcion claimed, hidden from God. This was the first great feat of micro-engineering.[14]

A different threat to the inclusive being of God came in monarchianism or 'identification theology' which kept plurality out of God and attributed all to an empty, identical God who, in different modes, did the work of father, son and spirit. This would not do because the relation of father and son had to be internal and not external to God; everything depended on it. No one knew the son without the father or the father without the son. An account of the being or substance of God was needed. While pictures of sun, ray and light could help, the basic image lay in the mind of the maker who thought and spoke. There was no picture for this, only the Stoic inner and uttered λόγος, and no explanation but the Stoic genre of relative disposition. God's substance is his unique, inclusive stuff: he is father, son and spirit.

From all this Tertullian simplified the rule of faith into the *sacramentum oikonomiae* or faith in the triune God. There were philosophical impulses. First, a criterion had to be simple, not complex. Truth is simple (*ap.* 23.7f.). Second, there were good reasons to telescope transcendent causes into one. This tendency, evident in Plotinus, negated profusely by Gnostics, later controverted by Iamblichus, resisted the multiplication of intermediaries. Third, talk about the substance of God is elusive. In modern times, empiricists once asked, 'What would it be like for "x" not to be the case? What would it be like for God not to be father, son and spirit?' Tertullian has the best answer of all. 'It would be like the divine subdivision by Marcion or the identification by Praxeas.'

There were also theological impulses. Not history, but God, father, son and holy spirit, was the object of faith. Tertullian put the truth of God's saving work within God. One God had lovingly created humanity, with the future man (*homo futurus*), Jesus, in

---

[14] Some years ago, when smoking was common, *Punch* portrayed a proud chemist with a bench full of elaborate apparatus through which a mixed-up gas was passed; glass tubing, retorts, valves, filter funnels, condensers, bubblers and a double helix reached almost to the ceiling. The caption was something like, 'How do I fit all this into one filter tip?'

mind. The same God had joined end to beginning on the cross and would be all in all when the son handed over the kingdom to the father. The entire dishonour of God was the Christian's only hope. Tertullian's mystery of the economy in God anticipates Gregory the Theologian's summing up of the trinity in one God.

This makes sense of the other things Tertullian wrote. A similar inclusiveness is expressed in prayer which is the heart of the Christian's life. Here the believer has a prayer which sums everything up; Tertullian describes the Lord's Prayer as an epitome of the gospel. Sin presented no surprise for one who lived with Heraclitean and Pauline tension. Tertullian clarified the problem of free will, of self-determined yet compulsive sin, through Adam's free choice and original sin. Yet sin within the church presented difficulties which he could not handle. The fulfilment of all things in Christ and the effectiveness of baptism required the absence of deadly sins from Christian lives. Won to Christianity by the heroism of Christian virtue, delivered from serious sin by baptism, he was driven to despair by the abundance of Christian sin. Forced to distinguish between sins which disproved the gospel and sins which did not, he found himself at variance with episcopal direction. This estrangement was no passing problem; in every age there have been as many repelled by a 'sordid' church as by the folly of faith.

Did he leave the church? It seems better to say that he did not.[15] Yet when Cyprian took up his ideas and made the classic pattern of the catholic church, Tertullian had to appear on the outside. Tertullian never looked like a statesman; nothing came easier than the promotion of his future disqualification. Yet present disagreements were temporary; all would be set right in the coming kingdom which the paraclete was bringing. He depicted the world to come with the detail and fearful imagery of the Apocalypse. When he came to ethics, he sought to reconcile love and fear, contingency and perfection.

With his ceaseless, anxious argument, he handed on a unity of antitheses and economy in one God. He saw the point at which many passed into one, so that father, son and spirit became a *tota*

---

[15] The question is both ambiguous and obscure; but David Rankin's negative answer stands up to objections.

trinitas, and a crowded recapitulation became divine unicity. Clement of Alexandria and the Platonic tradition could move (without moving) from the cosmic unity of the son as ὡς πάντα ἕν to the ineffable One. Tertullian's way was different. How does the summing up of all things reduce to a unity? Tertullian found the direct way from perfection to simplicity in the God who died to heal mankind (*Marc.* 2.16.3).[16] Gregory followed him with the simplicity of cosmic salvation. 'A few drops of blood recreate the whole world and draw human beings together into a unity' (*orat.* 45.29.36.664). No modern writer has put this more clearly than the philosopher and exegete who wrote, 'Jesus Christ clothed himself in all the images of messianic promise, and in living them out, crucified them: but the crucified reality is better than the figures of prophecy. This is very God and life eternal, whereby the children of God are delivered from idols.'[17]

At every point Tertullian defends the rational choice of Christian faith, which is grasped as *unica spes*: 'Lord, to whom shall we go? You have the words of eternal life' (John 6.68). Tertullian finds a natural sense of God in every human being, whereby Christ may be recognized for what he is. If we uncover the history behind the New Testament, there is no doubt that early Christian communities came to worship Jesus as divine, attributing divine titles and ultimacy to him.[18] If we read the Fourth Gospel, despite a unity of subordination between son and father, the word who was in the beginning dominates at every point until the cry of victory sounds from the cross: 'It is finished' (τετέλεσται) (John 19.30).

Choice is tied to vulnerability. Apologetic finds faith in no tranquil haven but in a world governed by the strife of opposites. Christian theology emerges to cope with vulnerability and to disarm false claims for immunity. All the people whom Tertullian attacks are concerned to vaccinate a vulnerable faith in a way which, he thinks, removes its ultimacy. The disciples of Athens want a Platonic or Stoic Christianity. Docetists want to soften the

---

[16] A recent influential exposition of trinitarian theology is similarly based on the death of Jesus. Jüngel, *Geheimnis*, xiv, 481 et passim.

[17] Austin Farrer, An English Appreciation, in Bartsch, *Kerygma and Myth*, 223.

[18] L. Hurtado, *One God, one Lord: Early Christian devotion and ancient Jewish monotheism* (Philadelphia, 1988), 11.

contradiction of an incarnate God. Marcion wants to remove the conflict between creator and redeemer, law and gospel, by attributing the two parts of the antithesis to two different gods: Tertullian replies that God is not God if he be not one and that the antitheses must be contained in one God. Praxeas argues that father, son and spirit are identical in one God who acts in each capacity: Tertullian argues that the mystery of the divine economy is hidden within the triune God, who alone deserves worship. Only a creator who is also redeemer is credible. Gnostic determinism separates, at birth, sinners and saints. Tertullian argues for human freedom tainted only by the sin which was chosen after Adam left his maker's hands. Indulgent bishops dispensed forgiveness to sinners within a sordid church: Tertullian protested, since it was the moral excellence of believers which had first turned him in the direction of faith. Hermogenes' matter explained the imperfection of the world: Tertullian claimed that it introduced a second god. Valentinians proposed a knowledge immune from rational attack: Tertullian claimed that such immunity made possible all kinds of nonsense. Spiritual resurrection or immortal souls might have answered objections to the vivid detail of Christian apocalyptic; but Tertullian found no hope in a God who abandoned his creation. Christian ethics were vulnerable because of their contradiction between affirming and denying the world; but this and other tensions were inevitable for right living.

Theologians have long looked for continuity in the development of doctrine from the New Testament to the creeds of the fourth and fifth centuries. They have ignored the fact that discontinuity is equally evident in any tradition of thought and have submitted to the desire for 'fictive concords with origins and ends'.[19] Immersion in the New Testament and second-century writers can breed a dislike for councils and creeds, with a readiness to reject 'the long period of dogmatic squabbling while the Empire was falling to pieces'.[20] This is a reasonable reaction to the almost universal

---

[19] 'Men, like poets, rush "into the middest" *in medias res* when they are born; they also die *in mediis rebus* and to make sense of their span they need fictive concords with origins and ends, such as give meaning to lives and poems.' Frank Kermode, *The sense of an ending* (Oxford, 1967), 7.

[20] Inge, *Platonic tradition*, 111.

attempt to interpret a putative middle in terms of a putative end, or to the assumption that second-century writers were unsuccessfully trying to answer fourth- and fifth-century questions, or to the belief that Chalcedon might be interpreted from the New Testament without thought for what has come between. The history of ideas functions neither by following the same agenda nor by building bit-by-bit a final scheme. Discontinuity outstrips continuity. To take a rough analogy, from Bach to Messiaen is as far as from the New Testament to Chalcedon. César Franck is not a bridge or stepping stone between these two points any more than Tertullian is a bridge from the New Testament to Chalcedon. Yet what the mid-term says is the way to understand the continuity and discontinuity between the two extremes. In a word, the middle is never merely a revision of the beginning and never simply an anticipation of the end, but a statement in its own right which may enable the move between the two designated extremes to be understood.

The assimilation of classical thought into Christian theology is to be understood in the same way. It is not present in the New Testament. By the time we reach the fourth century it is there.[21] Indeed, there is no evidence of positive interaction between philosophy and Christianity in the first half of the fourth century. If we are to understand the process, it will be through understanding the second century (Clement and Tertullian are the key figures) in its own right, neither as an afterthought nor as a prelude. If we are to understand the movement of European music, we have to treat César Franck and others in the same way.

No book should try to say everything. This study has taken Tertullian's arguments as exposition of his vocabulary and found that many common readings of his thought are questionable. Three points have emerged which need to be followed up elsewhere.[22] First, his argument was commonly creative, through metaphor, paradox and wit. Like all innovators he used old ways of arguing together with new ways of metaphor which broke the moulds. Second, his Stoic materialism has interest because of the

---

[21] This is evident in the recent study of Christopher Stead, who shows how deep the difficulties are. See his *Philosophy in Christian antiquity* (Cambridge, 1994).

[22] In fealty to Rorty and Davidson.

non-reductive physicalism which is so plausible at present and the common assumption that Christianity can be identified with Platonism.[23] Thirdly, Tertullian, more than Augustine, is the innovator.

As we rediscover Tertullian today, we acknowledge his historical importance, his alien setting and his strongly individual mind. It is plain that in him the Western mind ('der abendländische Geist') finds its first Christian expression. 'In Western Christianity everything seems to commence with Tertullian: the technical language of Christians, theology, interpretation of scripture and other manifestations of a religion which is in part already settled and in part still on the move.'[24] This continuity is qualified by our estrangement from his world, where a surfeit of gods gave him a setting which is alien to our secular scene.

Finally, what are the qualities of his mind which appeal today? First there is his originality. He is an intellectual Genghis Khan, who explores the bible and classical culture, yet manages to present antiquarian, scientific, medical and philosophical material in an original way. Far from the *florilegia* of Clement, there is a highly individual sparkle in what he says. 'For he wants to present things in his own words and not simply repeat the language of the schools.'[25] His humour gives colour to what he writes, through widening the scene; after all, it *is* easier to imagine a man (like Marcion) born without heart and brains than to imagine a man born without a body (*Marc.* 4.10.16). His personal piety is inseparable from his theology and from his style; every human being stands under a power which strictly orders what he should do and to which in an intense and imperfect way he is responsible. At the last day, Christ will own those who have chosen to own him. Individual choice determines all. 'No one is born for another, and he dies for himself alone' (*pall.* 5.4). 'Build your faith, brother, on your own foundation!' (*an.* 26.1).

[23] See R. Rorty's account of Davidson's non-reductive physicalism, in his *Objectivity, relativism and truth* (Cambridge, 1991) 113–25.

[24] C. Moreschini, Aspetti della dottrina del martirio in Tertulliano, *Compostellanum*, 35 (1990), 55.

[25] 'Denn er will mit den Worten charakterisieren, nicht Schulbildung an den Tag legen'. K. Holl, Tertullian als Schriftsteller, *Gesammelte Aufsätze zur Kirchengeschichte*, vol. III (Tübingen, 1928), 8.

Secondly, there is his openness which disappoints some who want comprehensive conclusions. He is forever on the move, seeking more of what he has found: one should be ashamed of intellectual inertia ('hic tantum curiositas torpescit', (*nat.* 1.1.3)). He uses exegeses and arguments in one place and denies them elsewhere; he praises and criticizes martyrs; and he extols the wonders of married life, yet sees a widower as relieved of a burden. Part of this is the logic of apologetic which is directed to distinct and separate problems. Part of it is the advocate who argues each case separately. Deeper still is his commitment to reason: he has to satisfy himself, not others, that a position is rationally justified.[26] This means that he does not always bring out the inner unity of his own position, because he is too concerned to set out a problem and to discuss every point.[27] He saw on his own side contradictions which others ignored and made things difficult for himself by raising problems (*bapt.* 12) which did not worry others. His anxious artistry[28] gave him courage and the ability to grasp a complex of ideas and to bring from each detail something which was useful to his case. The anxiety derived from the ease with which Christians compromised their unique hope. His Heraclitean love of opposites is a complex thing, ranging from a stylistic tic, which may infect those who read him, to his wide, inclusive humanity. Conflict is his life; opposites are his reality; and paradox is his intellectual delight. The poet, Robert Browning, captured a small part of this,

> Our interest's on the dangerous edge of things
> The honest thief, the tender murderer, the superstitious atheist...
> We watch while these in equilibrium keep
> The giddy line midway: one step aside,
> They're classed and done with.[29]

Thirdly, there is the coherence provided by one theme: the perfection of the divine economy in the crucified Christ. A profound unity springs from his final vocabulary or rule of faith.

---

[26] *Ibid.*, 10. 'Was er annehmen soll, das muss ihm auch denkbar sein.'
[27] *Ibid.*, 11. 'Das Problem ist klar zerlegt und jeder einzelne Punkt mit dialektischer Kunst erörtert, aber hat er es verstanden, die innere Einheit seiner Motive zum Ausdruck zu bringen?'
[28] *Ibid.*, 12. 'verzweifelte Kunst'. This gave him, I think, a courage of despair or 'Verzweifelungsmut'.
[29] *Bishop Blougram's Apology*, 395–401.

For the simple mystery of human salvation, God's economy, the summing-up of all things in Christ joins his prolific intellectual adventures. The superiority of Jerusalem over Athens derives from the order of the divine economy and recapitulation joins Alpha to Omega in credible ineptitude. To the soul naturally Christian, the long story of salvation brings recognition of the well-known God. Divine disgrace unites Marcion's antitheses or the divine trinity within the being of God. Saving history is summarized in the Lord's Prayer or extended in the bible. The church cannot allow post-baptismal sin which denies the sovereign power of Jesus Christ, son of God, saviour. The divine comedy is obscured by Valentinian fables. Apocalyptic affirms the coming kingdom of Christus Victor. Christian morals point to the mystery which at the end restores the divine likeness given in creation.

For us today, Tertullian's overarching theme raises different problems for different people. From the beginning the reconciliation of all things in Christ (Eph. 1.10, 4.13–16) meant conflict for believers fighting (Eph. 6.10–20). The antithesis of Athens and Jerusalem confirms and questions the exclusiveness of any monotheism. The paradox of incarnation is central but unacceptable to that total metaphysic,[30] for which God is not in the world. The strife of opposites suggests the pointlessness of progress and the 'God-shaped blank' grows blanker for some in a secular world. Antitheses in God raise questions about the ultimacy of evil and Christian use of the Old Testament. Since only a crucified God answers the primitive claim for divine credibility (a creator must redeem), how does this reinforce trinitarian belief? Do prayer and the bible exacerbate or illuminate problems of belief? Can the force of evil in human life be reconciled with human freedom and divine goodness? Why is the church itself so often an obstacle to faith? Where does Christian nonsense begin and how is reason important? What is the future of Jesus Christ? In morals can we reconcile world-affirmation and world-denial, fear and love of God, the natural and the new? All these questions are enlarged and better understood through Tertullian's argument.

His originality and openness made him an ecclesiastical failure,

[30] Wittgensteins's *Tractatus Logico-Philosophicus*, the reductionism of which continues in popular secularism.

for the church was offended by much that he wrote, even if it could never forget him because he so clearly belonged within its life.[31] That same originality remains his claim on our attention today, for we have learnt, from the pragmatists, that the one worth-while intellectual enterprise is to speak as though we are not rehearsing a previously written script.[32]

[31] Holl, *Tertullian als Schriftsteller*, 12. 'denn er war einer der ihrigen, und er war einer der Grössten'. Cyprian's 'Da magistrum!' must be remembered.
[32] R. Rorty, *Contingency, irony, and solidarity* (Cambridge, 1989), xiii.

Select bibliography

TEXTS AND TRANSLATIONS

Acta Martyrum, ed. H. Musurillo, *The acts of the Christian martyrs* (Oxford, 1972)
Die ältesten Apologeten, ed. E. J. Goodspeed (Göttingen, 1914)
Apuleius, *De philosophia libri*, ed. P. Thomas (Leipzig, 1908)
Aristotle, ed. W. D. Ross
  De Anima (Oxford, 1961)
  Metaphysics, 2 vols. (Oxford, 1924)
  Physics (Oxford, 1936)
Aristotle, *The complete works of Aristotle: the revised Oxford translation*, ed. Jonathan Barnes (Princeton, 1984)
Clemens Alexandrinus, ed. O. Stählin, *GCS*, 4 vols. (Leipzig, 1905–36. Revision by Ursula Treu: 1, 3 Aufl., 1972; 2, 4 Aufl. (L. Früchtel), 1985; 3, 2 Aufl. (L. Früchtel), 1970; 4, 1, 2 Aufl., 1980)
Clément d'Alexandrie, text and trans. S.C., ed. C. Mondésert
  Le Pédagogue: 70 (1960), 108 (1965), 158 (1970)
  Protreptique: 2 (1949)
  Stromate I: 30 (1951)
  Stromate II: 38 (1954)
  Stromate V: 278, 279 (1981)
  Extraits de Théodote: 23 (1948)
Clement of Alexandria, Stromateis 3 and 7, translated with notes by H. Chadwick in, *Alexandrian Christianity*, eds. J. E. L. Oulton and H Chadwick (*LCC*, London, 1954)
Clement of Alexandria, trans. W. Wilson, *ANCL*, 4, 12, 22, 24 (1882–4)
Diognetus, To, A Diognète, text and trans. H. I. Marrou, *SC* (1951)
Irenaeus, *Against heresies*, text, R. Massuet (Paris, 1710), *PG*, 7 (Paris, 1882)
Irenaeus, *Against heresies*, text, W. D. Harvey, 2 vols. (Cambridge, 1857)
Irenaeus, *Against heresies*, text and translation, SC, ed. C. Mondésert
  Contre les Hérésies:

I: 263, 264 (1979)
II: 293, 294 (1982)
III: 210, 211 (1974)
IV: 100 (1965)
V: 152, 153 (1969)
Démonstration, trans. 62 (1959)

Irenaeus, *Against heresies*, trans. A. Roberts and W. H. Rambaut, *ANCL*, 5, 9 (1883–84)

Irenaeus, *The demonstration of the apostolic preaching*, trans. J. Armitage Robinson (London, 1920)

Irenaeus, *Des heiligen Irenäus Schrift zum Erwies der apostolischen Verkündigung in armenischer Version entdeckt herausgegeben und ins Deutsch übersetzt von K. Ter-Mekerttschian und E. Ter-Minassiantz*, *TU*, 31, 1 (Berlin, 1907)

Justin, *Opera*, text, J. C. T. Otto, 3rd edn (Jena, 1876–9)

Justin and Athenagoras, trans. M. Dods, G. Reith and B. P. Pratten, *ANCL*, 2 (Edinburgh, 1879)

Justin, *Apologies*, text, A. W. F. Blunt (Cambridge, 1911)

Justin, *The dialogue with Trypho*, trans. A. Lukyn Williams (London, 1930)

Justin, *First Apology*, trans. E. R. Hardy, Early Christian Fathers, ed. C. C. Richardson, *LCC*, 1 (London, 1953)

Justin, *Saint Justin, Apologie pour les Chrétiens*, Édition et traduction, Charles Munier (Fribourg, 1995)

Origen, *Contra Celsum*, trans. H. Chadwick (Cambridge, 1953)

Origen, text, *GCS* 2, 3, 6, 10, 22, 29, 30, 33, 35, 38, 40, 41 (Leipzig, 1899–1941)

Philo, text, eds L. Cohn and P. Wendland, 6 vols. (Berlin, 1896–1915)

Philo, text and trans. F. H. Colson, G. H. Whitaker and R. A. Markus, *LCL*, 12 vols. (London, 1929–62)

Plato, text, J. Burnet, 5 vols. (Oxford, 1900–7)

Plotinus, text, P. Henry and H. R. Schwyzer, 3 vols. (Paris, Brussels, 1951–9)

Plotinus, text, P. Henry and H. R. Schwyzer (edn minor), 3 vols. (Oxford, 1966, 1977, 1988)

Plotinus, text and trans. A. H. Armstrong, *LCL*, 7 vols. (1966–88)

Plotinus, text and trans. E. Bréhier, 7 vols. (Paris, 1924–38)

Plotinus, text and trans. R. Harder, R. Beutler and W. Theiler, 12 vols. in 8 (Hamburg, 1956–71)

Plotinus, trans. S. Mackenna, 2nd edn London, 1956)

Plutarch, *Moralia*, text and trans. F. C. Babbitt *et al.*, *LCL*, 15 vols. (London, 1927–8)

Plutarch, *Moralia*, text, G. N. Bernadakis, Teubner, 1st edn, 7 vols. (Leipzig, 1888–96)

Plutarch, *Moralia*, text, C. Hubert, M. Pohlenz *et al.*, Teubner, 2nd edn (Leipzig, 1925–74)
Posidonius, text, E. Bake (Leyden, 1820)
Proclus, *Elements of Theology*, text and trans. E. R. Dodds, 2nd edn (Oxford, 1963)
Tertullian, *de anima*, text, J. H. Waszink (Amsterdam, 1947)
Tertullian, text and trans. E. Evans:
　Adversus Marcionem, 2 vols. (Oxford, 1972)
　Homily on baptism (London, 1964)
　Treatise against Praxeas (London, 1948)
　Treatise on prayer (London, 1953)
　Treatise on the incarnation (London, 1956)
　Treatise on the resurrection (London, 1960)
Tertullian, text and trans. *SC*, ed. C. Mondésert:
　A son épouse: 273 (1980)
　La chair du Christ: 216, 217 (1975)
　Contre les Valentiniens: 280, 281 (1980, 1981)
　De la patience: 310 (1984)
　De la prescription contre les hérétiques: 46 (1957)
　De la pudicité: 394, 395 (1993)
　Exhortation à la chasteté: 319 (1985)
　Le mariage unique: 343 (1988)
　La pénitence: 316 (1984)
　Les spectacles: 332 (1986)
　La toilette des femmes: 173 (1971)
Tertullian, trans. Peter Holmes and S. Thelwall, *ANCL*, 7 (1878), 11 (1881), 15 (1870), 18 (1884)
Tertullian, trans. W. P. Le Saint, *Treatises on marriage and remarriage*, *ACW 13*, London, 1951); *Treatises on penance*, *ACW* (London, 1958)
Tertullian, trans. J. H. Waszink, *Treatise against Hermogenes*, *ACW* (London, 1956)
Xenocrates, text, R. Heinze (Leipzig, 1892)

SECONDARY WORKS

Abramowski, L., *Drei christologische Untersuchungen* (Berlin, 1981)
　Der Logos in der altchristlichen Theologie, in C. Colpe *et al.* (eds.), *Spätantike und Christentum* (Berlin, 1992)
　Trinitarische und christologische Hypostasenformel, *ThPh*, 54 (1979)
Ahondokpe, A. Z., *La vision de Rome chez Tertullien*, 2 vols. (Lille, 1991)
Alès, A. d', Le mot οἰκονομία dans la langue théologique de s. Irénée, *REG*, 32 (1919)
　La théologie de Tertullien (Paris, 1905)

Altendorf, E., *Der Kirchenbegriff Tertullians* (Berlin, 1932)

Andia, Y. de, *Homo vivens, Incorruptibilité et divinisation selon Irénée de Lyon* (Paris, 1986)

Andresen, C., *Logos und Nomos, Die Polemik des Kelsos wider das Christentum, AKG* (Berlin, 1955)

Zur Entstehung und Geschichte des trinitarischen Personbegriffes, *ZNW*, 52 (1961)

Aulen, G., *Christus Victor* (London, 1953)

Ayers, R. H., *Language, logic and reason in the church fathers: A study in Tertullian, Augustine and Aquinas* (Olms, 1979)

Aziza, C., *Tertullien et le Judaïsme* (Nice, 1977)

Balthasar, Hans Urs von, *Herrlichkeit, Eine theologische Ästhetik* (Einsiedeln, 1962). ET *The glory of the lord* (Edinburgh, 1984)

Barnes, T. D., *Tertullian, A historical and literary study*, 2nd edn (Oxford, 1985)

Bauer, W., *Orthodoxy and heresy in earliest Christianity*, eds. R. A. Kraft and G. Krodel (Philadelphia, 1971), translated from the second German edition, ed. G. Strecker (Tübingen, 1964)

Beck, A., *Römisches Recht bei Tertullian und Cyprian. Eine Studie zur frühen Kirchengeschichte* (Halle, 1930)

Bengsch, A., *Heilsgeschichte und Heilswissen, Eine Untersuchung zur Struktur und Entfaltung des theologischen Denkens im Werk 'Adversus Haereses' des hl. Irenäus von Lyons* (Leipzig, 1957)

Benoit, A., *Saint Irénée, introduction à l'étude de sa théologie* (Paris, 1960)

Berthousoz, R., *Liberté et grâce suivant la théologie d'Irénée de Lyon* (Fribourg, 1980)

Bianchi, U. (ed.), *Le Origini dello Gnosticismo* (Leiden, 1970)

Bill, A., *Zur Erklärung und Textkritik des ersten Buches Tertullians 'Adversus Marcionem'* (Leipzig, 1911)

Braun, R., *Approches de Tertullien* (Paris, 1992)

Deus Christianorum, 2nd edn (Paris, 1977)

Tertullien et le Montanisme: Église institutionelle et église spirituelle, *RSLR*, 21 (1985)

Bray, G., *Holiness and the will of God* (London, 1979)

Brox, N., *Offenbarung, Gnosis und gnostischer Mythos bei Irenäus von Lyon* (Salzburg und München, 1966)

Campenhausen, H. von, *Ecclesiastical authority and spiritual power* (London, 1969)

The formation of the Christian bible (London, 1972)

Cantalamessa, R., *La cristologia di Tertulliano* (Freiburg, 1961)

Chadwick, H., *Early Christian thought and the classical tradition* (Oxford, 1966)

Countryman, L. W., Tertullian and the Regula Fidei, *The Second Century* (1982)

Daly, C. B., *Tertullian the Puritan and his influence* (Dublin, 1993)

Daniélou, J., *Gospel message and Hellenistic culture* (London, 1973)
The origins of Latin Christianity (London, 1977)
The theology of Jewish Christianity (London, 1964)

Décarie, V., Le paradoxe de Tertullien, *VC* (1960)

Di Berardino, A., and B. Studer, *Storia della teología*, I, *Epoca patristica* (Casale Monferrato, 1993)

Dillon, J. M., *The Middle Platonists* (London, 1977)

Dölger, F. J., ΙΧΘΥΣ *der heilige Fisch in den antiken Religionen und im Christentum* (Münster, 1922)

Duhot, J. J., Y-at-il des catégories stoïciennes? *RIPh*, 8 (1991)

Eynde, D. van den, *Les normes de l'enseignement chrétien, dans la littérature patristique des trois premiers siècles* (Gembloux and Paris, 1933)

Finé, H., *Die Terminologie der Jenseitsvorstellungen bei Tertullian; ein semasiologischer Beitrag zur Dogmengeschichte des Zwischenzustandes* (Bonn, 1958)

Fredouille, J.-C., Tertullien, *Dictionnaire des philosophes* (Paris, 1984), vol. II
Tertullien et la conversion de la culture antique (Paris, 1972)
Tertullien et l'empire, *REA*, 29 (1984)

Frend, W. H. C., *Martyrdom and persecution in the early church* (Oxford, 1965)
Montanismus, *TRE*, 23 (1994), 271–9

Gager, J. G., Marcion and philosophy, *VC* 26 (1972)

Gibson, A. Boyce, *Should philosophers be kings?* (Melbourne, 1939)

Ginzberg, L., *The legends of the Jews*, 7 vols. (Philadelphia, 1909–38)

Grant, R. M., *The Early Christian Doctrine of God* (Charlottesville, 1966)
Gods and the one God (Philadelphia, 1986)
Two notes on Tertullian, *VC*, 15 (1951)

Hägglund, B., Die Bedeutung der 'regula fidei' als Grundlage theologischer Aussagen, *StTh*, 12 (1958)

Hallonsten, G., *Meritum bei Tertullian* (Malmö, 1985)
Satisfactio bei Tertullian (Malmö, 1984)

Hanson, R. P. C., Notes on Tertullian's interpretation of scripture, *JThS*, NS 12 (1961)
The search for the Christian idea of God (Edinburgh, 1988)

Harl, M., *Origène et la fonction révélatrice du verbe incarné* (Paris, 1958)

Harnack, A. von, *Marcion, Das Evangelium vom fremden Gott*, 2 Aufl. (Leipzig, 1924)
Militia Christi (Berlin, 1905)

Heinze, J., Tertullians Apologeticum, *BVSGW.PH*, 62, 10 (Leipzig, 1911)

Holl, K., Tertullian als Schriftsteller, *Gesammelte Aufsätze zur Kirchengeschichte*, vol. III (Tübingen, 1928)

Holte, R., Logos Spermatikos, Christianity and ancient philosophy according to St Justin's Apologies, *StTh*, 12 (1958)

Horbury, W., Tertullian on the Jews in the light of De spectaculis 30.5–6, *JThS*, 23 (1972)

Hornus, J. M., Étude sur la pensée politique de Tertullien, *RHPhR*, 38 (1958)

  It is not lawful for me to fight, Early Christian attitudes towards law, violence and the state (Scottdale, Pa., and Kitchener, Ontario, 1980)

Huby, P., and G. Neal (eds.), *The criterion of truth, FS George Kerferd* (Liverpool, 1989)

Hurtado, L., *One God, one Lord: Early Christian devotion and ancient Jewish monotheism* (Philadelphia, 1988)

Inge, W. R. *The Platonic tradition in English religious thought* (London, 1926)

Jonas, Hans, *Gnosis und spätantiker Geist* (Göttingen, 1964, 1966)

Jüngel, E., *Gott als Geheimnis der Welt* (Tübingen, 1977)

Karpp, H., *Probleme altchristlicher Anthropologie* (Gütersloh, 1950)

  Schrift und Geist bei Tertullian (Gütersloh, 1955)

Käsemann, E., *Essays on New Testament themes* (London, 1964)

  Exegetische Versuche und Besinnungen, vol. I (Göttingen, 1960), vol. II (Göttingen, 1965)

  Jesu Letzter Wille nach Johannes 17 (Tübingen, 1967)

  New Testament Questions of Today (London, 1969)

  The testament of Jesus (London, 1968)

Kinzig, W., Καινὴ Διαθήκη, the title of the New Testament in the second and third centuries, *JThS*, 45.2 (1994)

Klein, Richard, *Tertullian und das römische Reich* (Heidelberg, 1968)

Kouri, E. I., *Tertullian und die römische Antike* (Helsinki, 1982)

Kretschmar, G., *Studien zur frühchristlichen Trinitätstheologie* (Tübingen, 1956)

Kunze, J., *Die Gotteslehre des Irenaeus* (Leipzig, 1891)

Kuss, O., Zur Hermeneutik Tertullians, *Neutestamentliche Aufsätze*, eds. J. Blinzler *et al.* (Regensburg, 1963)

Labhardt, A., Tertullien et la philosophie ou la recherche d'une 'position pure', *MH*, 7 (1950)

Labriolle, P. de, *La crise montaniste* (Paris, 1913)

Lassiat, H., *Promotion de l'homme en Jésus Christ d'après Irénée de Lyon* (Tours, 1974)

Leonhardi, G., *Die apologetischen Grundgedanken Tertullians* (Leipzig, 1882)

Logan, A. H. B., *Gnostic truth and Christian heresy* (Edinburgh, 1996)

Long, A. A., *Hellenistic philosophy* (London, 1974)

Lortz, J., Das Christentum als Monotheismus in den Apologeten des zweiten Jahrhunderts, in A. M. Koeniger (ed.), *Beiträge zur Geschichte des christlichen Altertums und der Byzantinischen Literatur, FS A. Ehrhard* (Bonn, 1922)

  Tertullian als Apologet, 2 vols. (Münster, 1927, 1928)

Maas, W., *Unveränderlichkeit Gottes* (München, 1974)

Markschies, C., Die Krise einer philosophischen Bibel-Theologie in der alten Kirche, oder: Valentin und die valentinianische Gnosis zwischen philosophischer Bibelinterpretation und mythologischer Häresie, in R. Berlinger and W. Schrader (eds.), *Gnosis und Philosophie: Miscellanea, Elementa*, 59 (Amsterdam, 1994)
    Valentinus Gnosticus? (Tübingen, 1993)

May, G., Marcion in contemporary views – results and open questions, *The Second Century*, 6 (1988)
    Ein neues Markionbild, *ThR*, 51 (1986)
    Schöpfung aus dem Nichts (Berlin, 1978)

Mayer, A., *Das Gottesbild im Menschen nach Clemens von Alexandrien* (Rome, 1942)

Meijering, E. P., *Tertullian contra Marcion, Gotteslehre in der Polemik* (Leiden, 1977)

Meis, A., El problema de Dios en Tertuliano, *TyV*, 21 (1980)

Milano, A., *Persona in teologia. Alle origini del significato di persona nel cristianesimo antico* (Napoli, 1984)

Minns, D., *Irenaeus* (London, 1994)

Moffatt, James, Aristotle and Tertullian, *JThS*, 17 (1916)

Moingt, J., Le problème du dieu unique chez Tertullien, *RevSR*, 44 (1970)
    Théologie trinitaire de Tertullien, 4 vols. (Paris, 1966–9)

Moltmann, J., *The crucified God* (London, 1974)
    Theology of hope (London, 1967)

Monceaux, P., *Histoire littéraire de l'Afrique chrétienne*, vol. 1, *Tertullien et les origines* (Paris, 1901)

Mondésert, C., *Clément d'Alexandrie. Introduction à l'étude de sa pensée religieuse à partir de l'Écriture* (Paris, 1944)

Monro, D. H., *Argument of laughter* (Melbourne, 1951)

Montini, P., Elementi di filosofia stoica in S. Giustino, *Aquinas*, 28 (1985)

Morel, V., 'Disciplina' le mot et l'idée ... dans les oeuvres de Tertullien, *RHE*, 40 (1944–5)

Moreschini, C., Aspetti della dottrina del martirio in Tertulliano, *Compostellanum*, 35 (1990)
    Temi e motivi della polemica antimarcionista di Tertulliano, *SCO*, 17 (1968)

Moule, C. F. D., Fulfilment-words in the New Testament: use and abuse, in *Essays in New Testament interpretation* (Cambridge, 1982)

Munier, C., Analyse du traité de Tertullien, de praescriptione haereticorum, *RevSR*, 59 (1985)
    L'apologie de saint Justin philosophe et martyr (Fribourg, 1994)
    Les conceptions hérésiologiques de Tertullien, in V. Saxer (ed.), *Ecclesia orans, Mélanges Hamman* (Rome, 1980)
    Petite vie de Tertullien (Paris, 1996)

La structure litteraire de l'Apologie de Justin, RevSR, 60 (1986)

Tertullien, in *Dictionnaire de spiritualité, ascétique et mystique,* vol. xv (Paris, 1990)

La tradition apostolique chez Tertullien, in Collected Studies Series CS 341, Autorité épiscopale et sollicitude pastorale, *L'année canonique,* 33 (Paris, 1979)

Muñoz, A. B., El antifilosofismo de Tertulliano y la fe como reconocimiento, *RET,* 36 (1966)

Murdoch, Iris, *The fire and the sun* (Oxford, 1977)

Metaphysics as a guide to morals (London, 1992)

O'Malley, T. P., *Tertullian and the bible* (Nijmegen and Utrecht, 1967)

Orbe, A., *Antropología de San Ireneo* (Madrid, 1969)

Osborn, E. F., Arguments for faith in Clement of Alexandria, *VC,* 48 (1994)

The beginning of Christian philosophy (Cambridge, 1981)

The emergence of Christian theology (Cambridge, 1993)

Ethical patterns in early Christian thought (Cambridge, 1976)

Justin Martyr (Tübingen, 1973)

The philosophy of Clement of Alexandria (Cambridge, 1957)

Otto, S., *'Natura' und 'Dispositio', Untersuchung zum Naturbegriff und zur Denkform Tertullians* (München, 1960)

Pfeil, H., Die Frage nach der Veränderlichkeit und Geschichtlichkeit Gottes, *MThZ,* 31 (1980)

Pohlenz, M., *Die Stoa,* 2 vols. (Göttingen, 1948, 1955)

Vom Zorne Gottes (Göttingen, 1909)

Polto, E., *Evoluzione del pensiero di Tertulliano sulla dottrina del peccato* (Biella, 1971)

Pouderon, B., Athénagore et Tertullien sur la résurrection, *REA,* 35 (1989)

Prestige, G. L., *God in patristic thought* (London, 1936)

Prigent, P., *Justin et l'ancien testament* (Paris, 1964)

Prümm, K., Göttliche Planung und menschliche Entwicklung nach Irenäus' Adversus haereses, *Schol.* 13 (1938)

Quispel, G., African Christianity before Tertullian, in *Romanitas et Christianitas, FS J. H. Waszink* (Amsterdam, 1973)

De Bronnen van Tertullianus' Adversus Marcionem (Leiden, 1943)

De humor van Tertullianus, *NThT,* 2 (1947–8)

Rambaux, C., *Tertullien face aux morales des trois premiers siècles* (Paris, 1979)

Ramos-Lisson, D., et al., *Masculinidad y feminidad en la patristica* (Pamplona, 1989)

Rankin, David, *Tertullian and the church* (Cambridge, 1995)

Tertullian's use of the word *potestas, JRH,* 19.1 (1995)

Rauch, G., *Der Einfluss der stoischen Philosophie auf die Lehrbildung Tertullians* (Halle, 1890)

Refoulé, F., Tertullien et la philosophie, *RevSR*, 30 (1956)
Rist, J. M., Plotinus on matter and evil, *Phronesis*, 6 (1961)
  Plotinus, the road to reality (Cambridge, 1967)
  Seneca and Stoic orthodoxy, *ANRW*, Teil II, Band 36, Teilband 3 (1989)
  Stoic philosophy (Cambridge, 1969)
Rorty, R., *Contingency, irony, and solidarity* (Cambridge, 1989)
  Objectivity, relativism and truth (Cambridge, 1991)
Rorty, R., J. B. Schneewind and Quentin Skinner (eds.), *Philosophy in history* (Cambridge, 1984)
Runia, D. T., *Philo and the church fathers* (Leiden, 1995)
  Philo in early Christian literature: a survey (Leiden, 1993)
  Philo of Alexandria and the Timaeus of Plato, 2 vols. (Leiden, 1986)
Scharl, E., *Recapitulatio Mundi* (Freiburg, 1941)
Schelowsky, G., *Der Apologet Tertullianus in seinem Verhältnis zu der griechisch-römischen Philosophie* (Leipzig, 1901)
Schlossmann, S., Tertullian im Lichte der Jurisprudenz, *ZKG*, 27 (1906)
Schoedel, W. R., and R. L. Wilken (eds.), *Early Christian literature and the classical intellectual tradition, FS R. M. Grant* (Paris, 1979)
Schoepflin, M., Servizio militare e culto imperiale: il 'de corona' di Tertulliano, *Apoll.*, 58 (1985)
Schöllgen, G., Ecclesia sordida? Zur Frage der sozialen Schichtung frühchristlichen Gemeinden am Beispiel Karthagos zur Zeit Tertullians, *JAC* Suppl. 12 (Münster, 1984)
  Die Teilnahme der Christen am städtischen Leben in vorkonstantinischer Zeit, *RQ*, 77 (1982)
Shortt, C. de L., *The influence of philosophy on the mind of Tertullian* (London, 1932)
Sider, R. D., *Ancient rhetoric and the art of Tertullian* (Oxford, 1971)
Siegwalt, G., Introduction à une théologie chrétienne de la récapitulation, *RThPh.*, 113 (1981)
Simonetti, M., Il problema dell'unità di Dio a Roma da Clemente a Dionigi, *RSLR*, 22 (1986)
  Il problema dell'unità di Dio da Giustino a Ireneo, *RSLR*, 22 (1986)
Skinner, Quentin, Meaning and understanding in the history of ideas, *HTh.*, 8 (1969)
Smallwood, E. M., *The Jews under Roman rule. From Pompey to Diocletian* (Leiden, 1976)
Spanneut, M., *Permanence du Stoïcisme* (Gembloux, 1973)
  Le stoïcisme des pères de l'église (Paris, 1957)
  Tertullien et les premiers moralistes africains (Gembloux, 1969)
Stead, G. C., *Divine Substance* (Oxford, 1977)
  Divine substance in Tertullian, *JThS*, 14 (1963)

Steiner, H., *Das Verhältnis Tertullians zur antiken Paideia* (St Ottilien, 1989)
Stier, J., *Die Gottes- und Logoslehre Tertullians* (Göttingen, 1899)
Stockmeier, P., *Glaube und Kultur* (Düsseldorf, 1983)
Strecker, G., *Eschaton und Historie* (Göttingen, 1979)
Striker, G.,Κριτηρίον τῆς ἀλήθειας, *NAWG: Phil. hist. Klasse*, 1 (1974)
Stritzky, M. B., Aspekte geschichtlichen Denkens bei Tertullian, *JAC*, Supp. 10 (1983)
Telfer, W., *The forgiveness of sins* (London, 1959)
  The office of a bishop (London, 1962)
Tibiletti, C., Vita contemplativa in Tertulliano, *Orph.*, NS 2 (1981)
Tremblay, R., *Irénée de Lyon 'L'empreinte des doigts de Dieu'* (Rome, 1979)
  La manifestation et la vision de Dieu selon Saint Irénée de Lyon (Münster, 1978)
Tully, J. (ed.), *Meaning and context, Quentin Skinner and his critics* (Cambridge, 1988)
Uglione, R., Il matrimonio in Tertulliano tra esaltazione e disprezzo, *EL*, 93 (1979)
Valentin, P., Héraclite et Clément d'Alexandrie, *RSR*, 46 (1958)
Vermander, J. M., Tertullien et les dieux paiens, *RevSR*, 53 (1979)
Viciano, A., *Cristo salvador y liberador del hombre* (Pamplona, 1986)
  Grundzüge der Soteriologie Tertullians, *ThGl*, 79 (1989)
  Principios de hermeneutica biblica en el tratado 'Adversus Judaeos' de Tertulliano, *Biblia y Hermeneutica* (Pamplona, 1986)
Wickert, U., Glauben und Denken bei Tertullian und Origenes, *ZThK*, 62 (1965)
Widmann, M., *Der Begriff*, οἰκονομία im Werk des Irenäus und seine Vorgeschichte (Dissertation, Tübingen, 1956)
  Irenaeus und seine theologische Väter, *ZThK*, 54 (1957)
Wiese, H., *Heraklit bei Klemens von Alexandrien* (Dissertation, Kiel, 1963)
Wilken, R., *The Christians as the Romans saw them* (Yale, New Haven and London, 1984)
Williams, Bernard, *Shame and Necessity* (Berkeley, 1993)
  Tertullian's paradox, in A. Flew and A. MacIntyre (eds.), *New essays in philosophical theology* (London, 1955)
Winden, J. C. M. van, An early Christian philosopher: Justin Martyr's dialogue with Trypho, chapters one to nine, *PhP*, 1 (Leiden, 1971)
  Idolum and Idololatria in Tertullian, *VC*, 36 (1982)
Wölfl, K., *Das Heilswirken Gottes durch den Sohn nach Tertullian* (Rome, 1960)
Wyrwa, D., *Die christliche Platonaneignung in den Stromateis des Clemens von Alexandrien* (Berlin, 1983)

Subject index

Citations from Tertullian

Citations from the Bible